Praise for *Buying, Selling, and Valuing Financial Practices*

David Grau Sr. has been listening attentively and working effectively with financial advisors since founding FP Transitions. This book reflects his profound understanding of our profession and what it requires to exit one's business with purpose, clarity, and effectiveness. Just as we don't believe there is a one-size-fits-all approach to financial planning, David does not believe there is only one way to approach your exit plan, and *that* is what sets him apart. The sooner you read the book the better.

**Elizabeth Jetton, CFP®, Former President of the FPA;
Cofounder, TurningPoint Vision**

As the leader of one of America's largest independent advisor groups, I have known David Grau Sr. and FP Transitions for the better part of 15 years. I have great respect for their vision, knowledge, and insight into the world of practice mergers and acquisitions. Once again, David Sr. and FP Transitions have published a book that every advisor should read.

At some point, every advisor will either be a buyer or a seller. This clear, practical, and expertly written book will help tremendously no matter what side of the table you are on. While reading the book alone will not prepare you for the complexity of constructing a thorough and appropriate deal, it is the best first step.

Bill J. Williams, Executive Vice President, Ameriprise Financial

David Grau Sr. and FP Transitions have written the consummate M&A guide for the financial services profession. Coupled with their first book on succession planning and building a sustainable business, this second book provides advisors with a set of bookends that provide a range of great options as advisors consider their future and plan accordingly. Advisors interested in buying, selling, or merging their practices now have a clear road map for developing and executing their plans. This is a practical, step-by-step guide that provides detailed insights on value and valuation, due diligence and documentation, even the financial tools for executing an M&A strategy such as acquisition loans and acceleration options. A must-read for those committed to mastering the process of buying, selling, or merging an advisory practice!

Chip Mahan, Founder and Chairman, Live Oak Bank

David Grau Sr. has written yet another outstanding book. He has a unique way of taking ideas that typically scare investment professionals away and capture their attention. So many in our industry wait until it is too late to develop succession plans and/or exit strategies. Grau does a great job of being blunt to get a professional's attention and then thoroughly educating them as to what they should consider doing. Succession planning, exit strategies, and M&A work is a detailed, thoughtful exercise. This book gives a professional the tools, language, and knowledge to begin the dive into that process.

Chris McAlpin, Senior Advisor, MBA, CMFC,
Sound Financial Strategies Group Inc.

David Grau Sr. and FP Transitions comprise one of the advisor industry's most skilled and sought-after matchmakers, bringing buyers and sellers together for more than two decades. In his new book, *Buying, Selling, and Valuing Financial Practices*, David manages to take the complex and often intimidating topic of mergers and acquisitions and deliver a powerful, yet simplified guide for advisors at every stage in their businesses. Whether in the market to acquire or sell a practice, advisors will benefit from David's insights on the buying basics, valuation fundamentals, and making the deal.

TD Ameritrade Institutional has worked with David and FP Transitions for more than a decade, and we've seen advisors put these ideas into action with great success. David goes beyond theory and provides advisors with a proven process and methods that have been tested in the trenches. This book is a must-read for any advisor who has ever said to themselves, "I know I need an exit strategy and I want to do what's best for my clients, but I don't know where to start."

Tom Nally, President, TD Ameritrade Institutional

The ability for financial advisors to successfully sell or transition their business (arguably their largest financial asset) is a huge challenge that the industry faces. Rather than just admiring this issue, David Grau Sr. and FP Transitions have evaluated the different causes of this problem and identified how advisors can apply these findings and solutions to their own firms, while recognizing that there's no one-size-fits-all approach to buying, selling, or valuing a financial practice.

Wayne Withrow, Executive Vice President,
Head of SEI Advisor Network

The "go-to playbook" for financial services professionals who are looking to grow through M&A activity.

**John W. Smith, ChFC®, CLU®, CASL®, MBA, Managing Partner,
Cardinal Pointe Financial Group**

This book describes everything you need to know for buying, selling, and valuing an advisory practice. A powerful read with many tools.

**Jonathon L. Myers, CFP®, ChFC®, CLTC, MBA, CASL®,
Private Wealth Advisor, Jon L. Myers and Associates**

Buying, Selling, and Valuing Financial Practices

The Wiley Finance series contains books written specifically for finance and investment professionals as well as sophisticated individual investors and their financial advisors. Book topics range from portfolio management to e-commerce, risk management, financial engineering, valuation and financial instrument analysis, as well as much more. For a list of available titles, visit our Web site at www.WileyFinance.com.

Founded in 1807, John Wiley & Sons is the oldest independent publishing company in the United States. With offices in North America, Europe, Australia and Asia, Wiley is globally committed to developing and marketing print and electronic products and services for our customers' professional and personal knowledge and understanding.

Buying, Selling, and Valuing Financial Practices

The FP Transitions M&A Guide

DAVID GRAU SR., JD

WILEY

Cover image: Alex Moan, FP Transitions
Cover design: Wiley

Published by John Wiley & Sons, Inc., Hoboken, New Jersey.
Published simultaneously in Canada.

For general information on our other products and services or for technical support, please
contact our Customer Care Department within the United States at (800) 762-2974, outside
the United States at (317) 572-3993 or fax (317) 572-4002.

Wiley publishes in a variety of print and electronic formats and by print-on-demand. Some
material included with standard print versions of this book may not be included in e-books or
in print-on-demand. If this book refers to media such as a CD or DVD that is not included in
the version you purchased, you may download this material at http://booksupport.wiley.com.
For more information about Wiley products, visit www.wiley.com.

Library of Congress Cataloging-in-Publication Data:

Names: Grau, David, Sr., author.
Title: Buying, selling, and valuing financial practices: the FP
   transitions M&A guide / David Grau, Sr.
Description: Hoboken : Wiley, 2016. | Series: Wiley finance | Includes index.
Identifiers: LCCN 2016015333| ISBN 978-1-119-20737-5 (hardback) | ISBN
   978-1-119-20739-9 (Adobe PDF) | ISBN 978-1-119-20738-2 (epub) |
   ISBN 978-1-119-20740-5 (obook)
Subjects: LCSH: Selling. | Purchasing.
Classification: LCC HF5438.25 .G723 2016 | DDC 332.6068/1—dc23 LC record available
at https://lccn.loc.gov/2016015333

Printed in the United States of America

10 9 8 7 6 5 4 3 2 1

To Oscar

Contents

Foreword

About 20 years ago, FP Transitions launched the open market concept for finding and matching the best of many interested and qualified buyers with one particular seller, confidentially, and everything changed.

Back then, we often introduced ourselves at speaking events around the country as "eHarmony for financial advisors," smiling as we said it. But today there is a 50-to-1 buyer-to-seller ratio. The high level of demand has resulted in not only a better value proposition for sellers, but also their ability to select the best of a large auditioning group of interested buyers to step in and take care of a loyal and trusting client base. That's turned out to be a great benefit for the entire industry—it has even increased the value of the buyers' practices as a result. Effectively, we empowered sellers to transfer their duties and responsibilities to someone else at the end of their career, and then created the systems and processes to help them do exactly that.

Fifteen years ago, we completed one of the first acquisitions in this industry that was funded entirely with an SBA-guaranteed bank loan, and today, we're working to help modernize and institutionalize the bank financing process that may yet again change the value proposition, and the payment structures, for an entire industry of independent owners. This could be a significant improvement in the mergers and acquisitions (M&A) space if together with our buyers and sellers we can make it work well from the clients' perspective.

Payment terms and tax structures in this industry have continued to improve as we honed our craft. We introduced the concept of a "shared-risk/shared-reward" payment structure to protect buyers and sellers, and to ensure that the post-closing "economic marriage" adequately supported cooperative and motivated parties to look after the clients who have always been the real focus of this M&A process. Ninety-five percent–plus long-term client retention rates and 2% default rates tell the rest of the story.

As we grew, our service offerings became broader because the business model we envisioned was expanding past what a small three- or four-person consulting practice could ever hope to offer. Like you, we wanted to make a difference. I was brought in about 10 years ago based on my experience as the COO of an international business brokerage firm that had valued and sold more than 2,000 practices and businesses every year of all types, all over the world. Together, we put the wrenches and hammers to a stagnant M&A market and a valuation system that wasn't adapting or evolving very effectively, even as the independent industry changed all around it, and continues to do so.

Ten years ago, it was obvious that buyers and sellers were struggling with a valuation problem as they sought to measure what they'd built, or sought to acquire at market value, and to precisely determine their next steps. There was simply no affordable, accurate, and practical method by which to make a value calculation for M&A purposes. At one end of the valuation spectrum was a multiple of gross revenue (GRM), which worked just fine for very small books with transactional revenue sold through an earn-out arrangement, but not much else. At the other end of the valuation spectrum was a full appraisal, such as the discounted cash flow (DCF) method, which was perfect for a courtroom setting or large, multiowner firms. But at $5,000 to $50,000 per valuation, only the largest and most motivated sellers could afford, were interested in, or had need of, this respected academic approach.

The independent industry needed another choice, a better choice, so our first order of business was to create the Comprehensive Valuation Report, an accurate and affordable value calculation that relied on FP Transitions' large and growing private database of comparable, closed transactions—without which this approach would have no credibility. It's all about the data! After eight years of closings (at the time), we had the "comps" to do the job right. Eight thousand valuations later, the handwriting is on the wall, so to speak, and along the way, the industry vernacular began to regularly borrow our valuation terms like "cash flow quality" and "transition risk." Answering one simple question—What would a competitive, strategic buyer pay for a specific revenue stream given standard and reasonable payment terms?— made all the sense in the world to most of the entrepreneurs in this industry.

But as it turned out, not everyone wanted to sell. Many advisors enjoyed what they did and wanted to sustain their lifestyle practices for as long as possible. Some advisors even had the temerity to want to create a legacy model, to build an enduring and transferable business that could outlive them and serve their clients and their clients' children and grandchildren. So we launched the concept of "equity management" in a white paper published in 2008 by Pershing, LLC, and championed the term "continuity planning" as separate and distinct from "exit planning." The related terms "revenue-strength" and "enterprise-strength" that we first shared in our work with Fidelity in 2009 have become common parlance in describing how practices or businesses are built and structured.

Along the way, FP Transitions led the shift from using basic revenue-sharing agreements, to earn-out arrangements, to today's use of a more sophisticated performance-based promissory note structure. We shared our concepts and thinking with hundreds, maybe thousands of practice management personnel at the various independent broker-dealer (IBDs) and custodians, sometimes gratefully, sometimes not. It turns out that independence is often more important during the recruitment process than upon an advisor's retirement, but we're going to champion the cause of the independent selling owner because in the long run, that's what is best for the clients who support this industry.

A few years back, FP Transitions literally wrote the book on building an enduring business and formally defined "succession planning" for this unique group of professionals for the very first time. Every year, we now help to create hundreds of new, first-time, "30-year-old" owners who are investing their money and their careers to build on top of an existing practice—to form a "successor team." We coined the terms "G-1, G-2, and G-3" to set up a succession strategy for next-generation advisors. Our original work with many of the large IBDs and custodians led to terms and concepts that are now commonly used throughout the industry. To do all this, we led the use of entity structures to create a chassis that is designed to last, and to serve well beyond the founder's career—a cutting-edge strategy in this industry. That's exciting and important work. And we continue to push the boundaries every day in order to keep advisory practices thriving and serving their client base for generations to come.

As this book is sent to the publisher, we have 40 staff members whose skill-sets include five JDs (lawyers), two CVAs (Certified Valuation Analyst), one of whom has also earned the designations of an ASA (Accredited Senior Appraiser) and MCBA (Master Certified Business Appraiser), ABAR (Accredited in Business Appraisal Review by the Institute of Business Appraisers), and MAFF (Master Analyst in Financial Forensics), and a CFA (Certified Financial Analyst) with several more CFA candidates in the wings. We also have compliance and regulatory skills to augment these credentials, important in this highly regulated industry. And along the way, we're building our own enduring, multigenerational ownership structure.

Today, there is no question that an advisory practice has value, but it doesn't seem that long ago that they didn't. Yesterday, we argued with industry "experts" and "pundits" fighting to establish that an advisory practice had any value at all.

The M&A space for the independent financial services and advisory industry has come a long, long way in a very short time because of great ideas like these and because of a really smart group of financial advisors/entrepreneurs who seem determined and destined to lead the professional services ranks in terms of value, transaction terms, and satisfied clients. And together, we're only just getting started!

Brad Bueermann, CEO, FP Transitions

Preface

FOR SELLERS

Rule No. 1: You get only one chance to do this right.

In our experience, sellers tend to be at a distinct disadvantage in the M&A process. That might sound strange given that there is, and has been over the past 20 years or so, a strong seller's market in the financial services and advisory industry. With a 50+-to-1 buyer-to-seller ratio, how can sellers not have the upper hand? The fundamental truths are these: (1) buyers tend to be more skilled in the M&A process, and; (2) the deck is usually stacked against a seller.

Advisors can buy many times, but selling tends to happen just once in a career, and unfortunately it often happens without a solid plan and without accurate and reliable information upon which to base any plan. It is hard to master a concept that you get to do only one time, especially if you learn mostly by word of mouth. Sellers have the advantage of scarcity, but buyers have the advantage of being able to repeat the acquisition process over and over again until they get it right. Buyers also have the support of their broker-dealers and custodians, whose goals align much more closely with those who stay than those who leave. Sellers, please read that last sentence over and over again.

For all these reasons, sellers need to pay very careful attention to the strategies in this book. Sellers need to understand that, while in the "driver's seat," they are not in control unless and until they command the entire transition process, from valuation to listing to documentation to taxation to closing, and then being able to deliver the clients—an overall process that often starts at least three to five years before most advisors think it does. Too often, sellers sit in the driver's seat full of confidence, but fail to understand that they're actually sitting atop a car-carrier and being driven along by someone else who knows where they're going and what they're doing. Sellers, be mindful of where you get your information and who appears to be helping you. Free information is usually worth just that, but it can sometimes cost a fortune.

Being prepared means planning ahead and relying on accurate, occasionally blunt information and data sources; do not make the mistake of relying on stories told by advisors who have gone through the M&A process one time as a seller and came out relatively unscathed, or by a practice management person at your broker-dealer or custodian whose job it is to make sure your clients/assets aren't lost to a competing broker-dealer, no matter what. Learn the basic facts and decide for yourself—but do the math.

Finally, sellers have a duty to place their clients' financial futures in the hands of the best person they can find, not the first person to walk through the door. Selling to a friend or someone who makes the process seem so easy is tempting, but stop and ask yourself this question: Am I doing what is best for my clients? The advantage of a seller's market does not lie simply in higher values; it lies in being able to find the very best match for your trusting clients. The goal is to find the perfect buyer, the perfect advisor to take over, which, in the end, creates and supports a fair value proposition for all. Starting with a one-to-one buyer-to-seller ratio, though, is rarely, if ever, the best way to achieve that goal.

Rest assured that buyers are reading this same material and are studying the very systems and processes that you're now learning. That's okay. You can always choose to keep working, at your pace, and not sell. In fact, trading in your exit plan for a long-term succession plan is a great idea if you start early enough and have the time and energy. This book is designed to put you in control of your future and to level a playing field now dominated by buyers of independent financial advisory practices. A level playing field is good for your buyers, too! But sellers, you need a plan and you need to execute it in a professional and learned manner.

And no matter what you choose to do in the end, don't forget Rule No. 1.

FOR BUYERS

Rule No. 2: Do it right—the value and terms you agree to pay as a part of today's M&A activity will affect the value and terms you'll receive tomorrow.

There is a lot of competition to acquire a financial advisory practice. Recognizing that acquisition allows you to substantially increase the size of your practice or business in about 90 days, paying for at least two-thirds or more of the acquisition out of the acquired cash flow over the next three to five years, there should be no surprise that there is a 50-to-1 buyer-to-seller ratio. But this book isn't just about how to fight your way to the front of that long line of interested buyers—it is also about how to avoid that line altogether by planning ahead and knowing exactly what you're doing and how to get the job done correctly.

In this book, you'll learn the basics of acquisition, including the legal, regulatory, payment structures, and tax aspects of the process. You'll learn how to look at sellers in a different way and how to sculpt your offer to reflect what the seller is selling and how they've assembled the pieces. You'll learn that there is no one single, formulaic method by which to value, construct, and complete every acquisition. You'll learn that in some instances, using a multiple of revenue is a perfectly acceptable method for valuing the book you're buying, and in other cases, that's about the worst thing you could possibly do. It all depends on what you're buying, and how the seller is constructed.

You'll also learn the difference between cash flow and equity value. For those of you reading this book that came from or learned the most important lessons in your professional life from the wirehouse side of the industry, there is a difference. Cash flow is obviously important and, day to day, captures the attention of every practice owner. But if you're going to build a business, or acquire a practice (and there is a difference between a business and a practice), you'll need to master and implement the concept of equity. This book will help you understand what it means to build a practice versus a business versus a firm. As a buyer, you need to know the differences because a successful acquisition strategy will depend on it.

Buyers, this book will also help you *get ready* for the next acquisition opportunity. Being prepared doesn't mean being very excited and willing to jump into the ring on a moment's notice when an M&A bout is about to begin. It means planning and building and valuing your own business ahead of time. Smart sellers can tell the difference between a well-prepared buyer and a mildly interested participant who thinks they can figure it out as they go and prevail through good intentions, enthusiasm, and even force of will.

Understand this simple fact: larger, stronger, durable businesses tend to acquire smaller, one-generational practices, books, or jobs. Where do you fit in this food chain? You need to know how things work in this industry and you need a strategy to succeed if you're serious about building a business designed for the sudden and explosive growth that accompanies an acquisition strategy. Your broker-dealer or custodian will gladly support your efforts to acquire and retain the clients and assets of every seller in their network. But will they help you first build a business model specifically designed for this purpose?

Today, you're the buyer. One day, too soon, you'll be the seller and will be dependent on the marketplace and values you're helping to develop, even the network you're working within. Plan and execute accordingly.

Acknowledgments

Writing a book is hard work. Most people probably intuitively understand that aspect of the process, but few have firsthand knowledge of what it actually takes—and the many people whose inputs and guidance are invaluable.

Of the many contributors, first, thanks must go to the clients who let us assist them, building and reshaping their practices, and sometimes calling it a day and selling or merging what they'd spent a lifetime building. The daily contact and connection with independent advisors, young and old, building and/or selling, is the lifeblood of a book like this. Not a night went by in the year of writing it that something learned by day didn't make its way into the manuscript. This daily connection is what separates a book based on theory and a book based on fact and observation—our goal has clearly been the latter.

The downside of writing through such a connection, on top of a day job, is that the book writing is mostly done at nights and on weekends, and that is why (along with three complete drafts) it took so long to complete. My wife, Penny, gave up all those weekends and gave me the endless quiet time to do what I needed to do. I'd like to say that she knew what she was getting into when she married an English major who became a lawyer who became a businessman who yearned to write, but most of us don't plan that far in advance. We just make the best of the world we find ourselves in the midst of, and she has done that without complaint.

I also had a great business team without whom this book would not exist. My longtime business partner and our company's CEO, Brad Bueermann, guided gently and patiently, telling me the truth whether I wanted to hear it or not. Laura Bueermann served as my personal editor and labored through draft after draft with me. It turns out that Stanford people are really smart. Laura saw things that I didn't and had the ability to add that one perfect word or two to each sentence and paragraph she touched, and the book is the better for it.

FP Transitions' valuation experts, Warren Burkholder, ASA, MCBA, ABAR, MAFF, CVA, and Ryan Grau, CVA, were incredible in helping shape the text and the messages in Chapters 2 and 3 on value and valuation, the most difficult chapters in this book to write. Eric Leeper, CFA, helped me think through the logic of various sections and double-checked the math throughout. As an English major, I have a lot of respect for our team of math majors.

Jeanie O'Reilly Northcutt, our longtime Listings Director, and Aaron Wells, Transactions Coordinator, serve as the anchors of our transactions section and helped maintain a steady flow of information from the daily activity of our buyers and sellers and contributed to the accuracy and strength of Chapters 5 and 6.

FP Transitions has assembled its own law firm over the years, and Rod Boutin, JD, our General Counsel, and Ericka Langone, JD, Assistant General Counsel, both contributed to the final draft, making sure that all the "t's" were crossed and the "i's" dotted. Rod and his entire team, in particular, helped shape Chapters 8, 9, and 10 and the forms in the Appendix.

Christine Sjolin, our Operations Manager, and Marcus Hagood, our head of EMS (our Equity Management System), each applied their special and gentle touches to various sections and helped keep me on track as earlier drafts occasionally wandered a bit . . . or a lot.

And last but not least, our marketing department, comprised of Elise Rogers, Marketing Director, Rachel Beckwith, Senior Marketing Strategist, and Alex Moan, Video Marketing Specialist, gets credit for everything artistic about this book from the cover to the graphs and illustrations.

Building a great business is about surrounding yourself with great people, and in that I have certainly succeeded. I am honored to work with those listed here as well as all of our many loyal and hardworking staff members every day of the week.

CHAPTER 1

The Basics You Need to Know

AVOIDING THE CRITICAL MISTAKES

There are two critical and common mistakes that independent financial advisors make in the mergers and acquisitions (M&A) space. One is to treat every sale or acquisition target the same way: applying the same valuation approach, the same set of documents, and a common set of payment terms or financing elements, regardless of the size or structure or sophistication of the opportunity. The second mistake is to equate exit planning with succession planning—the two concepts are completely different and advisors must understand the differences if they are to succeed in this arena and correctly structure a transaction, whether as seller or buyer.

The specific purpose of this book is to help advisors understand how to sell what they've built to someone else for maximum value and at optimum tax rates, and/or to successfully complete an acquisition and become someone's exit strategy, on the best possible terms, with minimum risk, writing off the entire purchase price over time. These are not disparate goals; they are connected in every way and part of a win-win-win strategy that must be the ultimate goal for the buyer and seller, the good of this industry, and the client base that serves as judge and jury over the outcome of the M&A process.

For most independent financial advisors, their book or practice or business is easily the largest and most valuable asset they own. Critical mistakes cannot be allowed to happen. The process of sorting out the issues, learning the basics, and then mastering the more complicated aspects starts right here, right now.

Exit planning results in a transaction with either an external buyer or an internal buyer, but the commonality is that the process is completed in one step—usually not suddenly, just completely. External buyers usually have a very similar practice model but are often much larger than the seller in terms of size and value, while an internal buyer is someone you've hired, know, and trust (maybe even a son or daughter), but who is often without the financial resources and the experience of the external buyer.

A succession plan is quite different; it is designed to build on top of an existing practice or business and to *gradually* and seamlessly transition ownership and leadership internally to the next generation of advisors. The founding owner in a succession plan is not a "seller"—they're a business partner or a shareholder, and long-term, sustainable growth powered by multiple generations of collaborative ownership is the number one goal. This book is not about succession planning. If that topic is of interest to you, please consider reading our first book, *Succession Planning for Financial Advisors: Building an Enduring Business*.

As part of exploring the various exit strategy options and how to structure those transactions, this book will also explain the different value and valuation techniques and their applicability given various situations. You'll learn the difference between an asset-based deal structure and a stock-based deal structure, as well as how to employ various financing methods such as a promissory note, performance-based or adjustable notes, revenue-splitting or revenue-sharing arrangements, and earn-outs. The element of bank financing will also be carefully considered because this is a powerful tool when used correctly. We'll also evolve beyond the basic concept of silos versus ensembles in the process toward a more sophisticated and accurate classification system.

One of the fundamental tenets of this book is to *not* treat all advisors the same as though one approach to valuation, contracts, payment terms, and contingencies fits all situations, sizes, and revenue models across the spectrum. In fact, there is no one single method, one single view of this unique industry that works every time for every buyer or seller. It depends on what you've built and how you've built it. Using your specific vantage point, our goal is to explain what works and what doesn't work, and how to do the job right, whether you're a buyer or a seller. In the end, we all need the best buyer to prevail, not the first on the scene or the one with the most money.

If you approach all M&A opportunities in this unique industry with one set of tools, one set formula, and just one valuation approach or method to be applied in every instance—the way most writers, consultants, and practice management personnel recommend—your view of the world will always be partly right, but mostly wrong, not unlike the blind men and the elephant from the Indian folktale told in a poem by John Godfrey Saxe:

The Blind Men and the Elephant

It was six men of Indostan
To learning much inclined,
Who went to see the Elephant

(Though all of them were blind),
That each by observation
Might satisfy his mind.

The First approach'd the Elephant,
And happening to fall
Against his broad and sturdy side,
At once began to bawl:
"God bless me! but the Elephant
Is very like **a wall!**"

The Second, feeling of the tusk,
Cried, "Ho! What have we here
So very round and smooth and sharp?
To me 'tis mighty clear
This wonder of an Elephant
Is very like **a spear!**"

The Third approached the animal,
And happening to take
The squirming trunk within his hands,
Thus boldly up and spake:
"I see," quoth he, "the Elephant
Is very like **a snake!**"

The Fourth reached out his eager hand,
And felt about the knee.
"What most this wondrous beast is like
Is mighty plain," quoth he,
"'Tis clear enough the Elephant
Is very like **a tree!**"

The Fifth, who chanced to touch the ear,
Said: "E'en the blindest man
Can tell what this resembles most;
Deny the fact who can,
This marvel of an Elephant
Is very like **a fan!**"

The Sixth no sooner had begun
About the beast to grope,
Then, seizing on the swinging tail

That fell within his scope,
"I see," quoth he, "the Elephant
Is very like **a rope!**"

And so these men of Indostan
Disputed loud and long,
Each in his own opinion
Exceeding stiff and strong,
Though each was partly in the right,
And all were in the wrong!

VALUATION: THE GREAT DEBATE

There is a lot of debate in the financial services industry as to the best approach and method to apply when valuing a financial services practice. Some feel an income approach (focused on earnings or profitability as espoused by the discounted economic cash flow method) is best. Others prefer to use a direct market data method that relies on market "comps" or comparable transactions between buyers and sellers of similarly structured practices or businesses within the same industry. Some buyers prefer a much simpler valuation approach, applying basic revenue splitting, revenue sharing, or earn-out payment terms to measure actual success over a period of years—a *wait-and-see* approach. Some buyers insist on using a multiple of top-line revenue or adjusted bottom-line earnings.

Buyers tend to use the one method that they understand, or a method that has worked well for them in the past, regardless of the size and structure of the acquisition opportunity. Sellers are often embarking on the valuation trek for the first time and sometimes have only a limited understanding of this crucial topic. Practice management personnel at the various broker-dealers and custodians have their own agenda and weigh in on the valuation debate with their own preferences. Each party to the process has a goal, and the goal really isn't about finding *the right answer*; the goal too often is to find the answer each party needs to be true to advance their own cause. As a result, there is a lot of unnecessary and unjustified confusion about how to value a financial services practice or business for M&A purposes.

The goal of valuation, aligned with the proper approach and method, should be to bring the parties together, not to serve as a wedge and to bludgeon the other side with an argument about who is right or wrong and why one party's approach is superior to the other's. Valuation in the financial services industry has become the single most divisive issue in the M&A process. Valuation disputes stop most deals before they even start. Let's end the debate with the goal of completing more transactions and taking better care of the clients who have placed their trust in an independent advisor.

The place to start is to fundamentally understand that there is no right or wrong answer to the question, "What is my practice worth?" The answer will vary depending on what is being bought or sold (a book or a business, assets or stock, a minority interest or a controlling interest, etc.), who the buyer is, why the valuation is being performed, the motivations of the parties, and even who's performing it. When the time comes for you to sell your practice, the first question shouldn't focus on which approach to use to arrive at a proper value. The appropriate series of questions leading to a valuation solution should be:

- What am I selling and why am I valuing my practice?

If you're a buyer, the focus should be on this question:

- What am I buying and why am I buying it?

Purpose Informs Value

In other words, you need to know what you are trying to solve for before you attempt to answer the question as to how to solve it. No one single valuation approach and method solves every problem, every time. There are many tools in the *valuation toolbox*, and as a buyer or a seller, you need to know at least the basics of how to use them and when to apply them, or at the very least, when to call for help and what questions to ask.

Of course, selling a relationship-based practice or business isn't like selling a fast-food franchise in which you hand over the keys and a *How-to-Run-It Manual*. In this M&A space, the clients get a vote, and most sellers care about what their clients think of their final act—something that buyers need to understand as well. Best price and terms should always take a backseat to "best match," another consistent theme in this book.

So what does all this have to do with elephants and blind men? Last year, I sat on a four-person panel where we were asked to discuss the intricacies of value and valuation as applied to independent advisors who were interested in acquisition or selling. Two of the panelists were practice management specialists, one with a large independent broker-dealer (IBD) and the other from a custodian. The other panelist was an investment banker. The investment banker was adamant that the discounted cash flow method his firm produced and sold was the single best way to perform a valuation in this industry, every time—anything else was just silly and a wild guess. Another panelist opined that for most of the thousand-plus advisors in his

IBD, what worked best on a daily basis was a simple rule of thumb, or a multiple of revenue or earnings. Over the length of his career, this method had proven to be practical, affordable, and good enough to do the job in most cases. The other panelist thought that it was simply a matter of "wait and see," paying value for what a buyer actually received using an earn-out arrangement or a basic revenue sharing approach; in his opinion, formal valuations or appraisals, even multiples of revenue, weren't even called for.

Each panelist was partly in the right, and *all* were in the wrong, but these points of view reflect what we hear and experience every day. There is no single valuation methodology adequately suited to the range of revenue streams and structural components now represented in this fast-growing and rapidly evolving industry. That is why buyers and sellers need to adjust and elevate their level of understanding and thinking about how to buy, sell, and value a financial services or advisory practice or business. On that note, another of our goals in this book is to help you understand not only how to determine value, but how to apply the payment terms so as to motivate a seller and to protect a buyer in order to ensure that the clients' best interests are never overlooked in the process of realizing or paying that value.

ASSESSING WHAT YOU HAVE BUILT (OR ARE ACQUIRING)

There's a clever use of terms and concepts in this industry. One good example is describing the organizational structures of independent financial practices as "silos" or "ensembles." The basic notion is that a silo is a single "book of business." The term "ensemble" is reserved for a business with multiple professionals who truly work together as a team, pooling their resources and cash flows, creating a bottom line, and then distributing profits to the owners of that business. These terms are certainly relevant in this industry, but they do not form a complete system to use in assessing what an advisor has built or seeks to acquire.

This binary system of categorizing all financial advisors as either a silo or an ensemble model does accurately reflect one critical element about this industry—the importance of organizational structure. For this contribution, we are indebted to our predecessors Mark Tibergien and Philip Palaveev, authors of *Practice Made Perfect* and *The Ensemble Practice*, respectively.

But the evolution continues and structural issues go well beyond just organizational elements and must include the choice of an entity (such as a C corporation, an S corporation, or a limited liability company), or not, as with a sole proprietorship, and the ownership level compensation system, which directly affects and supports growth rates and the underlying profit structure. These foundational elements, or the lack thereof, affect

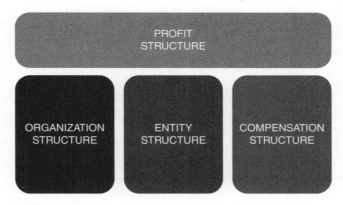

FIGURE 1.1 Structural Elements of an Independent Financial Services/Advisory Model

every advisor, broker-dealer, and custodian in this industry. More to the point, these basic foundational elements, whether weak or strong, dictate the structure, success, and value of every M&A transaction (Figure 1.1).

As you study and master the concepts and strategies in this book and begin to consider your exit plan or acquisition strategy, start with these basic questions:

"What have you built and are considering selling?" or,

"What exactly is it that you want to acquire?"

The answers to these questions require more descriptive and precise terms than just "silo" or "ensemble." We suggest you consider the following terms for classifying the levels of independent ownership in the financial services and advisory industry, which, in turn, accurately reflect how each level of ownership is built and operated:

- A job (or a book)
- A practice
- A business
- A firm

These descriptive terms, within the context of this M&A guide, also reflect how each level will likely be acquired, grown, or disassembled. These terms and the working definitions that follow form very practical tools that we have developed and use on a daily basis and contribute to help advisors understand the impact of the various structural elements of their transition plans. In other words, if or when you're thinking of selling, what you've built, and how you've built it, will often determine how you sell it and what you sell it for.

A *job*, often and appropriately called a *book*, exists as long as the advisor or financial professional does the work. Job or book owners are independent and "own" what they do, for the most part. W-2 or 1099, registered rep or investment advisor or insurance professional—it makes no difference—they can all fit equally well in this category. But when a job or book owner stops working and someone else starts, it becomes the new advisor's job; the cash flow attached to that job belongs in whole or in substantial part to the person doing the job. Of course it is about production; in fact, it is about nothing else. A job owner works under someone else's roof, owns none of the infrastructure, and has no real obligations to the business other than to produce and get paid while taking care of his or her client base. This is the basic definition of being independent.

The "value" of a job/book is tied almost entirely to how much money the producer or advisor takes home every year. Think in terms of gross revenues, or GDC, of less than $200,000 a year (although we do see cases of the "super producer," described in more detail in our first book on succession planning—that group has much higher production- or revenue-generation capabilities, but all other aspects still fit this defined category). In this industry, by our watch, about 70% of advisors are owners of a job or a book (Figure 1.2). Jobs or books are most likely to sell at the lowest price, and on the worst terms with the worst tax structure—at least when compared to practices, businesses, or firms.

A *practice* is more than just a job or a book, often involving support staff around the practitioner and the ownership of at least some basic infrastructure (phone system, computers, CRM system, desks and chairs, and so forth) usually within an S corporation or an LLC. But like a job, a practice exists only as long as the practitioner can individually provide the services and expertise. Practices are limited to one generation of ownership, after which someone else takes over. The practice may be sold outright, transferred through a revenue-splitting arrangement, or be dissolved with the clients finding their own way to another advisor. Practices have one owner, but often encompass one or more additional producers (usually categorized

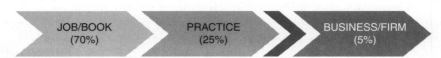

JOB/BOOK (70%)   PRACTICE (25%)   BUSINESS/FIRM (5%)

FIGURE 1.2   Industry Segmentation

as owners of a job or a book) with whom they share time, expenses, and support. About 25% of the advisors in this industry fall into this category.

Jobs/books and practices are "strongly held," a term we employ to reflect a single owner who dictates direction and results—the typical founder and entrepreneur. The focus for job or practice owners is entirely on revenue strength. There is little need for enterprise strength at these levels. There is also no significant "bottom line" or profitability at these levels (yes, we're talking about 90% to 95% of the industry at this level and below) and there doesn't need to be. No one invests in these models, at least in terms of becoming a formal shareholder or partner. Earnings are mostly paid out as compensation to the producers through some form of an eat-what-you-kill (EWYK) system or a salary/bonus structure tied in some way to top-line production, as opposed to actual profit distributions or dividends. None of this is written in stone—many practices have the ability to do much more, as is the case with jobs or books. It is simply that, historically, the advisor/owner takes home what was produced, a legacy of the wirehouse-brokerage model.

The more valuable practices tend to sell using a formal documentation process that creates and supports long-term capital gains tax treatment for the seller and write-offs for the buyer. Practices have a stronger value proposition than jobs/books, providing the owner with more options, a higher sales price on better terms and at better tax rates, and tend to have lower transition risk (see Chapter 3 for more information), an important element for buyers to consider.

If a practice is to grow and evolve into a business, it will need to enhance and bolster its organization, compensation, and profit structures along the way in order to facilitate a new generation of owners/advisors. Businesses and firms have or are implementing a compensation system that supports strong growth and sustainable profitability. Books and practices often have strong growth rates as well, but almost always at the expense of profitability, arguably irrelevant in a one-owner model. Revenue sharing or other EWYK compensation systems accomplish only the production and cash flow goals, leaving profitability and equity unattended to. In the end, these elements signal the divide between a job/book or practice on one side, and a business or a firm on the other side. We'll continue to build on these concepts and expand the thinking around revenue strength and enterprise strength later in this chapter because it effects every aspect of the M&A process.

A *business* has certain foundational elements in place, such as an entity structure, a proper equity-centric (or ensemble) organizational structure, and a compensation system that gives it the ability to attract and retain talent while generating a sufficient profit margin (i.e., 30%+) to reward and attract a multigenerational ownership structure. The revenue stream may be singular or diversified, but usually about 75% or more is fee-based. The business is built to be enduring and transferable from one generation to the next. It operates from a bottom line approach and earnings are used to reward ownership and encourage investment in the business. The ownership-level compensation system shifts to a base salary plus profit distributions. Continuity agreements are a given and take the form of a Shareholder Agreement or a Buy-Sell Agreement. A business gains its momentum and cash flow from revenue strength and its durability and staying power from its enterprise strength. Businesses tend to have a much stronger value proposition than practices, affording an owner a range of options, including retiring on the job, selling at maximum value with the best overall tax structure possible, or building a legacy, all with little to no transition risk. About 4% of independent advisors presently fall into this category, though this group is growing rapidly.

A *firm* is an established, multiowner, multigenerational business, and it got there through proper succession planning. It is built with a strong foundation of ownership and leadership by recruiting and retaining the very best people in the industry. It operates primarily from a bottom-line approach and earnings are the measure of success, at least as important as production and growth rates. Again, the revenue stream may be singular or diversified, but about 90% or more is usually fee-based. Continuity agreements aren't just a safety measure. They are a means of internal growth and strength. Anticipating the loss of one generation means planning for the success of the next generation. Collaboration among owners and staff is the rule. In a firm, the goal isn't to have the best professionals, but rather to have the best firm. Firms offer the best value proposition and are almost always supported with a strong internal succession plan that provides a culture of ownership, attracting and retaining the best advisors, who attend to multiple generations of clients. About 1% of today's independent advisors are owners of a firm and we expect this group to double in size in the coming years.

In this book, from this point forward, we will use the terms "job/book," "practice," "business," and "firm" very specifically and within the context of the preceding definitions. Depending on whether you are selling or buying a job/book, a practice, a business, or a firm, your choice of valuation methodology, financing, payment structuring, transfer mechanism (assets or stock), and even the paperwork to complete the transaction is often tied to the seller's level of ownership and what they've built—even how they've built it. This conclusion is reflected in the following section showing how advisors tend to leave or retire from each level of ownership.

Special Note: The ownership level of a *firm* tends to sell internally through a formal succession plan. As such, this book focuses on firms only with respect to their role in acquiring smaller businesses and practices and omits use of the term "firms" in most instances, including selling through an exit plan.

WHO IS SELLING? TRANSITION STRATEGIES BY OWNERSHIP LEVEL

So, who is selling? Where are the sellers? As a buyer, it is important to know where to look, and what to look for to make acquisition a reliable and profitable growth strategy. The numbers tell an interesting tale, one most advisors don't understand (Figure 1.3). What a seller has built, and how they built it, greatly influences their eventual transition strategy.

Each year, FP Transitions performs formal valuations on over a thousand advisors' jobs or books, practices, businesses and firms, a process that fuels a large and deep database. What advisors do next—once they know with greater certainty the value of what they've built—is simply a matter of observation. The data is clear. Across all ownership levels, we're seeing that about one in 10 advisors sell externally (to a third party), but the numbers vary significantly by ownership level. Perhaps the real story lies in what more than 8 out of 10 advisors do if they aren't going to sell.

Currently, the primary exit strategy for job/book and practice owners is attrition. Independent owners at these levels don't sell as a first choice, certainly not as often as they should. This is a surprising choice given that,

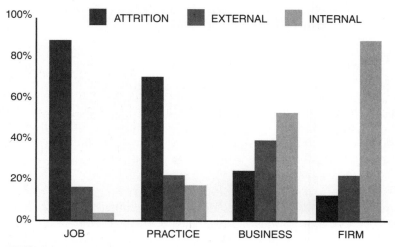

FIGURE 1.3 Transition Strategy by Ownership Level

for most advisors, their books or practices are usually the most valuable asset they own. Under the attrition route, these advisors enjoy their income streams for as long as they can while gradually working less and less, spending fewer days in the office and less time and energy on marketing and technology and then, one day, when there is nothing much left to sell, they call it a day. The work just dwindles to an end, and the remaining clients are given a few referrals to peers or friends and that's it. No cymbals clanging, no bells ringing. It just ends quietly.

This outcome is bad for the industry, and especially for the clients who look to their independent advisor for professional financial advice and mistakenly assume that their advisor will be serving them on a timeline tied to their lives and needs, not their advisor's planned (or unplanned) career length. And this really needs to change. But it would be equally incorrect to conclude that every job/book or practice owner needs or should attempt to create a succession plan.

Most books and many practices are not capable of generating a qualified internal successor because of how they are assembled. The primary culprit is the use of wirehouse-style employee-based compensation and reward systems that make production and sales achievements the pinnacle of a career. Durability and profitability are not the goals of book owners and most practice owners. As a result, it is far more likely that independent advisors will build one-generational books as opposed to an enduring business.

Think about it for a moment before we continue our discussion on transition strategies by ownership level. What would it take to prompt at least half of the job/book and practice owners (about 95% of the industry by our headcount) to either build an enduring business or, worst case, to sell their work at peak value to a business or a growing practice that could serve those acquired clients for generations to come? More knowledge of the M&A process? A better value proposition? Better payment terms, with a larger down payment and shorter or no seller financing? Could bank financing be the answer, allowing sellers to cash out more quickly and completely and with less risk? Would one or more of these things make the difference? We're about to find out because this industry is changing rapidly—whether it changes for the better, or worse, or just stays the present course, will be decided in large part by today's buyers and sellers and builders.

The next most popular strategy after attrition, at least at the practice level, is selling or transferring the cash flow to a third party. Those who do sell tend to be around age 60, though the sellers range in age from 40 to 70 in any given year. Sometimes the sale is prompted by an advisor who wants a good, old-fashioned, well-earned retirement. Sometimes the seller has no intention of retiring, at least not in the commonly used sense of the word. Entrepreneurs forever, many sellers have something else in mind and, once their clients are well taken care of, they use their time and energy (and money) to do something they've always wanted to do.

Take Glen Janken, for instance, who gave us permission to share his unique and fascinating tale. In 2010, we listed Glen's practice for sale. After 25 years as a financial advisor, Glen decided he wanted to become a math teacher. After using the open market system to find a handpicked replacement, Glen did just that. Today, he is in his fourth year of teaching math at the Notre Dame Academy in Los Angeles, California. Next year, he ups his game from teaching algebra to teaching calculus, and he couldn't be happier! Glen took care of his clients first, and then chased down his dream.

At the business level of ownership, transition strategies are a completely different story. Here, advisors have a full range of choices because they've taken the steps to plan ahead and take control of their futures—real control. The leading strategies at this level of ownership are to sell internally, sometimes completely and all at once to a son, daughter, or key employee (an exit plan), and sometimes gradually over many years to a team of internal successors (a succession plan), together comprising 75% of this group. Attrition is the least popular strategy.

In most cases, there is too much value at this level to just wind it down and get nothing out of the process. Attrition persists because the planning process sometimes starts too late or the concept of equity is just not understood or appreciated. Clients' expectations also weigh in heavily at this level. Have you ever been asked the question, "What happens to me if something happens to you?" Clients expect and deserve a good answer and business owners appear to have one, for the most part. At this ownership level, we are observing a rapid increase in building enduring businesses or selling them at career end to another business or a larger firm.

At the firm level, almost all transitions are through a succession plan where a team of successors gradually step in and take over, one at a time, learning on the job and earning their way up the ladder. Succession planning is about growth, and such growth depends on the firm attracting and retaining the best talent. To do that, equity must come into play. Advisors must have an opportunity to buy into ownership and to enjoy the benefits of *cash flow plus equity*. It's no wonder that firms are the most valuable and durable models.

In terms of considering an external sale, it is important to consider the role played by consolidators and "roll-ups," viable exit planning options in their own right. Though the terms have broad application generically, there are but a handful of enduring and reliable consolidator/roll-up models, at least on a national level. After 25 years in this space and seeing such models come and go on a regular basis, I'm reluctant to name names in a book with a shelf life that will extend beyond most of theirs. But occasionally these can be good and qualified buyers who offer an interesting and different opportunity to independent owners thinking of selling or merging or growing—with unique buy-in formulas that tend to keep the founding owner in place and in command but with additional support and capital.

Consolidators and roll-ups should be considered, but include regional models in your analysis as well. Start with a formal valuation of what you've built so that you have a center point from which to negotiate. Understand the realm of choices available to you and evaluate these unique opportunities comparing facts to facts. Consolidators and roll-ups can be the right answer, but only for a very specific group of today's practice and business owners.

Nothing in this section or the preceding graph should be taken as implying that there is a preordained fate that awaits you when it is time to sell (or buy) or internally transition. Armed with a good road map and accurate information, the future belongs to you.

OVERCOMING ATTRITION: PUBLIC ENEMY NO. 1

Most independent advisors who consider retirement wonder if they should sell internally or externally. The truth of the matter is that, at least at the job/book and practice levels, neither result is going to occur in significant numbers—not yet, anyway. The number one exit strategy, as you've now learned, is attrition.

Attrition is the process of enjoying the cash flow provided by the work for as long as it will last once the single owner stops investing their full time, attention, energy, and funds. Eventually, the book or the practice just dies, but not before providing an extra 5 to 10 years of gradually decreasing income and cash flow to the founder. The attrition strategy centers on the advisor's needs, goals, and career length. That is a problem because a client's needs will almost certainly extend beyond the longevity of a founding owner's career. Not only does this leave the clients to fend for themselves, possibly at a time and an age where such a transition is very difficult, but it also leaves a lot of money or value on the table from the advisor's perspective. In years past, we accurately identified this issue, attrition, as the independent industry's Achilles' heel. Nothing has changed.

From the perspective of an independent broker-dealer, custodian, or insurance company, the fact that more than 80% of their advisors' books or practices won't be selling at career end, possibly to a competitor, is often treated as good news. It's not. The data is clear that those same books and practices will stop growing and will decline in production, cash flow, and value *for about 10 years before* the practice actually dies out. They will gradually shed their clients to other advisors, perhaps within other networks. Imagine what the clients of this industry think . . . and decide on their own along the way. This is the toll of attrition.

But the news is not all bad. Slowly but surely, advisors are beginning to create formal succession plans that are designed to build a multiowner/multigenerational structure sophisticated enough to last for many years to come, and to acquire every book and practice in their path. Currently, the independent financial services/advisory industry looks something like Figure 1.4.

Interestingly, many practice management consultants employed by the various independent broker-dealers, custodians, and insurance companies focus almost entirely on not losing the 10% who will sell. All available resources are spent to make sure this 10% sells within the same network. Almost nothing by comparison is spent on helping those who are building, or who could build, an enduring business. These businesses, in turn, tend to acquire many, many jobs, books, and practices. Growth by acquisition is the foundation for most businesses' marketing strategies, and such growth demands the recruitment of younger, next-generation talent, that is, today's book builders.

We have been pressing the argument for some time now that the focus of the practice management personnel at the IBDs and custodians should be on the vast majority of independent advisors who do nothing but wither on the vine, who choose death by attrition, or who make no plans at all. The question(s) should be: How do we help these advisors and all the clients they serve? How do we get more advisors to sell to someone (preferably a business or a firm) who can serve their clients for more than one generation?

We don't think the answer, or the problem, centers on value or valuation, at least not in the sense that a higher value or sales price will cause every book and practice owner to sell. Independent advisory books and

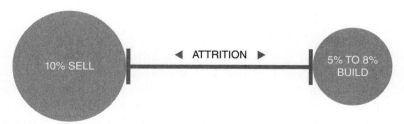

FIGURE 1.4   End of Career Transition Strategies for Independent Advisors

practices already command a value of two to three times that of most other professional service models. We think the problem is twofold:

1. The abysmal payment terms that create a total disconnect between the valuation opinion and the actual realization of that value years later.
2. The failure to create a formal, written, executable plan (whether an exit plan or a succession plan) early enough to benefit from it.

Slowly but certainly, advisors have been coming to grips with the notion that their practices have value, above and beyond the cash flow generated every month and every year—in many cases, a great deal of value. Most advisors have a plan to realize the cash flow element for as long as they can work, but most advisors do not have a plan for how to realize their equity value *and* ensure that their clients are taken care of for the rest of their lives as opposed to the career length of their advisor.

Revenue sharing agreements, one of the most commonly used "solutions" by book and practice owners interested in selling, deserve at least part of the blame. These simple two- or three-page agreements, provided by the practice management personnel at an independent broker-dealer or custodian at no cost, are a favorite of buyers. First of all, these buyers, with their broker-dealer or custodian's full support, bypass the competitive buyer-to-seller ratio in the open market, and enjoy starting and finishing with a 1:1 ratio. Second, buyers pay nothing down, bear no obligation to perform, and simply pay for what they choose to keep, sharing the revenue with the seller for a period of three or four years. Agreeing to pay 50% of everything earned from a seller's list of clients for four years might sound like a multiple of two times, but in fact, most sellers will only realize about 60 to 70 cents on the dollar, which represents the clients and cash flow the buyer elects, in his or her sole discretion, to retain and work with. Essentially, the buyer is able to cherry-pick the best clients and pay out on that select group only. Add in the fact that there is basically no liability or ongoing responsibility on the buyer's part. If something happens to them, whether a heart attack, stroke, car accident, early retirement, and so on, and they don't come back to work, the seller gets 50% of nothing.

With terms that belie the actual value proposition, perhaps it is no wonder that sellers simply retain control of their own client base and cash flow until they simply cannot do the work any longer. Selling what is left, or simply passing the remaining clients off to a friend or colleague is the attrition route.

A formal three- to five-year exit plan can help to ensure that a practice owner considers cash flow and equity, tied to realistic growth rates and profitability levels and tax rates. Armed with a solid plan backed up with good and reliable information and data can help independent advisors make good, long-term decisions and implement a transition strategy that not only meets their needs, but performs as it should. Whether an owner decides to build and grow, sell, or enjoy the cash flow for as long as possible as the practice winds down, that decision should be based on sound information and a plan.

One of the purposes of this publication is to help job/book owners learn what practice owners know and do, and how to realize the value of what they've built. In turn, practice owners can learn from what business owners know and do. In the course of our explorations, we'll examine practical, relatively easy steps to improve valuation results *and* the actual realization of those numbers through knowledge, planning, and execution.

We will also take the time to focus on the future and the major changes that are starting to affect the M&A process through the bank financing channel. Over the past 20 years, almost every transaction between a buyer and a seller of a book, a practice, or a business, has relied on seller financing. Imagine buying or selling a house if the seller had to extend a land sales contract to complete the sale. The marketplace would be fairly limited, but that is an accurate description of where things are or have been most recently in this industry. With the advent of bank financing options, many aspects of the M&A process are changing. Sellers now have the option to largely cash out and be done at closing if they have a plan and build properly and smartly for this purpose, and find a worthy buyer from a pool of qualified applicants.

In sum, there are many choices equal to or better than attrition. Learn, investigate, and make a decision, but don't let what you've built fade away because you think you don't have a better choice. You do. Remember, you pay good money to your broker-dealer or custodian. Demand that they support your efforts to build or to actually realize the full value you've spent a lifetime growing.

WHAT IS BEING SOLD?

In the 1970s, I was a teenager living in the Midwest and I was bored much of the time. I lived for the *Wide World of Sports* on Saturday afternoons. One such afternoon, I was introduced to a mesmerizing figure, a daredevil named Evel Knievel.

In 1971, Mr. Knievel made news, and my whole summer, when he announced his intention to jump a remote section of the Snake River Canyon on a rocket-propelled motorcycle—the X-2 Skycycle! Judging by the black-and-white pictures in the newspaper, it looked more like a rocket with wheels than a motorcycle. This was exciting stuff. All it needed was a fearless pilot and that slot was filled.

From the red, white, and blue leather jumpsuits to the Las Vegas–style production and choreography of his incredible feats, this guy was fascinating. He was brave. He was an entrepreneur. He was a modern-day superhero, and he could do things others only dreamed about. Or at least he could try. . . .

Sadly, nothing about the Snake River Canyon jump actually worked. ABC Sports declined to pay the price Mr. Knievel's team demanded, so the event ended up on closed-circuit TV, which in those days no one I knew could afford. And the X-2 Skycycle wasn't actually rocket-powered. Instead, it used a more pedestrian steam-powered concept. It was probably closer to a carpet cleaner than a rocket! Whatever it was, or wasn't, it didn't work. Fortunately, no one or nothing was killed—just my imagination.

The gap between those who own a job or a book or a practice on one side, and those who build a business or a firm on the other, is about equal to a leap over the Snake River Canyon, or so it seems. In fact, things have changed and for the better. We now collectively have the technology and the experience to succeed on a regular basis. Even better, there's a bridge not too far away from that launch ramp that will accommodate anyone who wants to make the trip in a more professional and conventional manner! It takes some time, but if you want to get to the other side, it can be done. Not everyone does, and that's okay, but understand that such a decision will affect your choices and options at career end.

The chasm between the ownership levels in this industry is best expressed and understood as the balance, or imbalance, between "revenue strength" and "enterprise strength." If you're selling or buying primarily revenue strength, you're selling or buying clients. If what you're selling or buying has a balance between revenue strength and enterprise strength, you're selling or buying a business. There is a huge difference. Which side of the canyon are you on? Are you building a book, or a business? What does the acquisition opportunity present? Are you sure?

By our estimate, more than 9 out of 10 advisors focus primarily or exclusively on revenue strength elements. The analysis of revenue strength covers an array of benchmarks, but focuses on the areas of revenue production, cash flow quality, and pricing competitiveness. The goal is relatively simple: increase the number of good clients (and recurring revenue, if possible) and hang on to all of it. (See Figure 1.5.)

Most independent financial service professionals understand how to build revenue strength. The challenge in building a practice to the level of an enduring business lies in creating a balance between revenue strength and enterprise strength. Enterprise strength is a term we use to refer to an advisory business's legal, organizational, compensation, and profit structures, all elevated to a high and sustainable level.

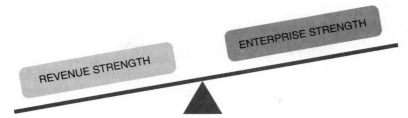

FIGURE 1.5 Most Advisors Focus on Revenue Strength Elements

Increasing both components (revenue strength and enterprise strength) may seem like a sensible and obvious approach to increasing value and equity, but the process can be quite challenging. For example, increasing the number of clients and retaining those relationships as a business's leadership ages may require a substantial investment in staffing, training, retention, and operational capacity, while pursuing a strategy of significantly increasing the revenue generated per client may require a change in culture, deliverables, skill-sets, and operational systems. In either case, any increase in revenue that is accomplished by emphasizing one strategy or the other does not directly correlate to an equal or proportional increase in the equity value of a financial services business, nor its ability to sustain the rate of growth and to realize that value upon transition. Sometimes, founders simply don't have the skill-set, the time, or the drive to make the change(s).

In fairness, almost every advisor must start out with a singular focus on revenue—a financial services professional, especially on the independent side, has to make money and grow in order to survive. The art of production, learning how to give great advice, and sell appropriate products and services is how advisors make a living, and for that reason, revenue strength is the principal component in determining the value of a privately held, independent financial services job/book or practice. Building revenue strength is almost intuitive to advisors, but rarely is it balanced by enterprise strength. (See Figure 1.6.)

A significant imbalance between revenue strength (usually the stronger of the two) and enterprise strength (often the weaker of the two) at career

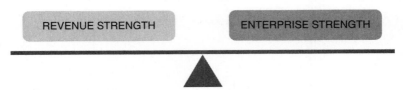

FIGURE 1.6 The Goal: A Balance between Revenue Strength and Enterprise Strength

end is best solved with an exit plan. In other words, sell the book or practice to a business or a firm where the imbalance can be quickly resolved and is an immediate value-add. A preference to build or enhance enterprise strength is best addressed internally with a succession plan.

This issue also bears on the valuation process. Revenue strength models (jobs/books and practices) have one owner and really aren't built for profits. The focus is on production. Accordingly, advisors need to take a different approach to determine value, especially when most buyers are twice the size in terms of value and cash flow of the sellers they acquire and, as a rule, purchase assets, not stock or profits. At this level, what is being sold is a revenue stream and not much more; the focus of a valuation should be on the top line. Businesses and firms, in contrast, are built for profitability and require a valuation approach that focuses on the bottom line. Here, what's being sold includes all the infrastructure, including expenses, liabilities, and even debt in some cases.

The first point to consider is this: if you're buying revenue strength and nothing more, you will value it and pay for it very differently than if you are acquiring enterprise strength *and* revenue strength. That is the difference between jobs/books and practices on the one side, and businesses and firms on the other side. Buyers, your acquisition strategy, valuation approach, and application of payment terms and financing must adapt to the opportunity and specifically to what you are buying. Sellers, understand what you're selling and factor the appropriate methods into your forecasted results.

The closing point is that sellers *can* build enterprise strength over the last 5 to 10 years of their career in order to generate better value and a wider array of choices at or near career end. Alternatively, prospective sellers can choose not to embark on such a journey and simply sell earlier, albeit for less value. Obtaining a formal valuation and learning from the process and talking to a qualified consultant can help you make a smart and practical decision.

ORGANIZING THE MARKETPLACE

In 1999, FP Transitions was founded to create a systematic way for a seller to find a buyer of a financial services or advisory practice and to efficiently handle the many details of selling, documenting, realizing value, and successfully transitioning the client relationships. Since its founding, FP Transitions has successfully sold and transitioned over 1,500 financial service or advisory books, practices, businesses, and firms. The marketplace is now organized and it works.

The part of this organizational effort that many advisors overlook is that selling, as a strategy, was the necessary first step to establishing and proving the concept of *value* in this industry. That was an incredibly important accomplishment. But while value has been proven, it still may not be *realized* because certain elements in this marketplace have conflicting agendas. Buyers and sellers need to be aware not only of where to find each other, but how the seller's choice of "selling venue" may also affect the realities of value and payment terms, for better or worse.

The seller's regulatory structure will likely shape the acquisition process and the venue or marketplace where they, as a seller, can be found. In other words, a fee-only seller will likely start their buyer search within their primary, current custodial network, even though RIAs/IARs might work with more than one custodian. A fee-based, FINRA-regulated seller with an independent broker-dealer (IBD) will tend to look for a buyer within the same IBD network. Being independent means having lots of choices and flexibility, at least theoretically. As a matter of practicality, however, these choices tend to be limited and center on one of these primary selling venues:

- An **open market** sale, defined as an unrestricted sale of a book, practice, or business that could take place, at the owner's discretion, either within the same IBD/custodian or outside of the seller's broker-dealer/custodial network. This venue provides a very competitive marketing opportunity for sellers to find the best strategic or economic buyer for what they've built and how they've built it, at best value and best terms. It is effectively a national search for the best qualified buyer, who may or may not be local.

  FP Transitions operates and continues to organize the open marketplace for independent advisors. It is what we do, at least in part. But FP Transitions also operates and supports several closed market systems because IBDs strongly prefer this approach (that's a kind way of saying that most IBDs do not like the choice afforded to sellers through an open market platform).

- A **closed market** sale is one in which a book, practice, or business is offered only to certain buyers because of a limitation imposed by a third party, such as a contractual agreement with a broker-dealer, or simply because that is the seller's preference. Typically, all of the potential buyers are with the same IBD or custodian, which ultimately means less competition and, at least conceptually, an easier and faster transition in terms of buyer selection, documentation, and client/asset transfers. This venue can also result in a lower price on less favorable terms when compared to the ultracompetitive open market process, but it really depends on how well it is run and who is running it, and the number of participants in the marketplace.

Handled professionally, there is nothing wrong with a closed market venue. The problem is, not all closed market venues are handled professionally or have sufficient scale to do the job right. The reality of the closed market and bulletin board systems discussed further on requires that we introduce a new term of art at this point, that of a "predatory buyer." Predatory buyers buy everything and anything with complete disdain for "market value" and professional deal terms. They're good at what they do and often employ static multiples of revenue or earnings and deal terms that create a "heads I win, tails you lose" approach. Worse, they have the blessing of their IBDs/custodians because they keep the clients and assets in the network, regardless of the monetary loss to an exiting/retiring advisor. Sellers need to be aware and understand that despite a long and close relationship with a single IBD, when it comes to selling and retiring, your agenda may no longer match theirs.

- A **bulletin board** is an online meeting place that typically provides few if any other benefits—no formal valuation (other than a free online system using a proprietary formula and with no supporting database), no documentation or qualified authority other than a list of third-party providers you can hire on your own. The point is to expose prospective sellers to prospective buyers, which is certainly important and relevant. The process may also be free of charge. Many IBDs and custodians operate their own bulletin board systems.

Bulletin boards tend to list everything and anything, and sellers usually list for free, so the sellers may or may not be qualified and properly valued or serious. Prospective sellers are the bait and they tend to attract a lot of paying, hopeful buyers. For the most part, no harm, no foul. But do be aware that some bulletin boards are run and organized by recruiters and predatory buyers, and confidentiality tends to be a low priority.

Sellers should be aware that many buyers within an IBD network, or within a closed market or bulletin board site, feel they should be entitled to special pricing because if it appears that an advisor "has to sell," the response might be that the buyer is doing the seller a *favor* by stepping in and helping out with a quick and easy sale. Once established, this dynamic can be quite difficult for a selling advisor to withdraw from, especially when engaged with a very experienced buyer.

- A **private transaction** is the case in which a seller decides to sell to a friend or an associate or someone provided by the IBD's or custodian's practice management team. It may also be the result of answering one of those acquisition-oriented letters you and everyone else at the practice level or above receives in the mail a couple of times a year. A private transaction represents a *handpicked* buyer in some sense and is almost always within the same IBD or custodial network. This is the process not of ending with a 1:1 buyer-to-seller ratio, but starting with a 1:1 buyer-to-seller ratio.

As a general rule, bigger buys smaller. Statistically, only about one fourth of the buyers are the same size or smaller than the seller they are acquiring, and private transactions make up the bulk of these sales. As you might expect, the value and payment terms are somewhat compromised when compared to those of a competitive buying environment, but this approach gets points for being quick and easy and "friendly."

Selling advisors tend to choose just one selling avenue until it is successful or the possibilities have been exhausted. The problem isn't that prospective sellers in this industry need more than one venue to achieve success—they don't. The problem is that too many sellers don't understand the limitations and end results of their choices. Speed, efficiency, and confidentiality are all important issues, but most sellers assess the ability of a chosen selling venue to deliver on these issues from unreliable sources, or sources with an agenda of their own. The continuing point that we'll make in this book, to every advisor and to their IBDs and custodians and the practice management personnel who are hired to assist in this process, is that sellers need support. They need a steady, reliable narrator to guide them on this onetime journey.

Buyers, don't despair. A smart and informed seller will succeed 100% of the time and that should mean more, good, affordable acquisition opportunities in which the clients are willing participants.

EXIT PLANS VERSUS SUCCESSION PLANS VERSUS CONTINUITY PLANS

It is common for advisors and practice management consultants to equate the terms "exit planning," "succession planning," and "continuity planning" and to use these terms interchangeably. However, these terms are very different, providing unique benefits and demanding different levels of preparation and investment to achieve the desired outcome. As an independent advisor, you need to understand and correctly apply the terminology to navigate this area and achieve your specific goals.

Here are the working definitions that apply to the independent financial services/advisory industry, each with a brief explanation.

Exit Plan

An **exit plan** results in a transaction with either an external buyer or an internal buyer, but the commonality is that the transaction is completed in one

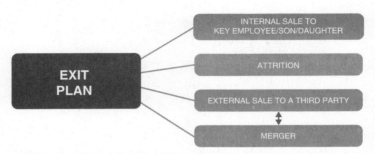

FIGURE 1.7   Exit Planning Strategies

step—usually not suddenly, just completely. External buyers usually have a very similar model but are about twice the size and value of the seller, while an internal buyer is someone you hired and trained, know, and trust. When sold externally, which is most common at the book and practice levels, the book/practice comes to an end, with a larger, similar practice or business or firm taking over the seller's duties and responsibilities. Documentation for a job or book is often a basic revenue sharing agreement, while an exit plan at the practice level typically revolves around an asset purchase agreement. There are four primary exit plans or strategies, as shown in Figure 1.7.

The most common exit plan involving transfer of ownership and control is a complete sale to a third party, and is often called a "merger" whether or not the legal and tax requirements support the definition of a statutory merger. Exit plans can be structured to last for five or six years, or be substantially completed in three to six months. These and other variations are explained later in this book.

Relatively few exit plans involve internal sales, which is best explained by the structure of the ownership levels. There just aren't many licensed and capable employees at the job/book or practice levels ready to step in and commit to the acquisition process. Internal exit plans at the practice level, if that is a choice, tend to be complete sales, all at one time, to one key employee, or a son or daughter. At the business and firm levels of ownership, internal sales are the preferred and common choice, but the methodology and documentation shifts to succession planning and follows a more gradual sale/purchase of stock or membership interest over many years.

Succession Plan

A **succession plan** is a design for growth and endurance. The process of succession planning builds on top of an existing practice, business, or firm and gradually and seamlessly transitions ownership and leadership internally to

FIGURE 1.8   A Succession Plan

the next generation of advisors, often called a "successor team" (Figure 1.8). The founding owner in a succession plan is not a "seller"—they're a partner or a shareholder, and long-term, sustainable growth powered by multiple generations of owners is the number one goal. A succession plan means your business or firm will continue after your career comes to an end. Most succession plans include the founder's continuing assistance and presence in the day-to-day operations for several years beyond the traditional retirement age. Documentation for a succession plan is more complex, but centers on a stock purchase agreement(s), or the equivalent for a limited liability company.

There are an infinite number of options available under the succession planning category, but all center on a gradual internal transition. No two succession plans are exactly the same. Like hiring an architect to design your dream house, the outside reflects the people on the inside and their unique goals, time frames, talents, and preferences. Every succession plan must be customized to fit the specific fact pattern at issue. It is a challenging process and it requires a skilled team of consultants to make it work. It is about building an enduring business.

Jobs/books and at least smaller practices do not need and probably cannot reasonably hope to construct a formal succession plan, absent a serious, long-term investment of time and money into the process. Larger, stronger practices, businesses, or firms can and should choose either an exit plan or a succession plan, perhaps both, depending on the circumstances. A succession plan certainly doesn't mean the business will last forever. It is a distinct possibility that the second or third generation of ownership (which came to pass through a succession plan) will choose to merge the business or sell it when the time is right. For this purpose, they will need an exit plan.

A sale of an advisor's book or practice results from the inability or failure to build a sustainable business. That's not bad, just reality. An airplane flight isn't a failure because it doesn't achieve orbit—that isn't what that vessel was designed to do. An exit plan should be required of almost every independent advisor who is not building an enduring business model.

The exit plans and succession plans discussed up to this point generally presume that the founder or primary owner(s) is alive, well, and capable of choosing what comes next—that isn't always the case, especially in an aging industry dominated by single owners. Sometimes life intervenes and the next

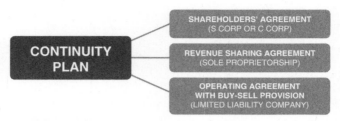

FIGURE 1.9   A Continuity Plan

step is a bit more sudden. Addressing death or disability is the role of a continuity plan, actually a subset of an exit plan or a succession plan for those who own a business or firm.

Continuity Plan

A **continuity plan** is usually a formal, written contract that assures a seamless transfer of control and responsibility in the event of a *sudden* departure from the practice or business of any of its owners, young or old, and whether by choice or through termination of employment, a partnership dispute, and certainly death or disability (Figure 1.9). The common terms applied to a continuity agreement are a shareholders' agreement (as with a corporation), a buy-sell agreement, or even an operating agreement (for use in an LLC). The event triggering a continuity agreement may be unplanned, but the solution should never be.

It is a bit of a misnomer to think of providing a "continuity plan" for a single-owner book or practice. Legally, when a one-owner model is transferred by a revenue sharing arrangement or an asset sale, it comes to an end. In reality, the continuity plan triggers a sale, which is a perfectly fine outcome regardless of the means. The clients, assets, obligations, and such may continue to be handled by a new advisor, but that advisor is not continuing what the former advisor built, at least in the sense of an ongoing enterprise. That is an important distinction and part of what separates books and practices from businesses and firms.

If you've already built a multigenerational business or are on the road to doing so, your continuity plan will derive from your succession plan. An internal ownership track, once implemented and in place, is the single best continuity plan available as clients' needs are addressed by the other principals who are invested in the same business. For the vast majority of advisors, it works the other way around—continuity is the first planning problem to solve because it poses the most immediate and serious threat to a lifetime of work, value, and the clients' well-being. For this reason, continuity planning is best thought of as a dress rehearsal for the exit planning or succession planning process.

Job/book owners and practice owners, groups dominated by a single advisor or single owner, often tend to enter into a very basic, even rudimentary, continuity agreement to address what happens to their clients and their value in the event of sudden death or disability. The solution set often exists in the form of a simple two- or three-page revenue sharing agreement provided by the practice management personnel at an independent broker-dealer or custodian. In the event of an owner's death or disability, the "buyer" or continuity partner will typically pay a percentage of every dollar received for three to five years and the "seller" or the seller's family/estate suffers the same disadvantages we discussed earlier under revenue sharing agreements: nothing down, all ordinary income tax rates, no guarantees. Sometimes, many times, this can be better than nothing, but that is setting the bar pretty low.

The bigger problem is that the IBDs and custodians often add "retirement" to the list of triggering events (in addition to the basic "death and disability" provisions), making this simple document set an *exit* plan as well and taking the book or practice off the market. If you're a willing continuity partner/buyer, good for you—you've just reduced a 50:1 buyer-to-seller ratio to 1:1 and now you can dictate price and terms to an eventual seller. That's smart, at least in the near term. If you're a prospective seller of a job/book or a small practice, this *might* be a good course of action, as your choices are limited, but do so with your eyes wide open. Remember, what's in your broker-dealer/custodian's best interest may or may not be in yours.

Let's shift gears and get back to what you can do to improve your end-game strategy. Whether you're considering an exit plan, a succession plan, or a continuity plan, the operative term is this: *planning*. We're not talking about an idea, or a developing thought in the back of your mind or, worse, an impulsive decision after a bad day or bad economic news report. Take the time to lay out a formal plan, do the math, and decide years beforehand what makes the most sense for you and your clients and your staff. Gather the information and expertise to evaluate your options and develop your best strategy going forward. Then execute that plan in a professional manner and adjust once a year or as needed.

A formal plan under any one or more of these umbrellas should include these fundamentals, all committed to writing and back-tested with a spreadsheet that assesses the plan on an after-tax basis tied to what you've built and how you've built it:

- A formal, annual valuation to assess and monitor equity value (and any decline in that value)

- A complete benchmarking analysis based on reliable data
- A review of current organization and entity structures and the impact on an eventual sale
- An assessment of the most likely payment structure and best tax strategy
- A review of the bank financing element and its possible application to your situation (covered in depth in Chapter 7)
- A plan for finding the "best match" and a determination of whether that is likely to be within the same broker-dealer network or not (for RIAs, the best choice or addition of a custodian)
- Preparation and retention of key staff members before the sale and after the sale
- A continuity plan to protect everyone's interests in the event of the death or disability of the owner before a sale or the readiness of an internal team of successors

I used to work for a curmudgeonly senior judge back in my law school days and one of his favorite expressions, especially to young lawyers who tended to overthink everything, was "This ain't rocket science!" Well, the combined legal, tax, regulatory, and cash flow structures that underlie an exit plan, a succession plan, and/or a continuity plan for a practice or business or firm worth a million dollars or more structured within an S corporation, a C corporation, or an LLC in this highly regulated industry—this *is* rocket science. It takes some real work, education, thinking, and planning to develop a sound and practical strategy. Give yourself time to do the job right. Don't be afraid to ask for help. And, above all else, do not expect to solve all of this with a three-page do-it-yourself form. Your clients deserve better, and so do you.

THE PLANNING CONTINUUM

So where to start? Begin with an accurate assessment of what you've built. Do you own a job or a book, a practice, a business, or a firm? Depending on what you've built to date, what is your goal for the future? Do you want to grow? Do you want to build your practice into a business? Do you simply want to earn a good living and sustain your current income as a book or practice owner for another 5 to 10 years without the complexities of taking on partners or new employees? Or do you want to retire on the job and make your business work for you? There is no wrong answer, only questions that go unasked. You can fix that.

For everyone not settling for the attrition route, let's put the planning process into context. In a perfect world, starting at about age 50, follow these steps to determine the best and safest path forward—steps that apply to both buyers and sellers:

Build or adjust supporting infrastructure (entity structure, organization, staffing, compensation, profitability) to support your goals

- Obtain a formal valuation (don't guess)
- Perform an annual benchmarking exercise to assess strengths and weaknesses
- Track your annual revenue growth rates on a five-year compounded basis
- Reassess your compensation structure if your profitability level is below 15% of gross revenue
- Assess regulatory environment/IBD status. Would a standalone RIA be a better model now, or in the future?

Protect what you've built

- Create a continuity plan
- Do not tie the buy-out valuation formula to a multiple of anything
- Don't settle for "better than nothing" as a solution to your continuity plan
- Provide for an adequate funding mechanism (life insurance/lump sum disability insurance/bank financing) to support your continuity plan
- Consider methods for improving the reliability and efficacy of your continuity plan (i.e., an internal ownership track)

Plan for transition of ownership and/or leadership

- Consider internal options (succession planning)
- Consider external options (exit planning)
- Consider a merger (an enormous field of possibilities, as you'll read further on)
- Consider advantages/detriments of an attrition strategy

Make a plan to realize value

- Attrition (cash flow only)
- Sale (equity only)
- Succession (cash flow + equity)
- Realize value at long-term capital gains tax rates at all levels of ownership

*Learn how to utilize bank financing and strategic debt
in a professional manner to support your planning
process*

- Fuel growth and support continuity planning with a working capital loan
- Utilize buy-in capital to support succession planning
- Consider acceleration options as soon as your team is ready

It is okay if you start the planning process later, maybe much later, than age 50. The takeaway is to start planning in a formal manner. Some exit plans can be laid out and implemented in 90 days, and some take five years or more. Just start planning and commit the process to paper based on accurate information as soon as you're able. Most advisors plan to work well past the traditional retirement age anyway, so start when you're ready. Just remember that the earlier you begin the planning process, the more choices you'll have when the time comes.

CHAPTER 2

Value and Valuation Fundamentals

AN OVERVIEW

Most independent advisors have some idea of what their practice is worth. Whatever the method used, the concept of value represents one of the largest, if not *the* largest and most valuable assets an advisor owns. Guessing at value is okay, right up until the time decisions and plans need to be made. There comes a time when plus or minus a hundred thousand dollars or so doesn't cut it. Engaging in any form of M&A activity is one of those times.

There is a lot of information in this chapter and the following chapter on value and valuation, some of it technical, some of it academic, and much of it practical. The goal of most advisors when the subject of valuation arises is to get to the *right* answer as quickly and inexpensively as possible and with the least amount of hassle. That goal is achievable, though the truth of the matter is that if you own anything larger and more complex than a book, you will likely need some help with the valuation process.

Valuations are performed for a variety of reasons. In addition to acquisitions, advisors might have a valuation performed for gift and estate purposes, for marital, partnership, or corporate dissolutions, for a sale of a minority interest in their corporation or limited liability company to a son, daughter, or a group of next-generation employees. Because of the differing objectives and standards of value for each of these situations, the valuation approach and methodology for each purpose can differ. Purpose drives value!

It is quite possible, even likely, that different standards of value and different valuation approaches and methods will produce different values when looking at the same target. That is okay and is how it is supposed to work. There is no one right approach, method, or standard that applies to every situation or that considers every possible circumstance. A valuation for the purposes of buying or selling an intangible asset such as a financial services or advisory practice will almost certainly provide a different answer, perhaps substantially different, than a valuation conducted for purposes of a divorce, a gift tax filing, or a shareholder dispute or some type of IRS-related filing. A firm that is acquiring the assets of a small practice, for example, and insists on using a discounted cash flow method under the income approach to value the acquisition opportunity, because that is the method it traditionally uses and has become comfortable with when selling equity internally, is likely making a mistake. In such an instance, the firm may be applying the wrong standard, approach, and method, as explained in more detail in the pages that follow.

This chapter is written to help advisors understand how the valuation process works from an analyst's or appraiser's perspective. The fundamentals, including standards of value, traditional valuation approaches, and the methods applied under each approach that are most applicable to independent financial service and advisory models, are a key component. Other key concepts include which valuation approach and method works best when buying or selling stock or a minority interest in a going concern, as opposed to executing an asset sale or absorbing a seller's practice into a buyer's business. We also will discuss how and when a rule of thumb approach (such as multiple of revenue or earnings) makes sense, and when it does not. Finally, advisors should become familiar with the credentials or designations that qualified analysts and appraisers earn so that qualifications can be quickly assessed. These value and valuation fundamentals will help every advisor in the M&A space understand what questions to ask, how things work, and why, in most cases, you *can't do this at home.*

Our goal here is not to teach advisors how to perform a valuation or even how to arrive at the specific value they might be willing to sell for, or buy for. The goal also is not to intimidate the average reader, though some of the information might do just that. Certain aspects of the valuation process are complicated, far more than most advisors know, and include a lot of assumptions and opinions—more than just the final number. The pages that follow are intended to provide insight into the actual valuation process. The end goal is to help prospective buyers and sellers of an independent model understand the basic but essential information needed to make decisions, create realistic plans, and to know what questions to ask.

Building on this information, Chapter 3 subsequently explains exactly how to value the assets of a book, practice, or business for the express purposes of buying it or selling it, as part of an advisor's exit plan. If you just want to know the right standard of value, the best valuation approach, and the best method to get the right answer for M&A purposes as a practice or business owner, skip to Chapter 3. And if you want to know the typical deal structures, payment terms, and the like that support this valuation method, Chapter 7 has the details. Consider this as a "fast map" to the specific answers some advisors want.

Principles of valuation have been constant for many years, but the independent financial services and advisory industry is changing rapidly all around us. This chapter and the next are aimed at bridging the gap between accepted tradition and practical solutions anchored by the reality of an active and efficient marketplace. The M&A space is still evolving, but it is much better organized than at any point in its history. Today, there is a proper way to value an advisory practice to determine its selling price and to quickly resolve the issue of valuation so that the parties can focus on the other critical attributes of a transaction and get the job done right the first time.

WHAT CREATES VALUE?

At its most basic level, the value of an independent financial services or advisory model lies in its client relationships. From this starting point, the discussion logically progresses to the revenue derived from those client relationships and, of course, the transferability of those relationships and that revenue. If, for some reason, the clients cannot or will not be transferred to another advisor, there is no inherent value from the buyer's perspective. These things are important, and fairly obvious.

So what *really* creates value? Why do 50 buyers line up for every book or practice to try to convince the seller that they're the right one? What is it that so many prospective buyers see when looking at a practice that another independent advisor has chosen to sell and walk away from? The answers to these questions suggest that "value" may include much more than a list of clients and the related trailing 12 months of revenue. The starting point is to look at the M&A process, certainly the valuation process, through the eyes of a buyer.

This industry is different from other professional service models. Independent advisory practices generally have predictable, recurring revenue, which creates predictable, recurring overhead. Sustainable growth rates tend to be in the neighborhood of 7% to 15% annually, sometimes higher. Overhead is not only predictable, it tends to be lower than in most other professional service models. Value, or selling price, is typically two to three times as much as in a similarly sized CPA, doctor, dentist, attorney, or architectural practice. Clients, especially when tied to a specific advisor and affiliated with an independent broker-dealer or custodian, are transferable, in a measurable and reliable way. These things add up.

As Senator Everett Dirksen (1896–1969) once famously never said, "A billion here, a billion there; pretty soon it begins to add up to real money." (Apparently, the senator once attributed the statement to having been misquoted, but thought it sounded so good he never bothered to deny it!) My father repeated the statement at the dinner table so often and so fervently that I knew it must be true. The point is, all these things do add up, and for an independent advisor, it adds up to a lot. But *the advisor* we're talking about here isn't the seller, it is those who want to be buyers.

Look at the average financial advisory practice as a *business* owner does, relying on the specific definitions from Chapter 1 in the process. By the time most *practice* owners sell, their revenue streams have often become stagnant. Real profitability is an afterthought since every dollar ultimately ends up passing through to the owner anyway. Clients, standing on a bedrock of trust, are loyal to the end. These same clients, however, often stop referring new business and investing additional assets as they see their sole advisor grow a little older and a little grayer. Practice growth tapers off, income declines, and when the markets become more turbulent than memory can recall, it becomes time to sell. So how does one measure the value of a practice that isn't growing, or may even be in decline?

One common way is to look to the recent revenue history, *take a snapshot* of the last quarter or the last year, and project that into the future. Common tools often include a multiple of revenue or even a more basic revenue sharing arrangement. Another common tactic is to significantly discount the seller's value and penalize him or her for not building a business of enduring value, or for not selling on the way up.

We have the benefit of observing the interactions between buyers and sellers on a national, open market platform, and every year we watch an increasingly large group of experienced buyers acquire one or two practices or businesses a year—basically, whenever they want to. These buyers know how to "buy value." Here's an example:

One buyer in particular acquires a practice through FP Transitions about once a year, usually a practice that has stopped growing, or may even be in decline. Within one or two years, they have it growing at 20% to 25% annually, every single time. Following the acquisition, the buyer's team meets with all of the professional advisors to the largest of the newly acquired clients and coordinates duties and roles with the clients' estate planning attorney, CPA or tax preparer, business or corporate attorney, insurance agent, and so on. In addition, the buyer's business creates a clear "value-add" by providing a choice of advisors to work with, and a larger staff and array of services than the smaller practice owner could ever have achieved. Having purchased the seller's assets, the seller's cost structure is eliminated in favor of the buyer's. In this example, the buyer recognizes that the cost of client acquisition justifies the price of purchasing a practice, even one headed for stagnation.

Experienced buyers provide one more important lesson: don't attempt to underprice the market or consistently offer substandard payment terms in an effort to find the best opportunities. In a competitive market full of smart and experienced buyers, sellers are quick to learn that when they receive a poor offer, there's another qualified buyer, or two, in line. Factor that into the process as the discussion moves to the technical aspects of value and valuation.

STANDARDS OF VALUE

Every appraisal report or valuation engagement should specifically identify and define the applicable "standard of value." The term "value," however, is relative to the circumstances and is not, as a single word or concept, considered to be specific enough when it comes to a formal valuation process. When you decide to sell your car, for example, the standards of value that you need to consider include trade-in value, suggested retail value, private party value, and certified preowned value, among others: one car, but at least four different values, depending on the purpose. Given the specific purpose, all four answers as to value are correct, even though all the answers may be different.

A valuation expert will need to determine the level, or standard of value, that a buyer or seller is seeking in order to properly consider the relevant facts and circumstances and to deploy the right set of tools (valuation approaches and methods) for the job. In the independent financial services industry, there are four common standards of value. The following list, while not exhaustive, is what most valuation analysts encounter on a daily basis when talking to independent financial advisors.

Most Probable Selling Price

MPSP is the standard applicable to the majority of the valuation work FP Transitions is hired to perform. This standard of value is defined by the International Business Brokers Association as "The price for the assets intended for sale which represents the total consideration most likely to be established between a seller and a buyer considering compulsion on the part of either buyer or seller, and potential financial, strategic, or nonfinancial benefits to the seller and probable buyers."[1]

---

[1] IBBA University, a division of International Business Brokers Association, Inc., Introduction to Pricing Small Businesses. Course 220 V2.1 2006.

This standard of value reflects the reality of the marketplace and is the standard or type of value applicable to books, practices, or businesses that might sell to a third-party buyer. This is the standard used in FP Transitions' Comprehensive Valuation Report, explained in detail in Chapter 3.

Fair Market Value

FMV is a standard of value set forth in IRS Revenue Ruling 59-60, and is defined as "The price at which the property would change hands between a willing buyer and a willing seller when the former is not under any compulsion to buy and the latter is not under any compulsion to sell, both parties having reasonable knowledge of relevant facts."[2]

Revenue Ruling 59-60 represents the 60th revenue ruling from 1959, which means that this ruling has been around for a long time. The relevance of this ruling is found in its clear and authoritative guidance on how to properly value privately held businesses. Revenue rulings are public administrative rulings by the IRS that are deemed applicable to particular factual situations. There are several important revenue rulings that relate to the valuation of business interests, but none are more insightful or widely cited and utilized by the valuation profession than Revenue Ruling 59-60. Even though this revenue ruling is now well over 50 years old, it is still authoritative as to the methods and factors to be considered in valuing the stock of privately held practices. Although initially presented for use in estate and gift tax calculations, its usage has spread and it is now relied upon in the valuation of privately held businesses.

However, it is worth noting that this standard of value is still more of an academic standard than the reality of what an advisor could expect to receive if they actually sold their practice or business to a third party. The goal in applying this standard isn't to find the highest or most probable selling price; it is usually to find a middle ground, a compromise of sorts. In fact, most buyers and sellers who are participating in an open marketplace *are* under some level of compulsion to buy or sell. If compulsion were not present, it stands to reason that a seller would never accept anything less than absolutely favorable deal terms at the highest value from his or her point of view. The inverse of this argument is applicable to buyers. Second, having knowledge of all reasonable facts is relative.

Investment Value

Investment value is value from the perspective of a particular buyer or investor, and may include both the value of the selling stand-alone entity as

---

[2] Revenue Ruling 59-60, 1959-1 C.B. 237.

well as the value created by the strategic buyer through synergies and other means. A strategic buyer is typically willing to pay the investment value for the business because, as a result of the acquisition, the cost of goods may decrease for both firms with the value of the acquiring firm thereby increased.

Investment value is closely related to the MPSP and is used when valuing a practice for mergers or acquisitions and in some states for divorce or other litigious purposes. The primary difference that sets investment value and MPSP apart is that investment value is built on the chassis of fair market value.

Fair Value

Fair value is a rational and unbiased estimate of the potential market price of a good, service, or asset for which a market price cannot be readily determined, often because there is no established market for the asset. This standard is typically a function of state law and is often applied to cases involving divorce, partnership, or shareholder disputes. This approach considers objective factors such as supply versus demand, replacement costs, and acquisition costs, as well as subjective factors such as cost of and return on capital, risk characteristics, and individually perceived utility. Commonly, there is a willing buyer but not a willing seller.

Fair value is the standard of value used by the Financial Accounting Standards Board (FASB) in its pronouncements pertaining to business valuation. For financial reporting consistency, FASB states, "Fair value is the price that would be received to sell an asset, or paid to transfer a liability in an orderly transaction between market participants at the measurement date."[3] Fair value is a market-based measurement, rather than an entity-specific measurement, and is determined using assumptions that market participants would use in pricing the asset or liability, including assumptions about risk. As a result, an entity's intention to hold an asset or to settle or otherwise fulfill a liability is not relevant in measuring fair value.

* * *

Advisors tend to think that "value" literally means "one value" and sometimes become frustrated with valuation analysts when things become a little more complicated and questions are asked about standards, approaches, and methods. Valuation, like financial planning and wealth management, is a professional, respected, and learned vocation; there's a right way to do it and a wrong way. People can now easily obtain free financial plans online, and sometimes they don't even need to talk to a human being to do so. This

---

[3] Financial Accounting Standards Board, "Statement of Financial Accounting Standards No. 157."

doesn't mean they obtain the right answers, just that they have some kind of answers that make them feel better. In sum, advisors would be wise to follow their own advice and admonitions, especially during one of the most important times of their career.

VALUATION APPROACHES AND METHODS

Traditionally, there are three broad valuation approaches used to determine value. These approaches include the income approach, the market approach, and the asset approach. Within each approach there are various *methods* for calculating value, as explained further on. Each method brings with it specific assumptions, benefits, and limitations. Depending on the purpose of the valuation, an analyst or appraiser may utilize more than one approach and provide each result with a weighting in order to arrive at a final conclusion.

That said, let's review the traditional approaches first, and then the common methods applied under each approach second, keeping in mind the specific scope of this book—M&A activity between independent advisors.

Income Approach

The income approach is commonly recommended for valuing a financial services *business* or *firm*. This approach seeks to identify the future economic benefits to be generated by an entity and to discount those benefits due to the risk that those benefits might not be received when expected or at all. The income approach is founded on the concept that future economic benefit streams, namely net cash flows, can be forecasted and then discounted back to a present value by applying a rate of return reflecting the uncertainty or risk associated with the projections.

From the income approach, an appraiser will then typically employ either a capitalization of earnings/cash flow method or the discounted earnings/cash flow method to determine value. Each of these income methods is designed for specific purposes. Since net cash flow is the economic benefit most sought by investors, it is the preferred level of earnings used to value a business in the financial services industry. Accordingly, for the remainder of this particular section, we will refer to each method on a cash flow basis.

The point of explaining these two methods in greater detail is to help advisors understand the actual valuation process and the number of assumptions and subjective judgments that are involved. In talking to independent advisors, large and small, all across the country, there seems to be a feeling that this valuation process is like a *black box*. Buyers or sellers know what information they put into it, and they can see the number that comes out of it, but in between is a complete mystery. The part that is clear is that someone smart is in charge of the *black box*, the process is complicated, the algorithms beyond comprehension, and buyers or sellers are charged thousands and thousands of dollars to complete the analysis. The assumption advisors make is that the process is sophisticated and reliable and must provide "the right answer." Advisors, whether buying or selling, need to know what is happening and understand that a certain level of subjectivity is involved.

Capitalization of Cash Flows   The capitalization of cash flows method is typically used when the business has attained maturity or is expected to grow at a uniform rate in the future. This method assumes that the nonincome related contributions to cash flow such as working capital, capital expenditures, and debt repayment will also grow at the same long-term rate proportionally to revenues. This method is not used as frequently as the discounted cash flow method to value businesses in this industry because the underlying assumption that all financial factors of the business will grow uniformly is simply not true in most cases.

Discounted Cash Flow Method   The most commonly used method from the income approach in the financial services industry is the discounted cash flow method, or DCF. The theory supporting the DCF method is that an entity's value is equal to its expected future cash flows, discounted at an appropriate rate (to accommodate the risks to receiving that cash flow, and including an appropriate return). The result is the present cash value of the business or firm. This method is used primarily when the valuator can estimate the known or expected future changes that are not uniform, may terminate or change after a period of time for specific elements of either income, receipts, or expenditures of the business. Said more succinctly, the short-term growth in net cash flow is not expected to grow uniformly at a single rate.

The steps for calculating value of nonmarketable equity using this method are summarized as follows:

1. Review, compare, and make normalizing adjustments to financial statements of the Subject Company.
2. Calculate adjusted net cash flow to invested capital (NCFIC).
3. Develop a risk-adjusted discount rate.
4. Determine the forecast period for growth to stabilize.
5. NCFIC is then calculated for the forecasted growth.
6. Discount forecasted NCFIC to its present value using a weighted average cost of capital (WACC).

7. Determine an applicable terminal value by capitalizing the NCFIC after the forecasted growth above using the terminal growth rate and the WACC.
8. Discount terminal NCFIC using a WACC.
9. Sum the present values of the discounted forecasted cash flows and discounted terminal value.
10. To this value, the present value of the deferred tax benefits of amortized goodwill needs to be added.
11. The resulting value is the present value of future net cash flows to invested capital on a marketable basis.
12. If the source of the discount rate is from the return on publicly traded stocks, the value needs to be discounted to account for the fact that this is a privately held company.
13. Subtract interest-bearing debt.

Each of the methods from the income approach generally relies on federal income tax rates applicable to publicly traded C corporations. As a result, a value that uses these methods may be artificially reduced. If an advisor's entity structure is anything other than a C corporation (i.e., a pass-through tax conduit of any type), an adjustment needs to be made in order to recognize the benefits of a pass-through tax entity. Furthermore, to arrive at a value that best represents the value of a privately held practice that is not as liquid as a publicly traded company, an additional discount may be justified. These two concepts are very important and are often overlooked by consultants or IBDs trying to apply this method.

The income approach to valuation is a thorough and robust analysis. It takes time and an expert to do the job right, and it costs more than the approaches and methods explained further on, but there are times when this is exactly what is needed. Common examples include selling equity to one or more employees of a business or a firm, preparing for an arbitration hearing, or a courtroom setting that involves a question of value such as for a marital or partnership divorce.

Market Approach

The market approach is one of the most commonly used approaches to value a financial services book, practice, even a business sometimes, because it is a relatively easy concept for the end user to understand and apply, it is inexpensive, and it is reasonably accurate *if there is private company data to support the conclusions*. The concept is that value can be determined by comparing one company to other similar companies that have previously sold.

The market approach to business valuation is rooted in the economic principle of a fair and orderly market: that in a free market buyers will not pay more for a business, and sellers will not accept less, than the price of a comparable enterprise. This approach is similar in many respects to the "comparable sales" method used in a real estate appraisal, even though a very different transaction.

The market approach relies on reported transaction data from public companies or private companies, or both, depending on the valuation method and assignment and available, relevant data. There are several commonly applied methods under the market approach that can be used to value a financial services book, practice, or business as listed next.

Guideline Transaction Method   Under the GTM, transaction databases are used to identify sales of businesses or assets that are similar to the business being valued. The presumption is that these transactions reflect valuation multiples or market multiples that can provide an indication of the value of the subject company. When the current common stock prices of freely traded public companies are used, the method is known as the "guideline publicly traded company method." When the method uses specific transactions of sales of all or at least a controlling interest in a privately held company, it is known as the "merger and acquisition method." In both methods, the prices used are only from a few (seldom more than eight) similar and relevant public companies or private companies. For determining the value of a closely-held or family-controlled business, there can be many adjustments needed to match the data to the ownership interest being bought or sold. As applied by most valuation analysts, the GTM uses both publicly traded companies and privately held businesses in its analysis, if both levels of data provide relevant and useful comparisons.

The steps for calculating value using this method are summarized here:

1. Review, compare, and make normalizing adjustments to financial statements of the Subject Company.
2. If available, obtain transaction data of relevant comparable publicly traded companies from available databases.
3. If available, obtain transaction data of relevant comparable privately held companies from available databases.
4. Make appropriate adjustments to the comparable transaction data to ensure the subject company data is being compared on a similar basis.
5. Develop a multiple of revenue or earnings, or a range of such multiples, from market data that will be applied to the company being valued.

The accuracy and reliability of the GTM depends on the thoroughness of the comparative data being reviewed (i.e., how detailed is it and how accurately was it reported?) and the number of businesses available that are similar, or very similar, to the subject of the valuation. Transaction databases that appraisers have access to provide a mixture of both asset-based sales as well as stock sales, and there are no consistent delivery requirements placed on the submission of data by private parties, often business brokers, or intermediaries. As a result, the prices and ratios reported from these transactions can vary and are often not fully disclosed. This can make it quite difficult for an appraiser to make an *apples-to-apples* comparison. Said in a more positive manner, the market-based approaches are only as good as the underlying database of information.

Direct Market Data Method   The DMDM method is similar in many respects to the GTM, except that it relies entirely on transaction data of similar, privately held practices and businesses. **The direct market data method involves the use of actual industry sales transactions.** This market based method tends to result in the most reliable conclusion when the comparable transactions were structured similarly to the anticipated transaction expected by the buyer or seller and *if* there is sufficient information available from the supporting database, which helps to explain why relatively few valuators use this approach.

The market approach and the DMDM method is used by FP Transitions in its valuation work in support of M&A activity between buyers and sellers who are trying to understand the market prices agreed to by others in similarly structured deals. With a large and complete database of private transactions between independent advisors, the DMDM is accurate and reliable in that it reflects actual and recent market activity. The database allows FP Transitions' valuation analysts to group transactions by size, location, revenue type, regulatory structure, payment terms, tax structures, and even the standard of value with a high degree of accuracy.

Asset Approach or Asset-Based Valuation Approach

This valuation approach focuses on a company's net asset value, or the fair-market value of its total assets minus its total liabilities. The asset-based approach basically asks what it would cost to reproduce the physical business. There is some room for interpretation in the asset approach in terms of deciding which of the company's assets and liabilities to include in the valuation, and how to measure the worth of each. This valuation approach consists of multiple methods, but the two most commonly used methods are book value and adjusted net asset value.

Book Value Method   Technically, this is an accounting concept and refers to the sum of the asset accounts, net of depreciation and amortization, less the liability accounts, as shown on a balance sheet.

Adjusted Net Asset Value Method   The adjusted net asset value method removes all of the business's assets and liabilities not being used to support operations from the balance sheet and the remaining assets and liabilities are restated to their fair market value. This method is applicable when estimating the value of a nonoperating business (e.g., holding or investment companies) that has a significant amount of capital invested in its assets or a company that will not continue operations into the future and will be liquidating its assets. The limitation to this approach is that it does not account for operating earnings, making it inappropriate to use when valuing intangible assets such as goodwill. Since the client list is the primary asset of a financial services or advisory practice, this method isn't of much use in this industry.

Methods from the asset approach are often appropriate in the following situations:

- The business is considering liquidating, or going out of business.
- The business has no earnings history.
- The business's earnings cannot be reliably estimated.
- The business depends heavily on competitive contracts and there is no consistent, predictable customer base (e.g., construction companies).
- The business derives little or no value from labor or intangible assets.
- A significant portion of the business's assets are composed of liquid assets or other investments (e.g., marketable securities, real estate, mineral rights).

For the reasons stated here, the methods from the asset approach are not often called for when valuing a financial services or advisory practice or business in the M&A space.

*   *   *

It is interesting to note that both the income and the market approaches look to a marketplace for data from which to make a valuation decision. If a valuation expert has a detailed and deep database of independent books, practices, and businesses from one particular industry, why would they look to publicly traded companies and then discount or adjust back to find value? Why not just look to the direct market data? The problem is, there is only one such database of sufficient depth and detail in this industry and FP Transitions owns it, and continues to build on it. In the end, both approaches require qualified analysts and good data—but one source of data is much closer to home than the other.

Consider Table 2.1 to help you understand the application of the various valuation standards, approaches, and methods, and the degree of

TABLE 2.1 Application of Various Valuation Standards and Methods

CHARACTERISTICS / PURPOSE	CVR	SBA LOAN	100% EQUITY	SMP MINORITY	TAX FILING 100%	TAX FILING MINORITY	DISPUTED 100%	DISPUTED MINORITY
Type of Report	Calculation	Appraisal	Restricted	Restricted	Restricted	Appraisal	Appraisal	Appraisal
Level of Certification	CVA	CVA, ASA	CVA, ASA	CVA, ASA	CVA, ASA	CVA, ASA	CVA, ASA	CVA, ASA
Hours to Prepare/Report	5	10	20	30	40	60	50+	60+
Client	Owner	Lender	Owner	Owner	Owner	Owner	Owner	Owner
Other Intended Reader(s)	Owner	SBA-buyer		G2s	IRS	IRS	Court	Court
Transfer Anticipated	Y		N	Y	Y	Y	Y	Y
Asset	Y	Y		N	N	N	N	N
Shares		N		Y	Y	Y	Y	Y
Excluded Assets								
Cash & Equivalents	Y	Y	N	N	N	N	N	N
Nonoperating Assets	Y	Y	N	Y	Y	Y	Y	Y
Acct Receivable	Y	Y	N	N	N	N	N	N
Acct Payable	Y	Y	N	N	N	N	N	N
Included Assets								
Noncompete	Y	Y	?	Y	?	?	?	?
Nonsolicit	Y	Y	?	Y	?	?	?	?
Consulting	Y	Y	?	?	?	?	?	?
Employment				?	?	?	?	?
Debt Assumptions								
Seller Note % Sale Price	70%	N	N	N	N	N	N	N
Seller Note Term	5	N	N	N	N	N	N	N
Interest Rate	6%	N	N	N	N	N	N	N
Economic Conditions								
National		Y	Y	Y	Y	Y	Y	Y
Regional		Y	Y	Y	Y	Y	Y	Y
Local				Y	Y	Y	Y	Y

Industry Factors							
RMA data comparisons	Y						
IBIS World/First Research		Y	Y	Y	Y	Y	Y
Bloomberg		Y	Y	Y	Y	Y	Y
Financial Analysis							
Adjusted P&L	Y	Y	Y	Y	Y	Y	Y
Adjusted Balance Sheet		Y	Y	Y	Y	Y	Y
Net Cash Flow Historical		Y	Y	Y	Y	Y	Y
Forecasted P&L		Y	Y	Y	Y	Y	Y
Forecasted Balance Sheets		Y	Y	Y	Y	Y	Y
Forecasted Net Cash Flow		Y	Y	Y	Y	Y	Y
Comparison to Industry		Limited	Limited	Detail	Detail	Detail	Detail
Market Debt/TC		Y	Y	Y	Y	Y	Y
Working Capital		Limited	Limited	Detail	Detail	Detail	Detail
Capital Expenditures		Limited	Limited	Detail	Detail	Detail	Detail
Methodologies							
FP Transitions DMDM - (CVR)	Y	Y	Y	Y	Y	Y	Y
Single Period Capitalization	Y						
WACC	Y	Y	Y	Y	Y	Y	Y
Discounted Cash Flow	Y	Y	Y	Y	Y	Y	Y
Private Entity Discount		Y	Y	Y	Y	Y	Y
Tax Pass Through Premium		Y	Y	Y	Y	Y	Y
DLOM (Liquidity)			Y	Y	Y	Y	Y
DLOC (Control)			Y	Y	Y	Y	Y
Non-FMV Factors in CVR		Y	Y	Y	Y	Y	Y

analysis applicable to each level. Covered in this table, from left to right, is the CVR or Comprehensive Valuation Report, a valuation for SBA loan purposes, a valuation of a 100% equity interest, a valuation of a minority ownership stake for use in FP Transitions' succession management program (SMP), a valuation for IRS tax purposes, a valuation for IRS tax purposes as a minority interest, a valuation of a disputed interest, and a valuation for a disputed minority interest. Under each of these headings is the type of valuation report that is produced, the level of certification needed to produce and sign off on the valuation report, and the estimated number of hours to prepare the valuation, among other things.

THE RULE OF THUMB METHOD OF VALUATION

A rule of thumb. A multiple of revenue. A multiple of earnings. A multiple of AUM. So many variations, and so many opinions. Are they reliable? Is one method more accurate than the others? Should they even be used at all?

Professionally, at least from the vantage point of a certified valuation analyst (CVA) or an appraiser, a multiple of revenue deserves little to no weight as a reliable and accurate valuation method. Let's start with the positive aspects of this valuation method and figure out if it can work for you—there are limited circumstances where it does make sense.

The best thing about using a rule of thumb approach is that it is simple. It is easy to apply and easy to understand. In the financial services or advisory industry, the most commonly applied rule of thumb is the gross revenue multiple, or GRM. Practically, this is a market-based valuation method and is assumed by many advisors to be reasonably accurate. A multiple of AUM is no longer a useful method for this industry because of the variations in fee structures currently in use. A multiple of earnings such as EBIT or EBITDA (earnings before interest, taxes, depreciation, and amortization) or EBOC (earnings before owner's compensation) really doesn't make sense at the job/book level because these one-owner models don't aspire toward profitability. It all goes home, one way or the other. The margin of error is simply too great at the practice, business, or firm levels of ownership for this or any other rule of thumb approach.

The multiple of revenue can work well for, and should be limited to, job or book owners who are buying or selling less than $50,000 to $75,000 of recurring gross revenue or maybe twice that amount of transactional revenue out of a sole proprietorship model. At these levels, the margin of error when coupled with reasonable payment terms is acceptable to most buyers and sellers. If an advisor is selling, or buying, a job or a book that has no entity structure and no profits to speak of, primarily using a simple payment arrangement such as an earn-out or a revenue splitting mechanism (more on this later) with little or no down payment, then a multiple of gross revenue is close enough and can be the right tool for the job, no pun intended.

Over the past five years, the GRM paid by buyers to sellers for every dollar of recurring revenue in an independent financial services book (fees and trails) ranged from a low of 1.40 to a high of 3.0 times trailing 12 months recurring revenue (TTMRR), after any applicable broker-dealer override (TTMRR-BD). (See Figure 2.1.) The multiple paid by third-party buyers for every dollar of nonrecurring revenue ranged from a low of 0.00 to a high of 1.60 × TTMR-BD. That means that for the average fee-based book in this industry, the range of multiples is from 0.00 to 3.00 × TTMR-BD. The recent average GRM for recurring revenue is about 2.36 × TTMRR-BD, but it changes or drifts from year to year and reflects the current sentiment of "the crowd" or, more appropriately, the open market and leans heavily toward recurring, fee-based revenue supported by standard deal terms. In other words, sellers don't get to realistically make up, or guess at, the multiple, *and* the payment terms, *and* the tax structure. Unfortunately, the way it usually works in the field is that the seller guesses at his or her value using a multiple, the buyer guesses at the payment terms and tax structure based on what he or she needs, and the result is considered an acceptable compromise. Playing a *guessing game* around $100,000 of value or more doesn't usually turn out very well.

Rules of thumb have some other significant drawbacks that make them inapplicable to practices, businesses, and firms. The various rules of thumb do not factor in risks that can materially impact value such as capital structure, regulatory issues, liabilities, profitability, growth rates, client demographics, and infrastructure, to name just a few. This method also does not

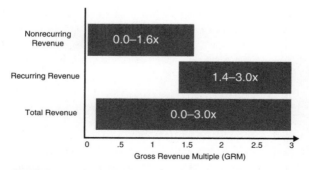

FIGURE 2.1 Gross Revenue Multiple by Revenue Type

consider the differences in cash flow quality or transition risk that might affect one book versus another. In other words, a rule of thumb treats every book as being equal to any other book except for the amount of revenue generated.

Rules of thumb are not empirical and have not been examined or tested to determine their validity. Rules of thumb, practically speaking, are often misstatements taken out of context and often applied incorrectly. Here are some specific examples: a multiple of 3.0 × TTMR is a great result at first glance, but not if the buyer insists on paying nothing down, and the entire balance on a fully contingent, earn-out basis over five years, which generates ordinary income tax rates to the seller; or perhaps a multiple of 2.25 × TTMR with 35% cash down, nonrefundable, and the balance seller-financed over just 24 months with one look-back provision (i.e., a performance-based promissory note) and all monies taxed to the seller at long-term capital gains rates. Which is the better deal? What about an offer of 1.35 × TTMR all cash and at preferential tax rates? Is the seller who sold at a GRM of 3.0 actually better off than the seller who sold at a GRM of 2.25, or even 1.35? Without all the underlying facts, and without knowing the final results years later, it is impossible to know.

When you hear about such multiples from a "successful" seller, or read about them in a trade publication, consider how much information is known and unknown. Even at the job or book level, the best advice is this: do not focus on *the multiple* without considering *all* the underlying deal terms, tax structures, and legal obligations, to support it. A simple multiple supported by simple paperwork often creates simply a mess.

For everyone else, specifically those advisors who own and have built a practice or a business or who seek to acquire such a model, a GRM is, at most, a starting point. Use a GRM to provide a *safety check* to the reasonability of a more formal and sophisticated calculation of value or appraisal, or a basic test to see if a more formal valuation is worth the time and expense. A GRM, for most practice and business owners, can be a decent place to start; it's just not a very good place to end. To be clear, practice and business owners should always progress to a more formal and thorough analysis on the issue of value.

APPLICATION OF STANDARDS AND APPROACHES

In this section, we compare the valuation results of two practices to illustrate the different levels of value that similar practices can have. The two practices used in the following illustration were valued for different purposes, utilized different standards of value, and employed different valuation approaches.

The purpose of this illustration is not to demonstrate which approach is "right" or "wrong" or yields the highest or "best" level of value, depending on a buyer or seller's perspective. Rather, it is to highlight value and valuation fundamentals: (a) that purpose informs value; and (b) randomly selecting valuation standards, approaches and methods to value a practice, or being *sold a one-size-fits-all valuation solution* without entirely understanding the process, can produce a value that is irrelevant.

Both practices in this illustration are Registered Investment Advisors (RIAs) with an independent broker-dealer (IBD) affiliation. They both are single-owner S corporations with relatively flat and stable growth rates and similar amounts of recurring and nonrecurring revenue. Both are located in or near a major metropolitan area. Table 2.2 provides a brief comparison of the two practices side by side.

Practice A is actually an example extracted from the previous, bestselling M&A book in this industry. Approximately 10 years ago, the authors of this book devoted an entire chapter to expertly explaining and working through a sample valuation process using both an income and market approach. While the purpose for the example wasn't made entirely clear (the subject matter was M&A activity), it was stated that the valuation results of **$567,000** are what a prudent investor would pay for Practice A's expected future income stream given the practice's specific risks. The authors placed an 80% weighting on the income approach and split the remaining 20% between two market methods, the *guideline public company method* and the *merger and acquisition analysis method*, which they said reflected recent merger and acquisition prices for reasonably comparable companies, noting

TABLE 2.2 A Comparison of Two Practices

Practice A	Practice B
Entity Structure: S corporation	**Entity Structure:** S corporation
Ownership: One Shareholder	**Ownership:** One Shareholder
Organizational Structure: Silo (one producer only)	**Organizational Structure:** Silo (one producer only)
Regulatory Structure: RIA/RR	**Regulatory Structure:** RIA/RR
$400,000 in annual, recurring, gross revenue	$365,000 in annual, recurring, gross revenue
$130,000 in annual, nonrecurring, gross revenue	$112,000 in annual, nonrecurring, gross revenue
$530,000 total, annual gross revenue	$477,000 total, annual gross revenue
Annual revenue growth rate: Flat (0% to 3%)	**Annual revenue growth rate:** Flat (0% to 3%)

that reliability of the underlying data was questionable, thus the reduced weighting. The resulting value was stated as the *fair market value* of a 100% interest in the common stock of the practice.

Practice B is an actual advisor who listed and sold on the open market in 2011. FP Transitions was hired for the purpose of performing a valuation to determine what a buyer would pay for the practice if it was listed for sale on the open market, assuming normal market conditions, a reasonable marketing period, and standard payment terms upon sale or acquisition, an example of the *most probable selling price* standard of value. Using a market approach and the direct market data method, relying on a database of over 1,000 transactions at that time, the value was estimated to be $1,009,000 (we will discuss the specific methodology in more detail in the following chapter). At the seller's request, the practice was listed for sale at $1.1 million and received 72 formal inquiries from interested buyers and three written offers. Within four weeks, the practice sold for **$1 million** with terms of 35% down, the balance seller-financed over four years using a performance-based promissory note. The buyer also maintained the seller's office lease and retained key staff members. One year later, a post-closing transition rate of 96% was reported (based on gross revenues received by the buyer). Note that Practice B was also about 10% smaller than Practice A in terms of gross revenue.

Table 2.3 contains a summary of the valuation results side by side.

The valuation results of Practice A may very well have been accurate given the choice of standard of value, valuation approach, and valuation method. It would also be uncommon for a buyer to acquire the stock of Practice A given its relatively small size and specific regulatory structure; it is far more likely to have been an asset sale. But that is comparing academics to the reality of the marketplace. In fact, if the same standard of value, method, and approach were applied to Practice B, the seller would have lost more than $400,000 in value. This isn't an isolated example, and it isn't

TABLE 2.3 A Summary of Valuation Results

Practice A	Practice B
Purpose: What would an investor pay for stock?	Purpose: Sale to third party
Standard of Value: Fair Market Value	Standard of Value: Most probable selling price
Approach: 80% Income—Capitalization of Earnings	Approach: 100% Market—Direct Market Data Method
10% Market—Public Company	**Valuation Results: $1,009,000**
10% Market—Public Company M&A	
Valuation Results: $567,000	

"merely academic" when the wrong approach is used on the largest, most valuable asset most advisors own.

The takeaway is this: the applicability of each standard of value, valuation approach, and underlying methodology is based on the purpose and circumstances of the practice to be valued, as well as the appraiser's understanding of all the relevant facts at hand. In most cases, one standard and approach is better suited for the job than the others, but no single standard applies in every instance. The process of valuing a dynamic, fluid, and personality-based practice or business like those in this industry is a more complex task than most advisors, buyers, or sellers realize. It is one thing to hire a valuation professional; it is another thing to let him or her take charge of one of the most important decisions of your financial life.

MAKING SENSE OF IT ALL

In summing up the valuation fundamentals covered in this chapter, suffice it to say that independent advisors have choices to make. Valuing a highly regulated, relationship-based practice or business is challenging work, but it isn't that hard, or expensive in most cases, to do the job right. Simple approaches and quick answers may be appealing, but they are rarely accurate and such inaccuracy tends to cost many times what a formal valuation or appraisal actually costs, to one party or the other.

The starting place for most advisors in the M&A space is the simple mantra: *purpose, standard, approach, and method* (Figure 2.2.). These are the key choices that need to be made. Work with a qualified analyst or appraiser to determine the best choices at each level for your particular circumstances. As an advisor interested in buying or selling, you don't need to know how to perform a valuation. In fact, a disinterested third party is a

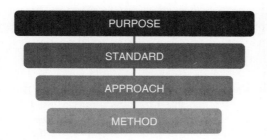

FIGURE 2.2 Valuation Considerations: Purpose, Standard, Approach, and Method

must, but you do need to help your chosen valuation analyst make the correct decisions as to the purpose, standard, approach, and method in order to obtain a reliable and accurate valuation result. There is no one set answer that applies to all situations.

For advisors who follow the general structuring techniques of an asset-based purchase or sale, with a meaningful down payment and common payment terms, the standard of *most probable selling price* is the best choice. If the other party in your transaction insists on a different standard, ask for their justification and consider the consequences. Remember that, while qualified analysts will not allow an advisor to *buy a specific valuation result*, choosing a less applicable or incorrect standard, approach, or method can have the same effect.

In a nutshell, the least appropriate of the traditional valuation approaches is the asset-based approach. Think of this as the value of the "bricks-and-mortar." This method is generally not applicable to financial services or advisory work at any ownership level because there are relatively few valuable tangible assets (computers, copiers, and file cabinets notwithstanding). In contrast, the real value of a financial services or advisory model lies in the strength of its client relationships, the quality of the cash flow generated by those relationships, and their transferability.

At the other end of the spectrum, the income approach analyzes the earnings of a given book, practice, business, or firm. Think of this approach as the value of the income stream that could be derived from the bricks-and-mortar. Earnings-based appraisals (think bottom-line looking up) using the discounted cash flow (DCF) or the capitalized-earnings method work best and should also be the primary method for *businesses* and *firms* in support of an internal ownership track where advisors purchase a minority interest of stock in a profitable and ongoing model. Recall that this group comprises just 5% to 8% of the industry at this time.

The income approach should also be used for any courtroom-based valuation activity such as a partnership dissolution or marital dissolution, and certainly for an arbitration-related issue. FP Transitions provides valuations using the income approach to advisors every day, but *not* for most of the basic, straightforward M&A activity that applies to prospective buyers and sellers.

Understand that when performed correctly, this approach requires an in-depth analysis of a business's or firm's financial performance and financial reports. This isn't a process that can be performed online or for free, if it is done right. The income approach requires a qualified, competent, disinterested professional to perform the analysis required to generate a reliable valuation result.

The market approach compares the practice being valued to other, similar practices that have recently been sold under similar, if not identical, circumstances. If an advisor is going to participate in the open market, as either buyer or seller, knowing what similar practices sold for as of *yesterday* is a fair, accurate, and relatively inexpensive way to determine the value of what you're selling today. If you're going to participate in the market, or seek to benefit from the market that supports valuation data, why not listen to the market data?

This approach is typically a "top-line, looking down" view that reflects the way most of this industry's ownership structures are operated on a day-to-day basis. The market approach is applicable to books, practices, and those businesses that sell externally to a third-party buyer. It has many positive attributes. It is accurate, inexpensive, and easily understandable, but requires one critical component to make it all work: *supporting data.* Without privately held transactional data in sufficient quantity and of sufficient quality, it's like comparing apples to lemons. This is the point of Chapter 3, "Solving Valuation."

Rules of thumb also deserve some attention here. Simply put, if an advisor does not understand how valuation works or doesn't see the need for paying someone else for the answer, they'll just multiply recurring revenue by a factor of two (or maybe a little higher) and trust that it's close enough and that the other party will not have, or insist on, a better answer. A multiple of revenue might work for the smallest and lowest-valued ownership level (jobs or books) because, even though it is really just a *best guess*, usually without any underlying factual basis. However, for these smaller advisories, it isn't *wrong enough* to warrant spending the time and money on a better answer.

In the end, choosing the correct path from a standard approach and method isn't a matter of which is better, or more accurate, or more expensive, or less expensive, it is solely a function of addressing the specific purpose of the valuation.

WHO IS QUALIFIED? (TO OFFER AN OPINION OF VALUE)

If you are in need of a formal valuation, be sure to work with a qualified individual. Refer back to Table 2.1 for a detailed, quick checklist of the different valuation approaches and methods, and the *competency standards* for each level. The field of valuation, like financial services and advisory functions, has its own professional designations and governing bodies. These regulatory bodies include the American Society of Appraisers (ASA), the Institute of Business Appraisers (IBA), the National Association of Certified Valuators and Analysts (NACVA), and the American Institute of Certified Public Accountants (AICPA). These regulatory bodies issue the respected valuation credentials, or designations, set forth in Figure 2.3.

If you are going to have a valuation performed, for any purpose, make sure the analyst or appraiser holds at least one of the following designations:

- Certified Valuation Analyst (CVA)
- Accredited Senior Appraiser (ASA)
- Accredited in Business Appraisal Review (ABAR)
- Master Certified Business Appraiser (MCBA or CBA)
- Accredited in Business Valuation (ABV)
- Master Analyst in Financial Forensics (MAFF)

In some instances this list might also include a Certified Financial Analyst (CFA). A CPA, even with a PFS, is not usually qualified unless one or more of the above designations have been earned. The same holds true for an MBA without one or more of the designations above.

In addition, some knowledge of this industry's regulatory or compliance aspects is helpful in the valuation process.

FIGURE 2.3   Valuation Credentials

Whoever you choose to value or appraise what you've built or seek to acquire, rely only on valuation analysts or appraisers who are certified and have earned the necessary and proper designations. If the person or company offering you an opinion has not earned one of these designations, you have an unqualified person telling you what they think about one of the most valuable assets you own, or will acquire. While everyone seems to have an opinion nowadays, this one matters.

To this end, it is highly likely that the practice management personnel at a broker-dealer or custodian have no special valuation training or qualifications or market transaction data upon which to base their opinions; answering hundreds of questions the same way does not equal qualification or certification. In addition, as well intentioned as they may be, these folks have a stake in the outcome. That is why most IBDs and custodians smartly do not wade into the value and valuation space. If one side of a transaction, either buyer or seller, relies on an unqualified opinion from an *interested* third party, he or she should be called out. We're being hard on this issue. The point is, credentials and expertise and experience matter.

VALUATIONS FOR BANK FINANCING

As you'll read later, more and more advisors are now able to utilize bank financing in their transactions to help implement an exit plan or to accelerate their succession plans. Reasonable and appropriate bank financing for acquisition purposes is a relatively recent and major step forward for independent advisors in the M&A space. While most independent advisors do not need a formal appraisal for their M&A activity, it is a distinct possibility that a specific type of valuation will be needed if or when bank financing is utilized to complete the transaction.

Since the financial crisis of 2008, bank lending standards have become noticeably more stringent. This is easily observed by visiting the Small Business Administration website and reviewing the ongoing changes made to their lending and processing standard operating procedures (SOPs), *SOP 50 10 5*, specifically. This SOP states the conditions that must be met by both the borrower and lender to secure and provide, respectively, an SBA 7(a) or 504 loan. (Bank financing is addressed in detail in Chapter 7.)

Since 2009, *SOP 50 10 5* has been updated annually with each iteration containing substantial changes. For example, in 2012, the entire *Change of Ownership* section for this SOP was rewritten, and in 2013, the SOP no longer allowed lenders to accept appraisals from certified public accountants (CPAs) without further valuation accreditation. According to the SBA, appraisals for a *change of ownership* must be completed by a "qualified source," which is defined as an individual who regularly receives compensation for business appraisals *and* is accredited by one of the following recognized organizations:

- American Society of Appraisers
- Institute of Business Appraisers
- American Institute of Certified Public Accountants
- National Association of Certified Valuators and Analysts
- International Society of Business Analysts

In addition to being accredited, appraisers must be independent and have no financial or other interest in the property being appraised; be capable of rendering an unbiased opinion; be hired and paid by the lender, not the borrower or the seller of the property or business; and be state-certified or licensed in accordance with the Uniform Standards of Professional Appraisal Practice.

In addition to the standards set forth by organizations such as the Institute of Business Appraisers (IBA) and American Society of Appraisers (ASA), qualified business appraisers must follow the Uniform Standards of Professional Appraisal Practice (USPAP), recognized as the official source of appraisal standards in North America.

CHAPTER 3

Solving Valuation

THE *BLUE BOOK* STANDARD

In 1918, Les Kelley parked three Model T Fords on a lot, put them up for sale, and thus started the Kelley Kar Company. It was to become one of the largest used car dealerships in the world. But in order to succeed, a method was needed for placing easily determined *and accurate* values on the vehicles. Solving valuation was the key step in the process.

In those days, new car dealerships didn't sell used cars, so Kelley bought vehicles that new car dealers took in trade. Sometimes the line of cars waiting to be appraised would wind around the block. During the Depression, there were times when the Kelley Kar Company bought the entire inventory of dealers who went out of business. As a frequent buyer and seller of cars, Mr. Kelley was tied into the open market on a daily basis, and his experience and opinions as to value began to hold increasing sway with others in the automotive industry, from individuals to banks to car companies. In 1926, Kelley published his first *Blue Book of Motor Car Values*, which quickly became a standard.

The title "Blue Book" was borrowed from the Social Register, a directory of names and addresses of prominent American families who formed the social elite, because, to Kelley, it implied that one could find valuable information inside. That was important, because this was a new concept, a new valuation tool. And not coincidentally, Emily Post had recently published her first book on how to do certain things properly, titled *Etiquette: The Blue Book of Social Usage*.

The *Kelley Blue Book*, as it came to be known, became the authoritative source for car values. It was certainly not an appraisal, and it was not intended to be. The *Blue Book* was not the approach that you would use if ascertaining the value of your 1962 Ferrari 250 LM, and it didn't try to be that. It was something else, something more. Of course, valuing a priceless Ferrari isn't the issue, or the challenge, that most people have. For the task at hand, buying and selling cars on a daily basis, the *Blue Book* did the job better, and more accurately, than any other method ever invented.

In the previous two chapters, the point was made that valuation is often a divisive issue. Buyers, sellers, and their IBD or custodian-supplied practice management support teams sometimes think that paying more for a valuation, or using a more complicated method, will allow them to *dial in* the result they're looking for. Somehow, somewhere, the right number is waiting to be found and proven. But what if the best source of information does not directly relate to spending $10,000 on an appraisal or obtaining a valuation report that weighs 2.5 pounds? Consider what the marketplace has to say.

LESSONS LEARNED

When FP Transitions launched the open market concept almost 20 years ago, independent advisors approached the M&A process in a rather unsophisticated manner, a kind way of saying that the market was unorganized and operated in a haphazard fashion, on a good day. The first problem to solve was convincing buyers (and even sellers) that a practice had any value at all. We fought buyers *and* sellers with our thinking, and we battled their CPAs and their attorneys. How could a new profession like independent financial advice command more value than the learned and time-honored professions of law, accounting, or even medicine?! New profession or not, the math was clear.

The industry pundits sat back and watched in amusement as FP Transitions sought to establish a beachhead and forever change the value proposition of this industry. It wasn't easy, similar to pushing a boulder up a hill. Sellers back then boasted that they were "irreplaceable" and proudly said as much to any interested but perplexed buyer (a term intentionally used in the singular).

In January 2000, we listed our first practice for sale, a fee-based sole proprietorship. We used a multiple of about 1.4 × TTMR (trailing 12 months revenue), an opinion extrapolated from the results of the discounted cash flow analyses that many at the time insisted held the right answer. But then a strange thing happened. Twenty buyer prospects threw their hats into the ring in the first week and the practice sold in eight days, at the full asking price, and with better terms than requested. Something seemed wrong, in a good way. The learning process had begun for the entire industry.

Still, with small down payments and long-term earn-out arrangements, it was hard to attract good sellers, so the second task was to figure out how to create appropriate payment terms to support a reasonable valuation opinion. Professional payment terms were also needed to create a "shared-risk/shared-reward" structure to motivate both parties to work together to ensure maximum success and client satisfaction. Those recurring successes, measured in the years after the sale was completed, or closed, led to a larger and more robust market that produced better results that fueled a database that supported higher values over time. Value and payment terms became inextricably linked together and it worked very well.

We learned this by simply watching buyers and sellers interact, and then tracking the data. We continually adjusted both value and payment terms to find the right balance that, years later, resulted in a win for everyone, especially the client base. We needed to work with both sides in a nonadvocacy fashion to gather the data, learn from it, apply the lessons, and learn some more. In the beginning, we learned that multiples of revenue worked well for small books organized as sole proprietorships when more than half of the revenue stream is derived from transactions (nonrecurring revenue). Coupled with an earn-out arrangement, it created a reasonably priced acquisition opportunity in which the payment terms rewarded a great seller effort, and still adequately protected the buyer from downside risk.

But this approach did not work well as small transactional books gave way to larger practices, practices with $300,000 to $500,000 in gross revenue, and the majority of it recurring (fees and/or trails). The problem was, classic appraisal techniques such as the discounted cash flow model didn't work, either.

First, the initial appraisals were just wrong, in hindsight. The opinions of value had no tie to the actual transactions being negotiated and constructed in the marketplace. Second, appraisers applied an all-cash value to assets (i.e., client relationships) that buyers would never consider paying all cash for. The parties were left to make their own adjustments or apply a "best guess discount" with little to no guidance. Third, the valuation experts failed to ascertain the value of embedded growth. Time and time again, we watched as larger buyers (businesses, for example) acquired smaller practices, retaining 95%-plus of the client relationships only to demonstrate a 10% to 20% improvement in annual gross revenues within a year or two from the acquired client base. Last, the valuations themselves were too expensive for the average advisor.

Given the cost and the inaccuracy, sellers simply changed course on their own, applied a multiple of revenue (or even a multiple of AUM in the early days), and waited the buyers out. Maybe a buyer would come along, maybe not. Attrition became the accepted alternative; clearly not a good path for a young and emerging industry. If the marketplace was to work well for buyers and sellers, easily determined and accurate values needed to be a part of the exit planning process.

One thing was clear. If values were to be clearly ascertained within the context of a reasonable payment structure that supported the long-term interests of the client base in transition, a new valuation approach was needed. So FP Transitions created one—the Comprehensive Valuation Report (or CVR). It was not an appraisal, by design. It was a completely new approach, for a completely new kind of financial services professional; the independent owner who was building a valuable, recurring income model, be it a practice or a business or a firm.

Did it work? Eight thousand valuations later, the handwriting is on the wall, as they say. More important, the great debate has shifted to *how much value* and on what payment terms, questions now fielded on a daily basis—a much more positive and productive discussion. Lessons learned.

A VALUE CALCULATION

In order to build a valuation tied to actual market activity, it was first necessary to build, organize, and operate a marketplace and gather the data. Everyone had to learn together what worked and what didn't. From the buying and selling activity, comparable sales data, or "comps," were amassed. These comps provided, and continue to provide, the guideposts to build and adjust a practical, sophisticated, real-time valuation system.

These comps are derived from actual sales in the marketplace, the largest such group of private transactional data in this industry at 1,500 and counting. This data is complete and comprehensive and is supported by access to the documents that provide all the details of the underlying transactions and payment terms. This data makes all the difference; it is what powers the Comprehensive Valuation Report.

The CVR is not an appraisal, and it is not intended to be. It is a *value calculation*. The CVR uses a very practical approach assembled in the trenches to provide answers to the questions and issues at hand. This is not an academic, ivory tower exercise designed for courthouses and combatants. The CVR is a seller- and buyer-oriented valuation approach because that is where and how the lessons have been learned. What were buyers willing to pay, and on what terms? What actually worked from the perspective of the acquired clients of those buyers in the years after the transaction was completed? What was the commonly negotiated tax structure that their CPAs or accountants supported? The CVR provides real answers to real questions.

Annually, we look back on the acquisitions that have successfully closed, and we make minute adjustments to maintain a high level of accuracy based on what has been actually happening in the marketplace.

Over the past several years, the value paid by buyers to sellers has generally been plus or minus 4% of the original CVR calculation, but it does vary, and the marketplace is constantly changing. This value calculation is designed to adapt and change with it over time.

The CVR was developed to solve these issues:

1. To provide an efficient, less expensive, and accurate tool for measuring value in this unique industry;
2. To function as a business management tool by helping advisors understand what drives value, and;
3. To take valuation *off the table* as a dividing or contentious issue in the M&A process so that the parties can focus on what really matters—determining the best match between buyer and seller.

One of the most important things we've learned over the years is that, in the vast majority of cases, valuation is *not* the driver for successful transactions in this industry. In other words, the skill-set of a valuation expert, or the valuation approach you take, is not what will make you a successful buyer or seller.

The role of a buyer of a relationship-based practice is not that of a bidder, but is more analogous to that of a *suitor*. The M&A process in this industry is less about negotiation and more about "dating," maybe even forming an "economic marriage." Buyers need to sell themselves to the seller. Being the high bidder simply doesn't work for most practice and business owners because the seller's clients are his or her friends, or certainly people with long-standing, respectful relationships. Professionals in this industry care, and that is a good thing, as long as the succeeding buyer also cares. These special attributes of this unique industry demand an equally adept valuation method, traditional approaches notwithstanding.

HOW IT WORKS

The Comprehensive Valuation Report is a "top-line, looking down" approach that reflects the way 95% of this industry's ownership structures are operated on a day-to-day basis. As such, the analysis in the CVR is based on the standard currency of the independent financial services market, that of gross revenue (or gross dealer concession or "GDC" under FINRA rules). This top-line, looking down approach also reflects the common practice of buyers in the competitive open market, and makes comparisons from one model to another far more accurate and consistent.

Here is how it works. Completing an accurate valuation of an independent, privately owned financial services practice is, in broad terms, a four-part process. We'll use the generic term "Subject Practice" for ease of reading in this section only.

Step 1—Analyzing Transition Risk

The first step in the CVR process is to assess the client base and associated revenue streams in terms of its transferability. The term "transition risk" refers to the likelihood that the clients of the Subject Practice will substantially transfer to a successor or buyer. It is possible, perhaps even likely, depending on the circumstances of a sale, that not all clients, accounts, and associated revenue will transfer to a buyer. In general, based on experience and observation of actual transactions in a competitive open market in which the buyer selected is the best match for a given seller, an average of about 90% to 95% of the clients of a financial services practice will transfer to, and remain with, a buyer or successor with similar or equal skills. That average, however, can be deceiving, as it is derived over many transactions with professional transition support and guidance, using standardized transfer and retention procedures. The term "best match" is necessarily derived from a very competitive marketplace environment in which sellers have many choices and can audition the field of buyers. The variance in the average retention rate is ultimately reflected in the *Transition Risk Index* for the Subject Practice.

Marketplace data also indicates that the number of clients who move to a successor or buyer during the transition period can vary substantially, depending on the specific transaction and circumstances surrounding the sale. Certain factors consistently reduce the risk of client transition and retention. These factors include: (1) whether the sale is internal (between family members, partners, or between an employer and employee) or external (involving a third-party buyer); (2) the time the clients have been associated with the existing advisor, and; (3) the amount of transition consulting time, or post-closing support, the seller and the seller's staff will provide to the new owner or successor. Additional factors are considered and addressed further on.

Step 2—Analyzing Cash Flow Quality

The second step in the CVR process is to assess the quality of the cash flow of the Subject Practice. Many factors play an important role in measuring and estimating the stability and long-term potential of the client revenue stream. Some of the cash flow quality factors evaluated in the

CVR include: (1) multigenerational planning; (2) revenue growth rates; (3) revenue generated per client; (4) client profile, including age and affluence; (5) the technology level of the Subject Practice; and (6) transferable referral channels.

Because the client base represents a future revenue stream, it is important to evaluate the client base in terms of its durability and growth potential. Obviously, there is a substantial difference between a client base comprised of 50-year-old entrepreneurs and CEOs at the top of their earnings cycle and one made up of mostly 70- to 80-year-old clients, even though both groups of clients may produce an equivalent revenue stream at the time of a valuation analysis. The ability to analyze and rank cash flow quality using a market-based valuation approach allows for an adjustment to value between two similarly situated practices or businesses. The outcome is reflected in the *Cash Flow Quality Index.*

An analysis of cash flow quality also addresses concentration risk, which can occur, for example, when a disproportionate amount of revenue is derived from a limited number of clients or households. Additional factors are considered and addressed further on.

Step 3—Analyzing Market Demand

The CVR also assesses and integrates market dynamics into the valuation equation, a measurement illustrated by the *Market Demand Index.* This step is accomplished by applying a market demand indexed capitalization rate.

The CVR uses a tiered schedule of gross revenue capitalization rates indexed to the size of the book, practice, or business. Over time, these capitalization rates are likely to change as the database of closed transactions provides additional marketplace-based data, especially in larger and more complex transactions.

From a methodology standpoint, the tiered capitalization rate schedule is applied to the client revenue base, which has been previously adjusted based on the *Transition Risk Index* and the *Cash Flow Quality Index.* The result is a "base price" for the Subject Practice, which may be further affected by the specific payment structure.

As with the previous indexes, many factors play a role in measuring and estimating the *Market Demand Index.* Some of the market demand factors evaluated in the Comprehensive Valuation Report include: (1) practice location; (2) practice size; (3) practice type; (4) current buyer activity in the area; and (5) practice niche, if any. A summary of the three valuation indexes is presented in Figure 3.1.

FIGURE 3.1 A Summary of Valuation Indexes

Step 4—Considering the Impact of Payment Terms/Taxes

Finally, the Comprehensive Valuation Report provides a specific value *within the context of set payment terms and even the anticipated tax allocation of an asset-based sale*, the norm for M&A activity involving a job/ book, practice, or business engaged in an exit plan.

A buyer's confidence and willingness to agree to a specific value for an intangible, professional services model is usually tied to the payment terms that support that value proposition. Payment terms or payment structuring represents the apportionment of risk in the transaction between buyer and seller. The payment terms that underlie the determined value in the CVR represent the most commonly and recently used payment structuring approaches. Very few practices or businesses are sold to third parties for an all-cash, noncontingent purchase price.

Consider this example: As a prospective buyer, would you willingly pay $1 million for $400,000 worth of fee-based income tied to 200 clients whom you've never met, and who have never heard of you? Without more information, probably not. But phrase the question within the context of the typical payment terms and tax structure provided by the CVR as reflected by marketplace activity and rephrase the question: As a prospective buyer, would you willingly pay $1 million for the Subject Practice on certain terms if it produced approximately $400,000 of fee-based revenue every year for the next five years, and you could write off or depreciate the entire purchase price? That's an entirely different proposition, but it reflects the close tie between the value proposition and the underlying payment terms and tax issues. Without considering and factoring in the terms of the payments and how they are taxed, the opinion of value is, well, purely academic.

So important are these issues, and their impact on the valuation process, that an entire chapter is dedicated to payment terms and tax structuring later in this book.

RECURRING VERSUS NONRECURRING REVENUE

From a buyer's perspective, nothing may be more important than the amount of recurring, predictable revenue. Fee-based income is what buyers covet. It is what they primarily value. Buyers almost always want more fee-based income and the clients who generate it. The 50:1 aforementioned buyer-to-seller ratio reflects seller listings in the open market in which the majority of the revenue stream is recurring, fee-based revenue.

Standards of value and most valuation approaches treat every dollar of revenue pretty much the same, but in this industry, there is a big difference. At the business and firm levels, the value of recurring revenue is heightened. Recurring revenue tends to generate predictable, recurring overhead. With skillful leadership and steady growth, such overhead can be controlled and minimized, which leads to higher profits and improved return on investment (ROI) for the founder and the next-generation owners who choose to build on top of the existing model. For businesses and firms, acquiring recurring revenue is a matter of building durability and long-term value. For book builders and practice owners, recurring revenue is a matter of convenience and predictability. Many times, for these two ownership levels, acquiring another book actually substitutes for a formal marketing plan.

Recurring revenue in the financial services industry is generally earned by applying a charge to assets under management (AUM), or trails derived through the sale of annuities, mutual funds, or insurance products. Transactional-based or nonrecurring revenue is generally earned from one-time transactions or a commission payment. From a valuation perspective and within the Comprehensive Valuation Report, these revenue categories form an important starting point for determining value. Regulatory changes may serve to further underscore the differences in revenue streams and their value to prospective buyers.

Since value is largely based on the assumption of a continuing stream of revenue into the future, it is important that the valuation analysis takes into account what proportion of the revenue is recurring versus transaction-based. Simply stated, recurring revenue is one of the single most important determinants of value of a financial services or advisory model. While the assessments used in the CVR are applied to both recurring and nonrecurring revenue, significantly more weight is usually placed on the recurring revenue component.

Transactional revenue is more elusive and difficult to predict, and while it may be *worth less*, rarely is it *worthless*. Transactional revenue can have value to a buyer, but it is essential to be able to show the propensity for additional revenue. In other words, if not recurring revenue, at least predictable revenue. Factors like the practice's historical revenue growth, length of surrender periods, and quality and depth of the relationships are instrumental in assessing the potential from transactional revenue. Insurance-based books and practices are assessed differently from a fee-based model for exactly these reasons.

The takeaway is this: If you want to maximize value, focus on generating recurring revenue. Every dollar of recurring revenue is worth approximately two to three times as much as every dollar of nonrecurring revenue. If your income model falls somewhere in between, predictability and reliability is valuable if you can demonstrate it over time and deliver it to a new owner. If you own a book, a practice, or a business, think like a buyer and evaluate what you are building based on the three indexes of value: *transition risk, cash flow quality,* and *marketplace demand.* How do you measure up?

ASSESSING TRANSITION RISK

Transition risk reflects the issue of transferability and retention of the client base post-closing. This is what keeps buyers and sellers up at night. Are the clients and the associated revenue stream transferable?

FP Transitions' Comprehensive Valuation Report assesses transition risk separately from cash flow quality. Transition risk is defined as the risk associated with transferring the clients, and hence the revenue stream, to a new owner or successor. Assessments are made based on actual experience as reflected in our comparable transaction database. Based on a given fact pattern and ownership level, it is possible to estimate the risk in transferring a given set of client relationships.

To be fair, the issue of transition risk can be accounted for in the income approach/discounted cash flow method, but most advisors never see this issue in terms of the specific assessments or a specific adjustment. The CVR allows an advisor to understand the logic and adjustments for assessing transition risk, the transferability of the client base, in plain English. Advisors need to know.

A number of factors, in addition to those listed earlier, are involved in accurately assessing transition risk, including:

- The tenure of the book, practice, or business
- The willingness/ability of the departing advisor to offer post-closing assistance
- The use of noncompete/nonsolicitation agreements for nonowner advisors
- Continuation with the same broker-dealer/custodian post-closing
- Client affluence level
- Client demographics
- Branding (personal versus corporate)

On average, experience dictates that in a well-structured, well-documented transaction at the practice level of ownership, the level of transition risk is around 5% to 10%, meaning that 90% to 95% of the clients and revenue should make the transition to the new owner and remain in place at least one year post-closing. Transition risk is typically higher for a book, and lower for a business, using practices as the measuring point.

In general, the longer the client has been with a given independent practice or business, the less likely that the client will leave following an ownership transition without significant cause. Long-term clients are much more likely to stay through an ownership transition (whether to a third party or internally to other partners, managers, or employees). This is particularly true if the assistance of the departing owner has been structured into the transaction or is part of an internal succession plan. This is a case of inertia working to the advantage of the transition.

A corollary factor for determining transition risk is the tenure of the financial advisory practice or business itself. The longer and better established the enterprise, the less likely the clients are to leave in the event of an ownership transition. A number of reasons may be attributed to this observation. In longer-tenured models, the clients may associate the services more with the practice or business and less with any one individual, thereby making a change in ownership easier and more natural. Longer-tenured firms also have acquired a marketplace reputation and position (often referred to as "goodwill") that carries through in the event of a well-structured and professionally executed transaction.

The degree that technology is used and maintained in the office also factors into transition risk, one important reason why this element is carefully tracked in our benchmarking studies. In models where there is a high technology level, and where owners have invested the time, money, and resources into this component, the common result is that client contacts and tracking are more automated and in many cases more systematic as well. In these models, the ownership transfer often experiences less disruption than when the contact, processing, and systems are not as highly automated. To the extent that technology produces a paperless or very efficient office structure, value is also positively impacted, reflected in part by much higher buyer demand.

Other factors that contribute to the transition risk assessment include the owner's willingness to grant noncompetition/nonsolicitation/no-service agreements upon their retirement or exit, and having similar restrictive covenants in place with licensed employees. Consider this issue carefully, especially if you are a potential seller and have surrounded yourself with "book builders" or independent contractors paid on a revenue-sharing arrangement. Further on, we'll cover this particular issue in more depth later in the chapter under "Fixing the Fracture Lines."

It should be noted that, in general, most of the individual assessment factors (other than the one exception just noted) do not tend to be very large, but rather result in incremental adjustments to value and, in sum, produce results that closely mirror the reality of the marketplace as we experience it every day.

MEASURING CASH FLOW QUALITY

The factors used to assess the cash flow quality index focus on the strength and durability of the revenue stream and include:

- Client demographics
- Asset concentration
- Revenue growth, separate and apart from new client growth
- Expenses
- Referral channels/referral fees
- Business niche

In assessing client demographics, it is statistically desirable from a value or equity standpoint to have the largest proportion of the client base in the 50 to 70 years of age bracket, while at the same time not having a large percentage of clients in the above-70 years age group. This is a recurring trait that we observe in the largest and most valuable businesses and firms. The 50-to-70 years of age demographic is desirable because this group, in general, is not only at the top of their earning cycle, but also is at the top of the saving cycle. "Event drawdowns," such as purchasing a home, paying for college tuition, or making business investments, are less frequent in this age group, while the urgency of saving as retirement approaches becomes more salient.

The demographics of those clients in the 30 to 50 years of age bracket are also important, contributing to a developing revenue base. In our benchmarking studies, this age group does not represent the majority or largest group of clients, at least in the most valuable models. The demographic group represented by those clients 70 years of age and older is often the wealthiest segment in a financial services practice or business. This group, however, is a less stable and less predictable source of long-term revenue because they are subject to event drawdowns for trust disbursements, gifting, living expenses, health issues, and, of course, mortality. In practices where the majority of the clients fall into the 70-plus age group, the result would be a lower cash flow quality rating, and, depending on other related factors, usually a lower value. Understanding these value drivers and knowing where you stand years ahead of time, is important and another reason for using a formal valuation as a management tool on a regular basis.

Asset concentration is another consideration in calculating the cash flow quality rating; it is measured by assessing the total percentage of assets under management owned by the largest top 10% of a practice's clients (ranked in order of fees paid). Most practices and businesses have at least some level of asset concentration.

Revenue growth and *net new client growth* are significant contributing factors to cash flow quality as well and are measured separately. In FP Transitions' analysis, average annual revenue growth over the 2005–2014 period was 12% (measured in at least five-year increments), with the middle 50% of the distribution curve growing by between 5% and 16% annually. The rate of revenue growth, however, is strongly influenced by market performance and therefore, by itself, is not a reliable indicator of the long-term strength of the cash flow. *Net new client growth*, on the other hand, provides an excellent proxy for determining the future growth potential of the practice, as well as helping to determine the quality and strength of the referral channels and the client development systems that the practice has in place.

In the end, it is cash flow quality that captures a buyer's interest. As such, this should be the starting point for every prospective seller thinking about an exit plan, a succession plan, and/or a continuity plan. Advisors often think about having a formal valuation performed and wonder why they need to know their "exact" value. *In fact, most advisors don't need to know their value at first—they need to know what drives and detracts from their value while there is still time to implement changes and improvements.*

FIXING THE FRACTURE LINES

The first generations of independent advisors are pioneers in their own right. Obviously, they got far more right than wrong. One important lesson learned from this group centers on compensation structures, a central element that defines and differentiates between owning a job/book, a practice, a business, or a firm.

Bluntly, here it is: all those compensation studies in years past missed the one key point by asking, "How much?" Interesting as it may have been, this was the wrong question. "How?" is the question we should all have been asking—*how* should an independent advisor pay, or be paid, in order to build a valuable practice or a business of enduring value. By overlooking this issue, and the importance of compensation structures, the independent industry has thus far created a culture of production and compensation instead of a culture of ownership and equity. Revenue sharing and other eat-what-you-kill compensation systems create one-generational models that die with the end of each career. This needs to be fixed, and it will be, but if you're a seller or a buyer today, the issue is more immediate.

The presence of fracture lines underscores a common trait of independent ownership: the strong propensity to build books rather than businesses. A *group of books* does not equal a business, though sometimes, it is hard to tell the difference. In fact, a group of books is usually portrayed to the clients as a single business and, after a while, the founder (sometimes an OSJ) starts to believe it is his or her business, especially when it is time to sell and implement an exit plan. The result is that sellers in these cases significantly overvalue what they can actually deliver, and buyers risk overpaying for value they can never realize.

Consider this example to better understand the problem from a valuation and M&A perspective: Advisor A is 63 years old and is the 100 percent owner of an S corporation (Figure 3.2). He hires and mentors Advisor B. Years later, Advisor A hires and begins to train Advisor C. The three advisors work side by side and enjoy each other's company and support. Advisor A gladly "shares" with his younger associates the bottom half of his client base and all new client referrals that are below his preferred minimum or who are just not a good personal fit. Advisors B and C are independent contractors but are treated like employees and, in fact, are often referred to as "partners" in front of the clients they serve. This fee-based practice is determined to have a current value of $1,250,000, but Advisor A is nowhere near ready to retire. He wants to work about five more years.

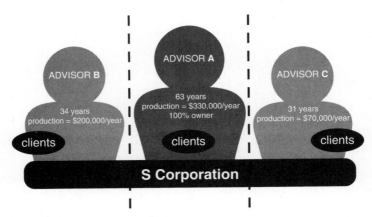

FIGURE 3.2 Identifying the Presence of Fracture Lines

Five years later, Advisor A receives an offer to sell his practice and the buyer is willing to pay him $1.75 million, on appropriate and reasonable terms. Advisor A decides to sell and fully retire. But there is a catch. The buyer (properly) requires that Advisors B and C cooperate and sign non-compete, nonsolicitation, and no-service agreements, and/or formal employment agreements with restrictive covenants so that the buyer knows they won't interfere with or impede the buyer's ability to control and retain *all* of the acquired cash flow and clients—except that they won't cooperate. And why would they?

All of a sudden, Advisors B and C, who are not shareholders, find that they are indeed owners of *something*, something quite valuable. In fact, Advisors B and C have quite a bit of value in the relationships they control, or could exert influence over if they chose to do so. Advisors B and C, together or separately, have veto power over Advisor A's transaction, or they'll cash out with him and take their share of the proceeds in exchange for cooperating. Advisors B and C own books, and books do indeed have value, as Advisor A has come to discover. In fact, Advisor A helped them build that value, shareholders or not. The fracture lines were built in long ago.

The presence of independent contractors, or book builders, or anyone on a revenue sharing compensation system, can signal the presence of fracture lines. It often takes a heightened level of review and expertise to spot the issue, and to provide a correct value calculation or valuation opinion and no one, or no company, FP Transitions included, is impervious on this issue. But if the valuation expert you're using is not familiar with this unique industry, or is otherwise unqualified or is trying to get you "your number" to please you and substantiate the cost of the engagement, spotting this issue is all but impossible.

Whether you are a prospective buyer or seller, it is critical that you identify these issues *ahead of time*, while there is still time to fix the problem. For those practices that have been built using revenue sharing, it is important to study and consider changing the revenue sharing model, as this may well be the key to a better, stronger value proposition when it comes time to implement, or be a part of, an exit plan.

THE PROFITABILITY ISSUE

There is an argument that pervades the M&A process in this industry that profitability is what defines "real value." The idea is that actual profits, or "normalized earnings," is the starting point from which value is, or should be, professionally determined. Even in the most simplistic sense, buyers attempt to use a multiple of earnings, arguing that a multiple of revenue is somehow *unsophisticated* in comparison. This brings us to the profitability issue, something yet again unique to the independent financial services industry and the valuation process, at least in terms of how the issue is created and resolved.

Most independent advisors make a good living, often a very good living. But there is a difference between *cash flow* and profitability, even if the former is $500,000 a year.

Every year, we have the opportunity to examine more than a thousand jobs/books, practices, businesses, and firms, collectively, from a financial statement perspective. Nine out of 10 are not profitable—in the literal definition, nothing, or next to nothing, makes it to the actual bottom line. However, most of these owners are indeed prosperous in terms of the money they take home as their reward every month. Their practice models certainly could be profitable, but they have set up an organization and compensation structure (sometimes an actual entity structure as well in the case of a C corporation) that is simply not focused on generating profits. Frankly, in a one-owner model where everything not spent on overhead gets taken home anyway, what does it matter?

In typical one-owner S corporations or LLCs, as well as sole proprietorships, profits are almost an afterthought regardless of how many additional advisors are in the office. The singular focus is on top-line cash flow, anchored by lofty production goals. The logic is that the best way to get every producer or advisor to *think like an owner* (without making them an equity partner) is to treat them like one. Said another way, the path to achieving double-digit growth rates year after year is to tie every advisor's compensation directly to their production, easily achieved with a revenue sharing arrangement or very large bonuses tied to production. This is part of the legacy of 50+ years of wirehouse compensation models.

Businesses, on the other hand, have a compensation system that supports not only top-line revenue growth, but also bottom-line profitability. Balancing the two aspects is challenging, but it is necessary if the goal is to build sustainability, because next-generation advisors can't invest in compensation. Younger advisors typically do not need to buy stock in the S corporation (or LLC) where they work to obtain a bigger paycheck. The point of investing money, energy, and a career into ownership, or equity, is to obtain the benefits of being an equity partner. If there are no profits, such as in the case of a C corporation that pays no dividends to avoid double taxation or an S corporation that "distributes" everything through a revenue sharing compensation structure, then what is the point of taking on the risk of ownership, especially at a minority level? Why invest if there is no ROI?

Profits, or profitability, is a game changer *if* you're building a business or want to take on equity partners. If there are no profits, there will be no next-generation advisor/investors. And profits need to be real, as in actual profit-distribution checks issued at least once a year to each equity partner, not an accountant's or valuation expert's attempts to normalize the income stream to create "profits" on paper.

So, a lack of profits also hurts value, right? No, not in all cases. Most buyers, at least of books or practices, are willing to focus on top-line revenue, not bottom-line profits. This reality is reflected in the Comprehensive Valuation Report, which reflects actual marketplace activity. Most buyers don't really care whether the seller they are chasing is "profitable." The acquisition of a book or practice is tantamount to a *marketing plan*, or more aptly, a substitute for a marketing plan. They view the book purchase as a client acquisition opportunity. ROI? That's an academic issue for the appraisers and sometimes a negotiation ploy by experienced buyers.

Now, let's put this in perspective. The lack of physical profit distributions or dividends does not necessarily hurt the value or the demand for most books and practices. Actual profits *do* matter if you're selling internally, or setting up a succession plan that involves next-generation equity partners. Lack of profitability may not always reduce value, but it is an early warning sign in almost every instance, and demands a closer look at the compensation system in use. It is very possible that the lack of real profits points to a book-building mentality rather than a single strong practice or business, and buyers should carefully consider this issue during due diligence.

Here's a quick walk-through, and further dose of reality, with respect to the various ownership levels and the issue of profitability in the M&A space and its impact on the valuation process.

- **Jobs/Books:** Acquisition of a job or a book has little if anything to do with a return on investment, at least in the commonly used sense of that term. This is about buying a list of clients and paying for them based on how successful the transition turns out to be, in hindsight. In these cases, profitability, or lack thereof, is usually irrelevant to both buyer and seller.
- **Practices:** At the practice level, owners start to pay attention to profitability. As revenue grows and owners utilize professional building tools and structures such as an S corporation or an LLC (generally some type of pass-through tax conduit), they also surround themselves with legal and tax counsel who gradually stress the importance of formalities in the practice operations. Profits at the practice level are typically around 10%

of gross revenue, occasionally up to as high as 15%. Most of the available profits are distributed, but not through the "compensation line" as with jobs or books—formal profit distribution checks are issued to the equity owner, usually once per year, or the owner's CPA makes an appropriate adjustment to balance wages and profit distributions at tax time.

If you're a buyer and you're evaluating a practice for sale, it only makes sense that you'll negotiate in your best interests, and penalizing the seller for not having greater profitability can be smart. If you're a seller, understand that a larger, more valuable third-party buyer is going to buy your assets and place your revenue stream into their existing overhead structure—their profitability is what matters, *not yours*. A different argument applies if bank financing will be used to complete the transaction, but even then, the income and expenses of both buyer and seller will be combined and examined by the lender. In these cases, actual profitability is relevant, but again, it tends to be the buyer's profitability that matters, not the seller's.

- **Businesses:** Profit distributions are one of the key aspects in rewarding owners and creating "owner-like behavior" tied to growing the top line in an efficient and sustainable manner. The goal of most business owners is (or should be) to generate profits of between 30% and 35% of gross revenue—that is the level it will take to support and finance next-generation ownership. Without the profit distributions at such a level, it is very difficult to create a multigenerational ownership structure that will enable the founders to maximize their value through an internal succession plan. Of course, that might be why the business is now for sale.

The point is, profits can affect value but not in exactly the same way as other components of cash flow. Failure to separate salaries and distributions or dividends on the profit and loss statement is not necessarily a red flag. In this industry, it is *normal* because of the use of compensation systems designed entirely around the goal of revenue production rather than the generation of profits. These books, practices, and businesses can still be excellent acquisition opportunities as evidenced by the high buyer-to-seller ratio almost every time one is listed for sale.

If nothing else, the goal here is that you, as a potential seller and even as a potential buyer, take the time to examine and evaluate your compensation structure. This is the real issue for most advisors. Are your "junior partners" on a revenue sharing plan? If so, you may be vulnerable to fracture lines in what you've built. Learn more. Obtain a Comprehensive Valuation and challenge what you think and what you've been taught. Understanding and solving the valuation issue early on might be the most important step you ever take.

CHAPTER 4

Building and Preserving Value toward the End of Your Career

My wife and I live on the edge of the continent, literally, on a basalt cliff 50 feet directly above the Pacific Ocean. At this latitude, the ocean often has an unpleasant disposition, even a bit of a temper. It's cold. It rages. You do not swim here. On a good day, the ocean is mostly mean, and always spectacular. And it is a great place to write.

A couple of times a day, a flight of brown pelicans comes through and time stops. There are lots of birds on the Northwest coastline, but none look like this one. A comically elegant bird with a six- to eight-foot wingspan, pelicans don't soar as much as they survey, gliding in low, surfing the wave tops, constantly on the lookout for fish beneath the surface of the ocean, always ready to strike.

The locals tell a story that pelicans live a magnificent life, plunge-diving into the ocean head-first in search of their next meal, eyes wide open, looking to stun and then capture unsuspecting prey. Time and time again they succeed, as they must, but they pay a price. Old age for a pelican is decided not by years, but by something worse. Diving repeatedly into the harsh and unforgiving ocean takes its toll. Pelicans, it is said, do not die of old age, but of blindness. Injuries suffered to their eyes over time render them unable to see and to hunt, and they eventually die of starvation. Such a sad and ironic story of nature.

As it turns out, this is a complete myth. Some pelicans do go blind, but it has nothing to do with the feats for which nature has designed them. Mercury poisoning and pesticides are the more likely culprits. Still, the myth persists here in the Northwest and it endears this species to those of us who look out across the ocean on a regular basis for inspiration.

There are lots of stories out there about what a practice is worth, or what someone recently was able to get for their book, or that there isn't as much value as you thought. M&A myths abound, especially in the areas of value and valuation. Sometimes, after reading various news items in the trade publications, I wonder if there aren't more myths than facts. But the stories are compelling and they are hard to forget. Over time, the stories actually start to sound like facts if they are repeated often enough, or they come from an otherwise credible source . . . or if you really need them to be true to support your plans and your thinking.

Let's separate fact from fiction and get to the task at hand—building or preserving the value you've spent a lifetime building as your career possibly nears the home stretch.

*   *   *

In a preceding chapter, we addressed the question, *What creates value?* In this chapter, we're going to answer a very different question, actually a series of questions, but all focused on one thing: What can you do in the next three to five years that will really make a difference in the value of your work, in a purely financial sense, as you contemplate an exit strategy? How do you increase value and ensure that you can realize it when the buyer requires a contingency based on client retention? If you have the time and the energy, tackle everything on this list. If you have less time, or less energy, start at the top and accomplish as many of these steps as you can, as best you can.

Remember that in most transactions, the buyer is larger than the seller— a business buying a practice, or a practice that is buying a book. This means that as a potential seller, you don't need to build the perfect model to be attractive and valuable to a buyer, and it is okay to let go of what you've built when the time comes. But until then, let's build on or preserve what you have. We'll stop halfway through this list to share a story about two advisors who custom designed their exit strategy and found a solution that best suited their needs as they extended their careers with the help of a strong and flexible buyer.

To be clear, this chapter will focus mostly on sellers. Buyers, however, can learn a lot by understanding what sellers are thinking and how they are preparing for this special event—an exit plan. Buyers can also learn what to look for as they evaluate the acquisition opportunity.

Much is made of "maximizing value" before selling, but for many owners who are in their late 50s, their 60s, or even 70s, the thought process isn't so much about doubling in value—that would take too much work and time. This chapter is about shoring up the past 20 to 30 years of work. It is about leaving no doubt that the practice is worth every penny being asked. It is about the seller being able to deliver valuable assets to the best possible buyer and having the entire client base welcome the seller's careful and exacting choice of the next advisor or business to step in and take over.

With these goals in mind, what can be done in the next few years, as a potential seller, to ensure that you can realize the market value of what you've built, on the best possible terms, at the best possible tax rates, to the best hand-picked buyer? Here are the 10 most important steps.

1. GET A POSITION FIX

In Chapter 1, we posed this question: "What have you built and are considering selling?" Read through the definitions again if you're unclear, but figure out which category of ownership you are currently in as a potential seller. Do you own a job or a book? A practice? A business, or a firm? Don't flinch. If you're not sure, go through the valuation process and ask for help. It could be the most valuable third-party opinion you'll ever receive. The answer will help you strategically plot your next move, but every plan requires an accurate starting point.

If you own a book, look at the definition of what it means to build and own a practice. If you've built a one-owner practice model, look at the definition of what it means to build a business. Does it make sense to expend the time, energy, and money to progress to the next level of ownership? Do you have time to do it? Assess where you're at and then decide where you would like to be at or near the end of your career. Another possibility, and perhaps the wiser course of action, is to determine which aspects of the practice or business-building process are within your time frame and skill-set and would have the most impact on value and the realization of that value post-closing.

It can be especially difficult to get an accurate position fix at the practice level of ownership. Practice owners are often surrounded by other producers or advisors who work for, or with, the practice owner on either a W-2 or 1099 basis. In other words, two or three advisors working under the same roof, side by side, but each using some form of production-first compensation. The common and critical mistake many practice owners make in the assessment process, and even in the valuation process, is to include the production of these nonowner advisors in their exit plans because the practice owner hired those individuals, trained them, even shared clients with them. If those other advisors own, or have cause to think they own, their books, there may well be a problem. These built-in "fracture lines" may seriously compromise the value the seller expects to receive.

As a practice owner, if you are thinking about an exit plan and there are other advisors with whom you work, or whom you employ, address the issue of separate books now. This issue is pervasive in our industry. An independent financial advisor can only sell and deliver what he or she can exert total control over. The fact that the seller's employees (or independent contractors) do not own shares in the overarching entity structure (corporation or LLC) does not mean that they don't or can't control the cash flows associated with the clients they individually work with. It matters, a lot, and every buyer is going to focus on this issue one day. It is a standard part of the due diligence process. The point is, a practice owner surrounded by three or four book builders does not equal a business and it cannot be valued or sold in the same manner.

2. FOCUS ON THE "M" IN M&A

In this book, we frequently use the term of art "M&A" or "M&A process" in place of "mergers and acquisitions." The funny thing is, almost everyone focuses on the "A" part and never even thinks about the "M" part. The merger strategy provides some very important benefits to independent advisors, especially those who want to take their practices to the business level later in their careers, or those who want to create a succession plan but lack the next-generation talent to support it.

Legally, a merger is the joining together of previously separate companies into a single economic entity. It is a statutory combination of two or more corporations in which one of the corporations survives and the other corporation(s) ceases to exist. This process can even work between a corporation and an LLC in what is referred to as a cross-species merger. In a true merger, the owners or leaders of the merged practices or businesses are typically retained for at least several years and this is why independent owners should consider a merger as an alternative to selling.

Consider this example. A practice owner who is 62 years old has his practice valued and is pleased to hear that market data supports a value of approximately $875,000. The reality is, the owner isn't actually ready to fully retire. There is a problem in that the advisor has no employees ready or willing to buy in or take over, and with some pending health issues, continuity planning is also an issue. The best this owner has been able to do is to continue working, enter into a revenue sharing arrangement with another practice owner across town who is 10 years younger and with the same IBD, and maintain his current client base. New clients are not as common as they used to be. A merger could be used to solve a wide range of problems and provide some great benefits.

A merger means that the practice owner will become an equity partner in a business, effectively exchanging the value of his practice for equal value in stock in a larger, stronger, more valuable business. As a part of a specific plan, this merger will necessarily include a continuity plan, a built-in succession plan, and even an exit strategy if that is what the practice owner wants. He can work for a couple of years, or maybe longer, and enjoy the benefits of ownership that usually include a base salary, profit distributions, appreciation of stock value, and a support team to help take great care of the client base, often a value-add in its own right. The new business entity would be obligated to buy back the practice owner's equity interest upon a well-planned retirement, or upon his death or disability.

Mergers can work in the other direction, too. A practice owner could also merge with a smaller, younger book owner who wants to build something bigger. A merger could provide each owner with time and resources in relatively quick fashion that would otherwise take years to achieve, if ever. The practice owner gets a succession and continuity partner. The book owner gets a mentor and an equity interest in a larger practice that he or she will one day own outright. For many independent advisors, a carefully planned and executed merger is smart business.

3. OBTAIN A FORMAL, THIRD-PARTY VALUATION

Is this the time to sell? Can you afford to sell? Before you can even start to think about preserving or building value, you need to know exactly how much value you have. Guessing, or applying a multiple of revenue or earnings stops being effective or accurate above about $100,000 in gross revenue (or GDC). An industry-specific valuation, such as the Comprehensive Valuation Report described in Chapter 3, will help you understand your value and what drives that value. In addition, this valuation process can provide diagnostic support when additional benchmarking elements are reviewed alongside it that can help you create a strategic and specific path forward.

Just to be clear, a "formal, third-party valuation" does not mean and explicitly excludes a free, online valuation tool—these are programs designed to spit out a number, not a carefully considered opinion of value. Whether this statement applies to your broker-dealer's practice management section's free opinion is up to you. Understand this—an accurate valuation requires a qualified individual who is impartial and is experienced in the valuation process. This isn't about best efforts, or coming "pretty close." This is about your future. Don't guess, or let others do the guessing for you. In terms of obtaining a formal, third-party valuation, it doesn't need to be FP Transitions, but it does need to be a similarly qualified, impartial, and experienced analyst or appraiser or you will not have a reliable answer from which to work and plan your next steps.

On the same tangent, the "value" of obtaining a formal, third-party valuation is about more than just receiving a number with a "$" sign in front of it. A thorough valuation takes work—quality in, quality out is how it goes—and most of the work is yours. You should learn almost as much completing the inputs and participating in the valuation process as you will from receiving the formal opinion of value. Accurately compiling all the data to support the valuation process takes some work, even some practice, so going through the drill a couple of times will improve the final results when you really need them. Your clients can find online solutions that will give them a "complete" financial plan for free, too. Would you tell them anything differently from what we're telling you?

Over the last five years or so of your career, obtain an annual valuation. This exercise will accomplish three important tasks. One, it will focus your efforts on sustaining your revenues and increasing value. Second, it will make you aware of when your value starts to decline and create a clear "sell" or "merge" signal. Finally, and perhaps most important, you will know what drives value and you will learn to look at your book, practice, or business as a buyer would look at it. At the very least, more experienced buyers will not be able to dissuade you from standing firm on the value of what you've built. Don't fall prey to the many myths surrounding value and valuation. Get the facts and do the job right.

4. UNDERSTAND THE IMPACT OF TERMS AND TAXES ON VALUE

As you contemplate selling your book or your practice, it is not enough to just know what your valuation result is. If you're going to make an informed decision, you need to understand how that value will be paid and what you can reasonably expect on an after-tax basis. How much of that value will be paid up front in cash? How and when will the balance be paid? Are there any contingencies? How will the proceeds be taxed, and what can you do to control or reduce the tax bill? How could bank financing improve the deal terms? These are just a few of the many questions that you need to have good answers to, and that is one of the purposes of this book.

A valuation result that does not tie value to payment terms and taxes is providing only part of the answer. It's similar to shopping for a mortgage and being told that, "yes, we can offer you financing. The term is 30 years." And then silence. If you don't receive additional details, you don't have enough information upon which to base a good decision, let alone sell your income stream and retire. As a prospective seller or merger partner, you need full and complete and accurate information.

Here are some important things to keep in mind. Selling assets does not create an ordinary income result for a seller, or at least it doesn't have to. If you are set up as a sole proprietorship, you can still obtain long-term capital gains tax treatment when selling your assets, if you structure your transaction correctly. This goes for book owners, too. If you're an S corporation or a limited liability company, stay the course. If you are a C corporation, you may have a conundrum, so keep reading. Selling an ownership stake of, say, 10% to a key employee/advisor doesn't foreclose your options going forward; it expands them if you have a good plan and construct the deal terms in a professional manner. Finally, avoid the use of revenue sharing and earn-out arrangements in your payment structure. In most cases, there are better and more professional tools for the task (see Chapter 7).

One more myth that needs to be destroyed that impacts the discussion in this chapter is the notion that selling advisors choose the highest bidder, as in an auction process. Nothing could be further from the truth, at least in our experience. As a seller, when the time comes, we expect and we know that you'll hand-pick the best buyer for your clients because that's not only the right thing to do, such motivation is built into the payment structure and you'll be rewarded for it. Start with "best match" and then focus on deal terms and tax structures—in that order. Sellers of an advisory practice cannot realize full value if their clients don't approve of the incoming team, year after year after year.

5. CONSIDER ALTERNATIVE STRATEGIES: SELL AND STAY OPPORTUNITIES

The Sell and Stay® strategy is unique and was pioneered by FP Transitions about 10 years ago. It serves to accomplish several goals. The Sell and Stay strategy blends or merges a smaller practice into a larger and similar business model in order to create an equity realization event, a continuity plan, and an ongoing employment opportunity with appropriate compensation and benefits for a seller who is in his or her last five years or so prior to a complete retirement, but who isn't quite ready to stop working. The chassis is usually an asset-based sale, which makes this approach different, legally, from a merger, but the term is still used and is generally applicable.

This strategy starts with a formal valuation of the subject practice. Once the value is determined and a "workweek trajectory" established for the practice owner, a search for a suitable partner is undertaken using either the open market system or a private listing process. The typical buyer or merger partner is usually a larger business that has at least one previous acquisition success. In addition, the buyer is well prepared, having put in place a formal continuity and succession plan supported with annual valuations and a culture of ownership, and is prequalified for bank financing should the acquisition process need to be accelerated.

A group of finalists is established and both buyer and seller begin the due diligence process. Once the best match has been determined and the details agreed to and memorialized in a term sheet or letter of intent, the practice owner sells his or her practice to the buyer under a special *Sell and Stay* arrangement and documentation package. The buyer typically agrees to pay a nonrefundable down payment and executes a promissory note for the balance, with payments beginning on the seller's full retirement or sooner. Most of these monies are taxed at long-term capital gains rates to the seller. The buyer also enters into a formal employment agreement with the seller and often hires key staff members as well. One of the key differences in the Sell and Stay process from a merger is that the seller does not become an equity partner in the acquiring business.

During the term of the employment agreement, the seller receives a base salary and incentive payments for new client referrals, but interest-only payments on the balance owed. The typical seller will work about 25 hours a week on average for a couple of years, or more, until full retirement is preferred. On the eve of retirement, the revenue of the seller's practice and client base is reviewed and a new valuation result obtained. The promissory note can be adjusted one time in most cases and then payments begin on the balance owed. Or, bank financing can be utilized to cash the seller out because, by this time, the seller's client base has been fully integrated into the buyer's business and transition risk is minimized or eliminated. This aspect also supports a great continuity plan in the event the seller has a health crisis or needs to step out suddenly for some other reason.

One caveat, and it is important in making this process work: Sellers will need to make some financial adjustments to accommodate this plan. A seller cannot continue to receive his or her past salary and benefits in full *and* maintain a similar level of control *and* be paid full market value for the practice. Something has to give, and this usually takes the form of a more moderate salary and control structure. Accordingly, this strategy is best used by sellers who are more than ready to "throttle back" to two or three days a week, or who already have reduced their time commitment, but are seeing a loss of revenue and/or value as a result. Those advisors in danger of falling into the attrition trap should seriously consider this model.

Taking Control of the Future: A Case Study

Alicia and Kerry had been in business for 11 years when the 2008 financial crisis hit. Like most advisors, they buckled down and worked their way through it alongside their clients and peers. But they also learned two important things. Next time, they would be better prepared, and they would not do it alone. They decided to explore a merger with a larger business or firm.

Alicia and Kerry, both in their early 50s, enjoyed helping their clients and providing financial advice. They did not like running the business and attending to the myriad details of operations, cash flow management, and staffing responsibilities. Some days the tasks were just a nuisance. As the business grew larger, the operational, technological, and regulatory aspects grew more daunting. They needed a comprehensive and permanent solution.

In May 2012, the search for a merger partner was commenced using FP Transitions' open market system. The process began with a formal valuation using a market-based approach and the direct market data method. The value was determined to be $2,385,000. Alicia and Kerry confidentially listed the opportunity in 2012 as follows:

> *Our business is located in the Northeast and has two branch locations in thriving metropolitan areas. This is a fee-only practice, with 100% recurring revenue. We have 50 clients with high net worth portfolios.*
>
> *Our business has two principals, both of whom are participating in their process. We have a high level of communication with our clients and communicate in person, through frequent phone calls, and newsletters. We conduct quarterly, in-person meetings.*
>
> *We would like to continue to work for the buyer/merger partner as employees after the merger to help aid in client continuity as well as to help grow the business, for a mutually agreed-upon period of time. The ideal buyer should be larger and organizationally stronger than our business and have the necessary ownership culture and staffing in place to readily absorb our operations and clients. We are not limiting this search to buyers only from the Northeast. We are open to diversifying geographically in order to complement our established locations. If necessary and desirable from the buyer's perspective, we can maintain our current office locations and leases. Our large cap growth style could either augment a buyer's similar style or, alternatively, complement an array of product styles as the buyer adds AUM.*
>
> *Terms: An asset purchase format, price $2,400,000 with at least 30% down, remainder negotiable and to include an ongoing employment agreement for each of the selling owners for a period of time to be determined.*

They were surprised by the results: 81 interested buyers responded in the first two weeks.

It took about 90 days to complete the due diligence process and to select a best match, and another 90 days or so to finalize the terms and the paperwork, but the transaction closed the same year. The sellers received 40% of the selling price in a down payment (nonrefundable) and a five-year adjustable promissory note based on the gain or loss of assets. The seller's office lease was maintained for two years while Alicia and Kerry worked from that location, and they now continue to work remotely.

The AUM at the time of the sale/merger was $141 million. Two years later, the assets under management had grown to over $152 million. Not a single client relationship was lost. The adjusted final sales price was $2.76 million. In addition, the sellers received a referral agreement that provided an additional four-year payout on all new referrals. Alicia is still working full-time as the relationship manager for the new owners. Kerry cut her hours back to spend time with her family and travel, though she is still co-managing her client portfolio with help from the new owners and staff.

As you approach the last years of your career, keep an open mind and rely on accurate and relevant information to guide your thinking and planning process. There are a lot of myths out there, so learn to separate fact from fiction. By doing so, you can take control of your future at this most important time in your life.

6. STUDY *RELIABLE* BENCHMARKING DATA

This is a great industry. Independent advisors own the most valuable of all professional service models. With recurring revenue, strong and sustainable growth rates, and low overhead, the typical practice owner is worth two to three times as much as a practice owned by a CPA, a lawyer, doctor, dentist, or architect. But this is a young and rapidly changing industry, too, and it hasn't quite solved all of its problems. One big problem is durability.

The ownership levels we defined as a job or book, and a practice, which comprise about 95% of the advisors in the independent space, are one-generation models. They are not durable. Simply stated, these models have not been built to last beyond the founder's career length and too many will follow the attrition route. The owners can and certainly do earn good livings while at the helm, but if realizing and maximizing value upon retirement is the goal, the entirety of this group may not be walking a path that you want to follow. So why would you benchmark against them? What will you learn?

There is a lot of benchmarking data floating around, and it isn't all good or useful. Remember what you learned in Step 1 when obtaining your position fix. If you own a practice and your goal is to try to build a stronger practice or even a business, or at least to move in that direction, studying benchmarking data obtained from practice owners who have surrounded themselves with book builders could steer you in the wrong direction. Be vigilant in your data sources and how you incorporate this information.

If you're going to use benchmarks as guideposts on your journey, especially over the last three to five years of your career, be sure you're getting reliable data to support your goals. Specifically, benchmark against businesses and firms, not practices designed for just one generation, unless that is your goal. There is a lot of data available to you in the independent financial services industry. As you review it, ask yourself these simple questions:

- What are your goals for the future? What do you want to build? Is it a valuable and enduring business? Is the goal to sell one day and maximize value?
- Who supplied the information you're thinking of relying upon—one-owner practices, or multigeneration businesses? Is the data reflective of practices below where you're at, or businesses twice your size?
- Did the owners in the benchmarking survey succeed in maximizing their value, or did they succumb to attrition?
- Have the owners of these practices or businesses ever accomplished what you are setting out to do?
- If you do exactly what "the crowd" did that supplied the data, where will you likely end up?

In that this is *The FP Transitions M&A Guide*, let's talk about how we do it. First, our database is extensive and accurate because we utilize information obtained during the formal valuation process. Second, our mission isn't just to help you sell what you've built; FP Transitions also endeavors to help advisors build an enduring business model, which means our benchmarking data contains information from those who are growing and balancing revenue strength with enterprise strength. Many have already achieved these goals. Third, FP Transitions benchmarks advisors against both their peer group and those twice their size. There is a lot to be learned from both groups.

7. CREATE A PLAN AND A DEFINITIVE TIMELINE

Have you ever said or thought, "I'll do this for about five more years, and then I'll think about selling." Or, "I have a plan. When I'm 75, or so, I'll hang it up and let someone else take over." Maybe something along the lines of "I'll do this forever. They'll have to wheel me out of the office on my last day." If any of these thoughts sound familiar, know that you're not alone. Unfortunately, you're also likely in attrition mode.

Most entrepreneurs do not retire at age 65. There is nothing traditional about the retirement process, especially on the independent side of the financial services industry. That also means that it is up to you to exert control over the process and create a plan that fits your needs and your lifestyle, and that serves your clients' best interests. In the next chapter, we'll show you how to time your final steps as an owner, but the takeaway here is to lay out a formal plan and commit your thoughts to paper.

For many advisors, a good starting point is to select the approximate age at which you want to be done working, and work backward from there. Set targets along the way, such as increasing value from the current $875,000 to $1.2 million, for example, or increasing the level of recurring revenue from 70% to 80%. Anticipate the impact of your plan on your office lease, and factor in lease renewal decisions. Another common strategy is to reduce or reshape the client base, transferring the smaller clients to a younger advisor, or discontinuing services to small or infrequent transactional-based clients. With reliable benchmarking data and annual valuations to track your progress, your practice can become much more valuable by doing some easy "pruning" along the way. If you have been considering a possible switch to a different regulatory format, such as a stand-alone RIA, now is the time to investigate how that change could affect your exit plans.

Setting up a formal entity structure, or refining the one you have, might also allow for the sale of a minority interest to one of your key employees, or to a son or a daughter. This step might produce an internal buyer, an internal successor, or just someone to assist an external buyer later. Nonetheless, consider this option while there is time to build a strategy that has a positive impact. An internal ownership track is often the best continuity plan money can buy.

The next time one of your clients asks the question, "What happens to me if something happens to you?," have an answer. Have a plan of action that has been carefully constructed and thoroughly tested on an after-tax basis fueled by reliable data. Think of it as a five-year plan and adjust it as you go, but do not confuse an idea with a definitive plan.

8. HAVE A BACKUP PLAN

An exit plan is supposed to be a well-planned, even joyous event—a moment of triumph and relief. But sometimes life intervenes and a health issue or something more serious, or sudden, occurs. Independent advisors need a backup plan, commonly referred to as a continuity plan. A continuity plan, prepared correctly and in the form of a continuity agreement, can address the clients' needs and help your family realize the value of your work in the event of your sudden death or disability.

Businesses and firms do not struggle as much with this issue as do practice owners and book builders. Having multiple owners within an entity structure drives the solution. Single-owner models have a much harder time solving for this issue. One common solution (do not confuse the word "common" with "good") is to use the free, broker-dealer or custodian prepared forms that set up a three-, four-, or sometimes five-year revenue sharing arrangement with another advisor within the same network in the event of your death or disability. Yes, this is better than nothing, but not by much. Even if you follow the first seven steps in this section and still discover that this route is in your future, be forewarned. Most of these "better than nothing" forms include "retirement" as a trigger event, which means that you have also effectively taken your practice off the market already (and for zero down payment, no guarantees, and at ordinary income tax rates). If you do decide to utilize one of these forms, use them solely for the emergency solution and *not* for your well-earned retirement.

There is an alternative to consider. Early on, FP Transitions designed an emergency continuity solution now called the Practice Emergency Plan, or PEP. The process requires that an advisor perform an annual, year-ending valuation so that there is a current and accurate picture of the practice on file. If something bad happens to the advisor, and upon notification by the spouse or designee (such as the family attorney), FP Transitions has previous instructions to list the practice for sale and to use the open market to quickly find the most capable and experienced buyer available in the area. In situations such as these, this process can be completed in as little as two weeks, which preserves most of the client relationships and, of course, much of the value. The process is carefully coordinated with the advisor's broker-dealer or custodian to help ensure a smooth and professional transition within their network if at all possible. Many practice owners implement this solution by including such instructions in their will. The process works well because of the many, many prequalified buyers ready to step up in a *heartbeat*, if necessary.

Continuity planning is often looked upon as a dress rehearsal for the exit planning or succession planning process, and for good reason. Don't overlook this element, especially toward the end of your career.

9. SELL ON THE WAY UP!

It almost sounds silly, but this is one of the most common mistakes that prospective sellers make. The problem is, most advisors convince themselves that they should sell only after things begin going badly in their work or in the national or global economy. It's like wanting to get out of a plane as it starts to fly through a violent thunderstorm. The result is too often that advisors don't sell and find themselves choosing the attrition route. Despite misgivings, it is still better to sell a lifetime of work even if at less than peak value than face a greater loss through attrition.

Our benchmarking process tracks growth rates using two different metrics. First, we obtain a five-year history in every valuation we perform so that we can determine the annual gross revenue growth rate over that period of time, but we also look separately at the net number of new clients in the past 12 months. This process is most effective during the last three to five years of an advisor's career when accompanied by annual valuations to closely monitor the trends in the data.

For financial professionals between ages 58 to 60, the *net new client acquisition rate* tends to level off and then, year by year, starts to track negatively. This is true, even though in a good to strong economy, the top-line revenue numbers will still track positive and may even look strong, or at least stable. For the group of owners over age 65, in a one-owner book or practice, both data sets are typically flat or even negative. This all helps to explain that the average age of advisors who sell on the way up is around age 60.

The leading cause of these declining growth trends is obvious—as advisors get older and achieve many of their personal financial goals, they simply don't invest the same amount of time and energy and money into their book or practice as they once did. The practice is put on "cruise control" while slowly losing speed and momentum. The effort to stay on top of modern technology and each new software release begins to wane. Owners take Friday afternoons off and then the entire day. Three-day weekends no longer require an official holiday. As entrepreneurs and independent owners, this is a well-deserved benefit and reward, but this is also where the one-owner model is vulnerable. These trends, left unchecked, will ultimately hurt your value and the ability to sell in the future if you don't monitor and address the issues beforehand.

Comparing these two different growth rates provides an *advance warning system* to prospective sellers. Don't be fooled by stable to slowly growing gross revenue numbers—your buyer won't be. Understand that, as a potential seller, it is not necessary that every aspect of the practice be fixed, polished, and in tip-top shape. Buyers don't expect that, especially those that are larger and own sustainable businesses. Focus on growing recurring revenue and taking good care of the clients who help you do that. Monitor your progress carefully over the last five years and be prepared to act appropriately.

10. FOCUS ON YOU

It almost seems that an apology might be in order at this point in that we've put "Focus on You," the advisor, as the last item on this important list. But that's how it is, isn't it? As a self-employed entrepreneur, everyone else's needs come first and you, the hardworking and diligent professional, come last on the list of priorities. Depending on your age, it has probably been that way for a long time. As you consider an exit plan, maybe it's time for a change.

In that we're focusing on the last three to five years of a career well spent, focusing on you and your needs means asking some tough questions. You often ask these or similar questions of your clients. Take some time to review them in the context of your personal and family life.

- What's next? What will I do if I don't have a place to go to every day and people who depend on me?
- What is my passion in life? Where would I devote my time if making a living wasn't at or near the top of my priority list every day?
- Will my social or business circle change significantly when I retire and leave the business world?
- What will I do with my extra time and energy?
- Will I be happier doing something else? Is there something else I want to do, if only I had the time?
- Can I afford to sell my practice?
- Does my family support my decision and my thinking?

Over the past decades we've observed that women in this industry often deal with career-changing decisions better than men do. As we speak to hundreds of advisors in detail about their plans every year, it seems clear that women have an easier time "calling it a day" at the end of their career. The women, it seems, become a part of the business where they work. While with many men, the business has become a part of them; it is who they are and they could no more separate from what they do than they could cut off their arm. While this may seem to be a generalization, it points to one critical task: Spend some time envisioning your next chapter, even if continuing to run your practice is the right answer. It never hurts to peer around the next corner. Just know that it is okay to let go. You've earned that right.

In this chapter, admittedly, we likely raised more questions than we've answered, and that is exactly the point. It is important to raise these questions and issues now while there is still plenty of time to address them and come up with good answers and solutions. Equally important is for you, as you consider an exit planning strategy, to understand which questions to ask.

CHAPTER 5

Preparing to Sell

For advisors thinking that an exit plan via a sale may be the best option, this chapter will lay out many of the important considerations including where to start, what to expect, and how to succeed. As a first step, give yourself time to do the job right. It is possible to find a great buyer and obtain full value, or something close, on short notice but the exit planning process is easier, more enjoyable, and more professional, especially from your clients' point of view, if you lay out a plan and follow it.

Buyers, this may be the most important chapter of this book for you. Smart buyers are well prepared and understand exactly what their counterparts are thinking and doing in preparation for such an event.

Even with a good plan, every independent advisor will need to decide on his or her own when the time is right. At least half of this decision is personal, bordering perhaps on emotional—an independent practice is something that advisors have painstakingly built and letting go can be hard even if it is the correct and logical choice. The other half of the decision process tends to be dictated by outside issues such as health, the economy, escalating or changing tax rates, regulatory issues (which never seem to get easier or be reduced), or sometimes even partnership struggles. Most sellers don't sell solely because they want to "get rich" or "cash out." There is almost always something more to it than that.

Historically, outsiders viewed the process as "selling and walking away." As a qualified intermediary, a better articulation is that we help sellers sell and walk in a direction of their own choosing, at a time that is right, leaving an advisor's clients in the hands of a highly trusted new advisor team of equal or greater capability and capacity. Taking control has to be about more than just working in one profession forever until the owner or the practice dies. In fact, there are some great alternative choices to consider and with time and a good plan, almost anything is possible.

WHAT'S YOUR PLAN?

When the time comes, most advisors don't need to look too far for buyers—prospective buyers are all around in the form of peers, competitors, consolidators, banks, CPA firms, and the like. Wholesalers and broker-dealers and custodians are more than willing to provide potential sellers with a short list of potential acquirers, regardless of the quality of the fit. The easy part is creating a short list of possibilities. The real challenge is in finding a *great* buyer, maybe the perfect advisor or firm to take over, pay market value, and retain all of the clients. The challenge, from the point of view of an advisor contemplating an exit strategy, lies in finding a buyer who can meet most of the goals on the following checklist. Does the potential buyer have:

❑ The same investment philosophy and a similar regulatory structure as the seller
❑ The capacity to take on many new clients in a short time frame
❑ The ability and willingness to pay market value and on reasonable, professional terms
❑ The willingness to structure the transaction to provide the seller with beneficial tax treatment
❑ A strong and loyal staff (and perhaps the ability and willingness to take on the seller's key staff members)
❑ The experience, education, and credentials needed to quickly earn the clients' trust
❑ A complementary location or geography given the seller's needs and circumstances
❑ The same level or a higher level of technology
❑ A culture or personality compatible with the seller's
❑ The financial ability and stability to handle the acquisition costs, even in a down market in years to come
❑ The ability to provide "added value" to the acquired client base, offering services or benefits that the seller could not or did not provide
❑ A continuity and succession plan of their own
❑ A larger, stronger business model with a younger team of owners/advisors so that capacity is not an issue, and that sustainability and durability are given attributes

Advisors, as independent owners, can elect to shorten this list and to accept a buyer who can check off at least some of these items. But for advisors who are taking the time to study the process and want to know how to create a high-quality and valuable exit strategy, the best advice is: do not deviate too much from this list. It is possible, even likely, to attain most of these goals. Your clients are depending on it. That's the power of the current strong seller's market—it isn't about receiving 50 offers; it is about narrowing the field of candidates to the best two or three and then letting those prospects prove they can solve all or most of these issues. It often takes a competitive selling position to accomplish this task.

Advisors considering an exit plan have choices to make. Advisors can sell internally to a son, a daughter, a key employee, or a group of the foregoing people. If this group is ready, and the clients are ready for them, bank financing can help to close the gap financially with external buyers, which, in many ways, comprises most of the other choices. In terms of external buyers, advisors can initiate a limited search starting with someone they know. You can take a more proactive approach and post a confidential search on the open market, casting a wider net and giving yourself even more choices, perhaps better choices in a competitive setting. More thoroughly, you can also initiate a private, targeted search to quietly and confidentially search for a prospect who can "check all the boxes," or a merger partner, or even a next-generation advisor (think book builder) who is willing to join a more senior advisor's practice or business and work his or her way up the ladder. While you might still elect to sell to someone you know, that decision should be able to withstand the scrutiny of a wider and deeper search.

Figure 5.1 provides an illustration of the range of exit planning choices, including the process of searching for buyers, selecting the best buyer, and completing the transaction.

Most sellers believe that the exit planning process starts with finding a buyer, even the first one that comes along, and working from there to *get what you can get*. Given the strong seller's market that exists at this time, and has for the past 10 to 15 years, this approach has become outdated and outmoded for most practice owners. In this industry, the phrase "finding a buyer" more closely fits a homeowner, or someone who is selling a retail

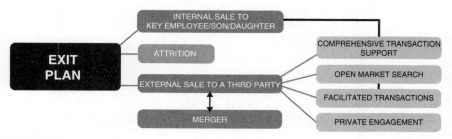

FIGURE 5.1   Exit Plan Options and Paths

business or franchise. In a highly regulated, relationship-based, professional services model, most independent advisors cannot risk putting a "For Sale" sign out front, or spreading the word through a group of peers and hoping for the best. Regardless of the method, this approach leads to a 1:1 buyer-to-seller ratio and it puts the buyer in the position of strength. Casting a wider net is a better way to find the best match and obtain full value while still taking proper care of the trusting client base.

Advisors who are thinking about retiring or slowing down need a plan. For those readers who are very literal, "a plan" doesn't mean that you need to pay $25,000 for a 50-page memorandum and commit to a multiyear process. For most advisors contemplating an exit strategy, it's actually the opposite. A good plan can be set up and ready to execute in fewer than 60 to 90 days, easily. Later in this chapter, we address the situation of the *quick sale*, which can be accomplished, and often is, in 60 days or less (not including post-closing support).

A formal exit plan, once value and valuation issues have been resolved, centers on three key aspects:

1. *Searching* for the best match
2. *Framing* the deal
3. *Closing* or completing the transaction

Figure 5.2 illustrates the basic exit planning process.

These plan elements are presented in order of difficulty, not necessarily what comes first. Ideally, the first step is to determine what the ideal plan is

SEARCHING	FRAMING	CLOSING
• Family	• Continuity Plan	• Documentation
• Friends	• Exit Plan	• Deal Terms
• Peers/Associates	• Internal Sale	• Tax Structure
• Private Searches	• External Sale	• Contingencies
• Open Market	• Merger	• Seller Financing
• Closed Market	• Complete Sale	• Bank Financing
• Banks/Credit Unions	of Assets	• Transition Plan
• Bulletin Boards	• Complete Sale	• Regulatory Issues
• IBD/Custodian	of Stock	
	• Partial Sale of Stock	
	• Sell and Stay	
LEVEL OF DIFFICULTY **LOW**	LEVEL OF DIFFICULTY **MEDIUM**	LEVEL OF DIFFICULTY **HIGH**

FIGURE 5.2   Basic Exit Planning Process

or should be and then, second, to find the best people to support and carry out that plan.

Searching could be the easiest part, or so it seems. If advisors help the process along by signaling tentative interest, perhaps posting on a bulletin board or calling their IBD or custodian, buyers will start showing up on their doorstep, literally. Number of buyers certainly plays a role, but if those buyers don't know what the selling advisor is looking for, the result may be a hundred buyers who are not a good fit. More likely, if confidentiality is not carefully maintained, competitors and clients will eventually find out, too. The goal should be to search broadly, but with pinpoint accuracy, and to do so in a quiet and professional manner.

Framing the best plan is largely a matter of experience and facts. Each advisor's fact pattern will help to select the best range of plans as a matter of course, and then it is a matter of personal preference. If more time is available prior to retirement, typically more options can be considered. If less time is available, most of the major goals of the exit plan can be achieved, but some of the details may require a compromise.

Closing the sale is the hardest part, and if the first two elements of the plan are not implemented to support the third step, it is even harder. Unprepared deals often get sent out to the lawyers, one for each side, who step in at the eleventh hour to try to weld together the pieces of a practice owner's dream while battling the other side's counsel even as the meter continuously runs. The better way is to start the entire process with good information, a steady hand to guide the journey, and the experience and expertise to actually complete the task as designed. Being an independent advisor and an entrepreneur is a thrilling and meaningful career choice. *It should end* with cymbals clanging and bells ringing in triumph and celebration.

Just as you worked through the 10 steps in the previous chapter to assess your current position and contemplate your trajectory, these elements also provide a road map. In this case, you are perhaps a bit more dependent on personnel and team members to assist you. This is a good time to start building your team and to identify who can help you achieve your goals.

FINDING THE VERY BEST MATCH

Being an independent financial advisor implies a commitment to a profession that surpasses a single career. The element of "planning," or at least focusing on the future, implies that an independent advisor is starting something that will not and should not end with his or her own career. No one expects an advisor to live forever, or provide endless services, but it seems reasonable enough to expect that every advisor will leave his or her clients in a better position than they found them. That's the point of an exit plan.

Starting with *a view from 30,000 feet*, the basic choices include buyers who are best summarized and properly categorized as:

- Strategic
- Financial
- Internal

A strategic buyer is thinking about the *synergistic effect* of the acquisition. Merging is a commonly used word and strategy for this group of buyers. Strategic buyers expect to get more value out of the acquisition than the intrinsic value of the book, practice, or business being acquired. As a result, strategic buyers are sometimes willing to pay a higher price for the opportunity. Strategic buyers may include banks, CPA firms, a credit union, a law firm, even a competitor in the same space, or an out-of-state advisory firm that wants an immediate footprint in a new or adjacent state. A strategic buyer is almost always an external or third-party buyer prospect.

The synergistic effects are more pronounced for an unrelated business such as a CPA firm or a bank or a law firm where a cross-selling strategy can be implemented. As a result, the common assumption is that these groups will pay more, sometimes a lot more, for an acquisition or merger opportunity. Firsthand experience over the past several decades illustrates that CPA firms and banks are competitive, but no more so than any other strategic buyer. While such opportunities are always intriguing, the reality of mixing two different cultures on a permanent basis is often very difficult and the results sometimes disappointing.

A financial buyer is focused on the financial return from their investment. The best example is a well-organized, well-capitalized consolidator. In past years, names like National Financial Partners, Focus Financial Partners, and United Capital come to mind. Financial buyers certainly don't overlook the strategic aspects of the acquisition, but they have systems and processes in place that work for them and they prefer to largely repeat those proven processes over and over—it's why they're successful. In this category, sellers tend to adapt to the buyer, not the other way around. Financial buyers tend to want the seller (as an individual) to remain in place and often to maintain an ownership position. Acquiring *a business*, as defined in Chapter 1, is the main target of a financial buyer, though larger practices are targeted as well. A financial buyer is primarily an external or third-party buyer prospect.

An internal buyer works with or for the seller, and may be an individual or a group of key employees or fellow owners/shareholders (in the same entity structure), perhaps even a family member. Remember that there is a difference between a succession plan and an exit plan—while this book focuses on the latter strategy, it is important to note that a business succession plan typically involves a "successor team" as opposed to one individual, and the team buys out the senior owner(s) *gradually* as the business continues to grow. As a result, this group of employees can offer a lucrative retirement strategy to the founding generation that may well surpass either a strategic or a financial buyer. The catch is, the succession planning process takes time, sometimes 10 to 15 years or more. In an exit plan, an internal buyer usually purchases the book, practice, or business all at once. In the past, internal candidates have lacked the financial resources that a strategic or financial buyer brings to the table, but with the advent of bank financing, that is not necessarily the case any longer. Now it is primarily a question of readiness and willingness on the internal candidate's part.

As a seller contemplating an exit strategy, always start the search for "best match" by looking at the internal prospects. If that is not an option, the open market often provides the next best opportunity to find an external buyer, whether strategic or financial in nature. The open market helps make it possible for an independent advisor to find his or her best match from a large pool of applicants—more times than not, the buyer pool contains both strategic and financial buyers. The high buyer-to-seller ratio allows an advisor to act in his or her clients' best interests by providing a hand-picked replacement of equal or better quality. If an advisor is going to sell their book, practice, or even business, the argument stands that every independent advisor has a duty to find the best possible replacement.

Some of the most basic advice FP Transitions offers to prospective sellers and buyers has remained the same for the past two decades, and it is as true today as it was back then.

1. Focus first on finding the best operational and cultural match between buyer and seller. Successful sellers tend to find buyers who are a mirror image of themselves, at least in terms of client base, revenue streams, regulatory structure, and investment philosophy but larger in terms of cash flow and value.
2. Second, focus on the issue of "geography." Sometimes this means selecting a buyer who is close by, and sometimes it doesn't. A seller who wants to keep his or her office open, the staff employed, and the same bricks-and-mortar operation in place will often prefer a buyer who does not currently have a local presence. A seller with four months left on his or her lease and with no intention of signing another lease will usually prefer a strong local buyer.

3. After satisfactorily resolving the first two issues, then and only then, focus on price and terms. If advisors get the first two steps right, this step will largely take care of itself.

Most advisors readily accept the concept of "best match" but often default to looking toward a friend or colleague as the easy or obvious answer. There is nothing wrong with selling to a friend or buying a practice from someone you know, but keep the words and strategies on the pages of this book in mind. You might sell your home to a friend, too, but would you forgo knowing what the market value actually is, give up the tax benefits of the sale, and take on all the risk because it seems easier? Many financial advisors do exactly that at the end of their careers, thinking they have few better alternatives. Most of the time, they're wrong.

WHEN TO SELL: TIMING THAT FINAL STEP

When should you start developing your exit plan or succession plan? The short answer is, start the planning process early. For succession planning, this is a 10- to 15-year process, so more time is definitely better. For advisors who want to sell using an exit strategy, ideally start the planning process three to five years before you think you're ready to actually sell. Monitor your equity value annually during those years to make sure you're not already in attrition mode and bleeding off value before you sell. But these are general rules, and most advisors require more precise information when talking about an exit plan designed to safely transfer hundreds of trusting client relationships and hundreds of thousands, perhaps millions, of dollars, in value.

One way to determine when to start the exit planning process is to first lay out your own "workweek trajectory." In other words, after reflecting on how much cash flow you need in retirement and whether you're ready to pursue some new interest or livelihood, consider a much simpler assessment tool: forecast the amount of time you would like to spend *in* the business, or are willing to spend *on* it, in the years to come. Realistically, what would you like to do? Use a graph like the one in Figure 5.3 to plot your own workweek trajectory. The example provided here is one advisor's preference to completely retire in about seven years, gradually reducing the hours spent at work along the way.

Start your trajectory with an accurate assessment of the average number of hours you now spend in the office each week, and working diligently on office-related matters from home. Then plot how many hours you'd like to be working in two years, four years, six years, and so on, or similar increments to fit your fact pattern.

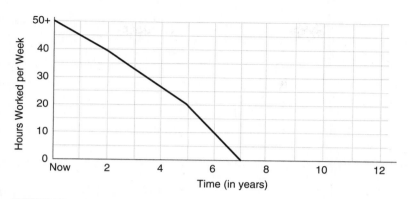

FIGURE 5.3 Workweek Trajectory

Next, draw a horizontal line at the 30-hour-per-week level as illustrated in Figure 5.4. This line is called, or represents, the "30-hour threshold." The 30-hour threshold provides an important lesson for founders and exit planners. Very few practices can operate efficiently with the founder and primary rainmaker consistently working fewer than 30 hours a week. In time, as younger competitors work hard to build their practices and continually invest time and boundless energy in marketing plans, technology, staffing, new clients, and such, older advisory practices with just one owner working less than full time, despite having years of experience, eventually begin to slip. The client demographics become worse than average, and then much worse. Growth rates decline. Fewer new clients come through the door. The practice soon finds itself in attrition mode.

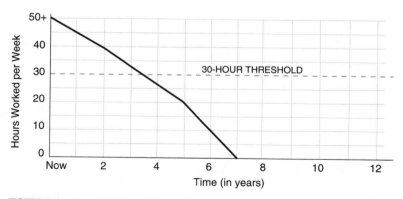

FIGURE 5.4 The 30-Hour Threshold

Without a formal exit plan (or succession plan), falling below the 30-hour threshold (or about 60% of your normal workweek) for a sustained period of time is a recipe for attrition and a continuing loss of value and cash flow. Sustaining the current or past growth rate, and equity value, is usually not possible for an indefinite period of time with a declining workweek trajectory.

Advisors should start the formal exit planning process three to five years before they anticipate breaking the 30-hour threshold. Carefully track and plot the valuation results from year to year and correlate any effect on value with the declining workweek trajectory. Next, develop a formal plan based on your workweek trajectory such as an external exit plan (sale to a third party or a merger), as illustrated in Figure 5.5, or an internal exit plan (a complete sale all at one time to a son, daughter, or key employee(s)), as illustrated in Figure 5.6. Use this planning process to create action steps on an annual basis.

As a quick reminder, a succession plan may be the better choice if you'd prefer to perpetuate your income for the rest of your life/career and you don't clearly see a "hard stop" at any point in your work—that is the purpose of this planning process. An exit plan brings your work and your practice to an end, or at least a *safe landing*, transferring control to a larger and sustainable business or firm. Almost every advisor, given a choice, will

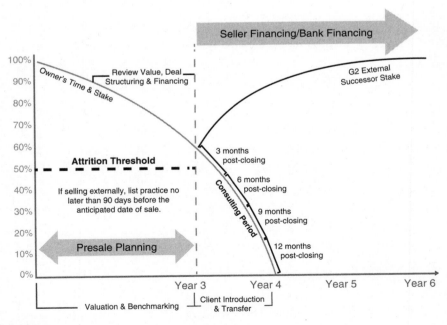

FIGURE 5.5 A Sample External Exit Strategy

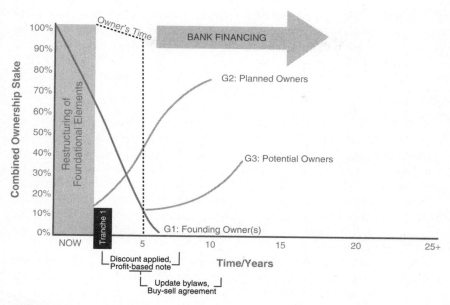

FIGURE 5.6 A Sample Internal Exit Strategy

prefer a perpetuation strategy, but not everyone has the energy or the time to pursue this path. But be sure not to confuse a perpetuation strategy with the attrition route. The determiner for advisors considering a perpetuation strategy is the owner's available time and energy, and of course, availability of next-generation talent.

Timing the "end game strategy" is hard. The suggestions in this section and elsewhere in this book are guidelines that each advisor will need to consider and adapt for their own use. There is no perfect answer or scientific method for pinpointing the right year or the right time except, perhaps, in hindsight. Acknowledge this limitation and create semiannual action steps while you ponder your trajectory. As you work through these steps and monitor your workweek assumptions, you will have moments of insight. These will help home in on the timing for an exit.

IN A NUTSHELL: HOW TO SELL YOUR BOOK, PRACTICE, OR BUSINESS

In most respects, what you've built, and how you've built it, will determine how you sell it. Let's consider how to implement your choice of an exit plan based on each level of ownership. In other words, how do you tend to sell at each level? How do you find the best buyer? What are the common mistakes to avoid? In addition to this information, Chapter 7 has more details on payment structuring, financing and tax allocation strategies, and Chapter 8 addresses the documentation process.

Jobs/Books

Relatively few jobs or books are sold, at least in percentage terms. Fewer than 1 in 10 owners at this level currently sell their book. Nonetheless, this is the most populous category of independent owners by a headcount with about 70% of all advisors. In terms of the sheer number of books for sale, this is still the largest group and buyers should take notice. With some advance planning, preparation, and knowledge of the possibilities, many more books could easily be sold directly or on the open market. This would be a major improvement to our industry as a whole, and a benefit to many hardworking solo advisors.

Most of the books that are sold are not listed on any formal exchange or website—they are simply transacted after a buyer and a seller "find" each other. Some of the time, the seller is introduced to a "preferred buyer" through existing channels at the seller's broker-dealer or custodian. Other times the seller and the buyer are friends, or at least respected colleagues. The introduction could start on a broker-dealer's or custodian's bulletin board or website. The closest thing to an internal sale at this level is a complete sale, all at once, to a son or daughter, or to an OSJ in the broker-dealer network.

Sellers beware: Predatory buyers dominate at this level of ownership because sellers are typically not well prepared and do not tend to appropriately *value* what they've built (in every sense of that word). It shows up in the final results, and, indirectly, in the 9 out of 10 books that never sell. Most negotiations between buyer and seller are at a 1:1 ratio, safely insulated from the competition of the larger open market. This 1:1 buyer-to-seller ratio might sound easy and appealing, but data indicates that the final realized value at this level, using the current selling and payment methods, is very low (.60 to .70)—not what's promised or implied, just what is actually delivered in the years following the transaction. The more competitive buyer-to-seller ratios mentioned earlier are common to the open market where sellers purposefully look through a large pool of interested buyers to find the best match and, ultimately, the best price and terms. The open market approach should work just as well for job or book owners.

Technically, this is an asset-based sale or acquisition, though the use of a formal asset purchase agreement is rare. If there is anything *below* an asset-based transfer, it is a simple *cash flow transfer*, and that is an accurate way of assessing the payment or financing mechanism employed in sales or acquisitions at this ownership level. Understanding that jobs/books range from solos to silos, the use of a stock-based transaction will most likely never enter into the discussion.

Independent broker-dealers and custodians routinely hand out short-form contracts (two or three pages in length is typical) to their advisors at no charge. These agreements, often called something like a "Business Continuity Agreement" or an "Agreement for Assignment of Accounts," allow a seller and a buyer to agree on terms of sale in the event of an advisor's death, permanent disability, *or retirement*. Adding "retirement" to the list of trigger events makes this a combined continuity agreement and exit plan. It essentially takes the seller off the market. The end result is a situation in which the M&A activity and deal structure can be tightly controlled and made to work in favor of the buyer, who will keep the seller's assets in the same broker-dealer or custodial network. This simple but powerful document is often used as a complete transfer device—it purports to value, transfer, and structure the payment or payment structure and (often unwittingly) establishes a tax structure for a job or a book. This is the most common method for transferring a book.

If you're preparing to sell your book, consider this: despite a relatively smaller total price, you can still easily maximize the payment terms and the tax advantages enjoyed by practice owners by structuring a formal asset sale. Too often, the parties simply agree to a revenue sharing arrangement without investigating what it would mean and what it would cost to *step up one level* of sophistication in a purchase agreement. Perhaps *especially at this size*, it is worth the extra effort in order to maximize an extra 10% to 15% of value to the seller, and at preferential tax rates.

Practices

Approximately one in five practice owners currently choose to sell what they've built through an exit plan, making this the next-largest group of advisors on the market. Practice owners who choose to sell have many options to consider.

Practice owners are highly sought after and many receive regular, unsolicited correspondence from interested buyers, consolidators, recruiters, even banks and credit unions. Another choice is to enter into a continuity plan with a local advisor who shares the same broker-dealer or custodian, a plan that may eventually turn into an exit plan. Mergers are a possibility at this level as well and create a wide variety of structures and options. Many practice sellers choose to conduct a broader and more thorough search for the best candidate regardless of broker-dealer affiliation, listing their practice on the open market. The closest thing to an internal sale at this level, as with a job/book, is a complete sale, all at once, to a son or daughter or key employee, or to an OSJ in the broker-dealer network.

Because of the choices that practice owners have, buyers should expect to work harder to successfully acquire at this level. Sellers should be able to produce an appropriate third-party valuation demonstrating the logic behind the price they ask and should demand to receive that value. Sellers should also be prepared to select the very best match in terms of personalities, regulatory structure, and culture, and then to support that choice, post-closing, until the clients are comfortable with the transition.

Financing and payment terms involving practices are commonly structured using a formal Asset Purchase Agreement complete with reps and warranties, covenants and conditions, even venue and dispute resolution mechanisms. Ancillary documents include a post-closing consulting agreement, a noncompetition/nonsolicitation agreement, and usually a performance-based promissory note if seller financing is involved. The goal isn't to produce a pound of paperwork for every million dollars of practice sold or acquired, but at this level, simple two- or three-page revenue sharing agreements are simply incapable of successfully transferring a professional service practice with an appropriate tax strategy.

There is a high level of "document pollution" that still occurs at the practice level. As mentioned earlier, as an industry, we're only about 10 years past the point of arguing about whether a practice even has any value at all. The result is that practice owners at the lower/smaller end of this spectrum sometimes still think they're selling their client lists and nothing more. The short-form revenue sharing agreements handed out by a broker-dealer's practice management team *do not apply* to practice owners, whether buying or selling.

Remember, if 50 prospective buyers want what almost every practice owner has built, this group has done something right. A practice sale should generate, at a minimum:

- An asset sale
- Long-term capital gains tax treatment for the seller, and write-offs and depreciable assets for the buyer
- A significant and nonrefundable down payment (25% to 35% is the range in most cases)
- A buyer match capable of retaining at least 90% to 95% of the client relationships
- A buyer with an enduring, stable, and valuable business of his or her own

It is easy to settle for something less, especially if you accept the first buyer who knocks on your door. Don't settle. If you're a seller, or thinking about it, you get to do this only once. It's okay to sell to a friend or someone you trust, but before you sell to that friend or to your OSJ or a preferred buyer who's *done this 5 times before*, find out what the market has to offer—you're likely to be pleasantly surprised. You can always say "No," but give yourself the power of choice, the power that comes with being an independent practice owner and an entrepreneur. Your choice of a buyer will directly affect your ability to not only give your clients what they deserve, but also to realize the proper value for what you have built over the course of your career.

Businesses

About 4 out of 10 businesses are transferred internally, usually gradually and as part of a long-term succession plan. Another 3 out of 10 businesses are sold externally, or merged with a third party. Understand that actual, true mergers do occur, but in most transactions, "merger" is simply a code word for a sale and acquisition and post-closing seller support.

In terms of sheer number of sellers, there aren't a lot at the business level that are up for sale at any given time, though these will be among the most valuable of the M&A opportunities. The interesting aspect at this ownership level is that buyers don't tend to find the sellers; the sellers often find the buyers.

Businesses have many choices in terms of who they sell to, how, and when. The goal with this group usually is not to maximize the number of buyer inquiries. Instead, business owners tend to prefer a *private listing* process where handpicked buyer prospects are meticulously screened and introduced one at a time with signed nondisclosure agreements having been exchanged in advance. If the seller is serious and the intermediary capable, one of the first three buyers introduced should be a fit and should succeed.

The buyers in this pool are well prepared and tend to have done their homework. Successful buyers of businesses will have built a sustainable business or even a firm that is valuable and has the valuation records to prove it; they will have a current buy-sell or shareholders' agreement in place for protection will have laid out a long-range succession plan for growth and prosperity and begun to implement it. A buyer like this will likely be the last stop for the seller's clients and most of the seller's key staff members.

Business owners receive plenty of unsolicited "offers" from buyer prospects just as practice owners do, except at this level most are just ignored.

Business builders and owners tend to dictate the terms and the timing of a transaction, not the other way around. It is still a seller's market and business owners know how to use it and not be used by it. As such, owners at this level tend to shun the help and support of their broker-dealer or custodian and fully expect to go it alone—that's likely been their path over the past 10 years, anyway. Don't expect to see a business for sale on a free bulletin board service. Businesses also tend to be fee-based, with less than 10% of their revenue stream from securities or annuities products or services, and they have at least one foot in the RIA circle.

Business owners have enough size and value that they attract, and are attracted to, professional valuation and transaction support. Professional advisors look to other professional service providers for high-caliber help. Attorneys, CPAs, business brokers, intermediaries, even investment bankers are common participants at this level.

Continuity planning provides an easy and early path to acquisition at the job/book and smaller practice levels because those models have little choice but to look outside for their back-up plan; most don't have licensed employees or staff, or fellow shareholders to turn to. That is not the case in a business. Businesses solve most of these problems internally. As a result, a business is generally well prepared for the sudden departure of one of its owners. However, this does not always translate into an enduring model or a succession plan. Exit planning may still be a part of the process.

Sales of a business to a third party are commonly structured using either a stock purchase agreement or an asset purchase agreement, each with supporting documents that include a post-closing consulting agreement for the founder, employment agreements for the key staff members, a noncompete/nonsolicitation agreement for the seller(s), and usually a performance-based promissory note financing structure. Payment terms include a significant down payment (20% to 50% of the purchase price is the range), which helps to motivate the buyer and to offset the risk in selling to a business or firm that the client base is likely unfamiliar with. Revenue sharing arrangements or earn-outs should never be used at this level.

Firms

Much of this book, from valuations to tax strategies to payment terms, applies to firms, but not all of it. Firms are different. Because of their size and level of sophistication, owners of firms demand special and private-level services to accommodate the needs of the multiple generations of talent and the unique aspects of what they've built and how they've built it. More than 75% of independent advisory firms are sold internally, usually to a team of successors and in a very gradual manner—a classic succession plan.

Only about 15% of firms sell externally and utilize an exit planning strategy along the lines described in the pages of this book, a number that appears to be gradually decreasing as enterprise sustainability becomes the focus.

THE LISTING PROCESS

The listing process describes how an advisor places their book, practice, or business up for sale, confidentially, to a national or regional audience of interested buyers and focuses on finding the best match for the seller's client base. The process can be conducted within the network of a cooperating and supportive IBD or custodian (a closed market), or across the entire spectrum of IBDs and custodians at one time (an open market)—it is the selling advisor's choice. At no point is this a *do-it-yourself process*, or a free online bulletin board—professional, one-on-one guidance should be provided every step of the way.

Buyers and sellers who participate in this process using the FP Transitions organized marketplaces (both open and closed markets) are prepared and qualified by the Transaction Team before the matchmaking process begins. Among the thousands of buyers who have indicated an interest in purchasing an advisory practice, hundreds are ready and able to move quickly and appropriately. All prospective buyers are asked to complete a detailed *Buyer Acquisition Profile* as a part of the get-to-know-you process, long before they are introduced to any selling advisor who lists their practice for sale (a sample Buyer Acquisition Profile form is included in the Appendix to this book). The listing process utilizes a marketplace of competitive buyers who agree to observe certain formalities and confidentiality requirements.

Stepping back from the details of the listing process for a moment, let's put this into perspective. Why consider *listing* your book, practice, or business for sale in an organized M&A system? What's in this for you, as a prospective selling advisor? Isn't there an easier or better way?

Independent advisors, whether working as registered reps under an IBD, as investment advisor reps (IARs) under an RIA of their own or someone else's, or in a hybrid model, *always have the ability to choose*. Independence means that an advisor can work with or under any broker-dealer or custodian(s) during the course of their career, and then sell to another rep or advisor with *any* broker-dealer or custodian at the conclusion of their career. What advisors have traditionally lacked until relatively recently is a confidential system that allows them to implement their ability to make these choices.

The idea behind the launch of FP Transitions' open market system almost 20 years ago was to create an efficient web-based platform that could provide independent financial advisors with the means of monetizing their ability to choose by providing access to the widest group of talented and motivated buyers. A closed market listing is handled in the exact same manner, but with a smaller, more limited group of buyers such as those within one particular IBD. Figure 5.7 illustrates the open market system.

The listing process creates a competitive setting that levels the playing field. Sellers have the advantage of numbers in terms of buyer demand. Buyers have more experience in the process in most cases and the support of their IBD/custodian. Generating an average of 50 interested buyers from which to select the best match provides a selling advisor more choice, control, and fairness in the process of transitioning an intangible, professional services model. By providing the seller with reliable and unbiased information, an accurate assessment of selling value, and the tools with which to realize that value, the listing process is probably the most effective way to find and provide the best talent for the client base in transition.

A typical listing contains some very basic but important information such as city and state (sometimes county and state if the city is smaller than a major metropolitan area), the underlying revenue streams (including recurring versus nonrecurring revenue), regulatory structure, assets under management, licenses held, a brief description of the client base, and the asking price and requested payment terms, among other things. The listing is prepared by the FP Transitions Transaction Team and is reviewed with the seller for accuracy. An example of a seller listing was provided in Chapter 4, "Taking Control of the Future: A Case Study," where Alicia and Kerry listed their merger opportunity to a national audience and found the perfect partner about 1,000 miles away.

The primary steps in both an open market and a closed market listing process are these:

1. Determine value (using the *most probable selling price* as the standard of value).
2. Conduct one-on-one interview with the seller (usually by phone) and a member of the Transaction Team to develop clear goals and expectations.
3. Prepare listing to explain to buyers the opportunity at hand and the seller's expectations.
4. Send notification out to all registered buyers, either nationally or locally, based on seller preference.
5. Review buyer inquiries and create a "short list" based on seller criteria and buyer information on file.
6. Organize direct interview process between seller and buyer prospects.
7. Obtain written offers from buyers who are the best matching candidates.
8. Upon acceptance of an offer, open escrow and commence due diligence process.

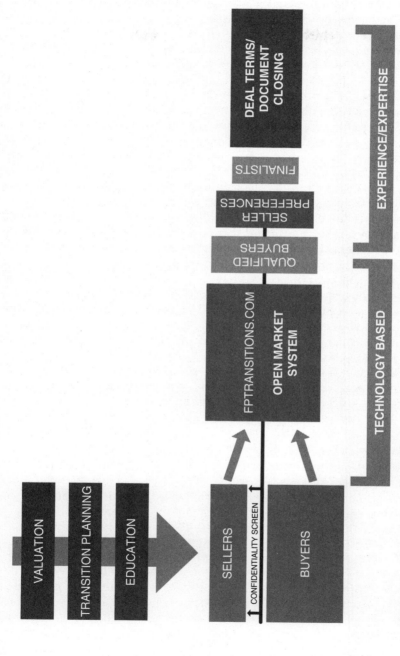

FIGURE 5.7 The Open Market System

9. Prepare and review necessary documentation to complete transaction.
10. Conduct closing.
11. Initiate client transition plan.
12. Monitor post-closing results and make any necessary adjustments to maximize transition rates and client satisfaction.

Many selling entrepreneurs find the listing and buyer inquiry process to be enjoyable, the pinnacle of a career spent building something of value and now searching through an enthusiastic and large pool of prospects who *want what you've built* and are willing to prove that they are the one you should select. Other advisors find the process overwhelming and prefer to stay in the background until the pool has been reduced to a qualified group of finalists that meets predetermined criteria. Either way, the system is designed to adapt to the seller's needs and the group of finalists.

In the following chapter, we'll discuss "interested buyers" versus "qualified buyers" in more detail. For now, understand that both are important to the overall process. It is a seller's market for certain, but on either seaboard, the tendency is for the buyer interest levels to swell by 50% or more above the current levels of buyer demand. Of course, interest is one thing—the buyers to whom you'd sell and offer seller financing to is quite another. As a general rule, every 12.5 to 15 buyer inquiries will generate one legitimate full-priced offer, with varying payment terms. Offers are what count in the end, but the competitive process supports fair and strong offers from which to choose.

The listing process requires not only the technological aspects of a web-based platform, but also the human and consulting element. One of our senior team specialists has worked with buyers and sellers for almost 20 years. Read on for her perspective on the entire process.

As a "matchmaker" and intermediary, I need to get to know the seller and spend time understanding this person and learning how we can help them. In addition to appreciating their motivation for selling, I need to know what they want versus what they need, what their goals are, and what worries them. I ask about family, hobbies, and the future, and then I listen. In time, I share information and stories—things that they need to know. Having good information and an experienced guide solves many of the problems. I try to make sure the process isn't overwhelming. I let sellers know that we'll take the lead and do most of the upfront work, but we obviously need their full support to be successful.

There are many reasons someone sells: illness, burnout, retirement, a desire to have more control over their time as they get older, relocation, going back to college for an advanced degree, industry change. Sometimes advisors are just plain tired, especially of compliance and regulations. At the point I speak with a seller, we've already done a valuation on the seller's practice, and the seller has indicated that they want to list, so the math part is clear. That part's simple, really. Finding the best matching buyer—that's the hard part.

Most sellers want to go in search of a buyer who is just like them, and that can be a good starting point. But once the facts are laid out with the value and related payment structure better understood, it becomes clear that what most sellers actually need is someone who is not just like them. Sellers tend to need a buyer to be larger and stronger. Issues of capacity, collateralization or security, continuity and succession, providing a value-added transfer all necessitate that job/books sell to a practice, practices sell to a business, and businesses sell to a firm. Sometimes that larger business or firm is someone the seller knows, sometimes it is a bank or a consolidator, sometimes even a competitor. If the seller brings us a buyer who has already indicated interest, we can simply act as deal coordinator. We have a special program for just that situation.

Buyers who are successful in this competitive, open market system don't just show up and make an acquisition. We work with them well in advance to prepare them for the opportunity. We perform a complete valuation on their practice or business, not so much for the purpose of determining what they're worth, but to understand what they've built, how they've built it, and who they would be a good match for. That, and having gone through the valuation process and learned what drives value helps them understand how to properly value the seller listings they come across, and set up the proper payment terms to ensure success in the long term. This is really important. By the time we start working on documentation, I want both parties to understand how the other side operates and how the entire transaction is in balance, especially since the seller almost always stays on to help transition the clients. It is what makes this system different, and special. It is why we're so often successful, if the seller is serious and dedicated to the process—and that's part of our job too.

We know that sellers get one chance to do this right. Our job is to guide them, counsel them, and hold their hand all the way through the process if necessary, and as necessary. We are a nonadvocate, but that does not mean we don't listen, care, and help. We just do it for both sides because there can't be any losers in this process.

There are other ways to sell your practice. The open market process may not be the right tool for everyone. A great argument can be made, however, that every independent advisor should endeavor to leave their clients in the hands of the best qualified candidate—selling for value and on fair terms has to take second place to the clients' best interests, though the concepts are inextricably tied together. The open market facilitates a seller's choices and control. Selecting from the widest group of potential candidates just makes sense, even if only to affirm that an advisor's first choice, perhaps local choice, or friend, is indeed the best of all possible successors.

MAKING A QUICK DECISION TO SELL

It is absolutely possible to sell an independent financial services or advisory book, practice, or business to a complete stranger, qualify them as the best fit and the best match, do the paperwork, obtain market value, structure preferential tax results for both sides, and close the deal quickly with minimal preparation in about 45 days. Sometimes, that is the plan. Chapter 7 discusses the details on how to structure the transaction and obtain the best tax results. Moving quickly does not require compromising on the basic payment structures and motivational aspects of the financing method.

In terms of speed, let's separate urgency from efficiency—two very different issues for would-be sellers. Urgency, the need or potential need to sell quickly, is best handled through one of two avenues: (1) a local buyer within the same IBD/custodial network who has previous acquisition experience, using basic but proven payment terms and documentation (see Chapter 7), in a nonadvocacy format; or (2) a written continuity agreement that is designed for exactly this issue and executed years in advance.

Don't confuse moving swiftly and certainly with a panic sale, or a sale to the first and only offer ever received. Some prospective sellers, after a few poor years and a very bad month, receive a letter in the mail or a phone call from an interested buyer, followed shortly thereafter by an offer. One of the biggest mistakes sellers make can be summed up with this simple monologue: "I've got an offer in hand. It's in the ballpark. I may not get another one, and I'm tired. I'm worn out. I think I'm going to take it."

Some advisors are firmly convinced that the first buyer who presents a reasonable offer should not be passed up—that it might well be the only offer. Therefore, "first buyer" often translates to "quick sale." That is possible, depending on what the advisor has built and the circumstances under which he or she is considering selling. Regardless, always start with a formal valuation of your own using the standard of *most probable selling price*, the *market approach*, and the *direct market data method* and judge from that standpoint.

In order to sell quickly, and at the best value to the best match, advisors need to be prepared and will need help—this isn't do-it-yourself territory, even though some buyers will advocate for quick sales and short contracts.

At the very least, sellers can protect themselves with information in order to be prepared. Know the facts by obtaining a formal valuation every year over the last three to five years of your career to eliminate vulnerabilities on this point. If the offer is still *in the ballpark* (and remember, ballparks are very large places), the payment terms and tax structure are competitive based on factual data (not hearsay), and you still want to sell after thinking about it, go for it. There may be other offers, but they're not likely to get significantly better. But an offer that meets these criteria, stemming from a 1:1 buyer ratio, is rare. Obtaining one or multiple offers of this nature from a pool of 50 or more buyers, where offers are tailored to meet your needs as a seller, is not only likely, but expected.

Negotiating with only one buyer not only means a lower selling price, it also almost always means that the seller has not chosen the best match. The process of finding "best match" requires that the seller search and interview and weigh one prospect against another. It is also possible that selling to someone you know and trust is as good as, or better than, the "best match" from a crowd of auditioning, competing advisors, large and small. Maybe, but test that premise. List the practice for sale and see if the first buyer stands up to the competition.

Highest selling price is not, and should never be, the determining factor when selling a book, practice, or business, nonetheless, it does matter. First, if you're selling to a buyer who is shopping for the best deal in town, is that really who you want to present to your clients? Second, balanced deal terms create a "shared-risk/shared-reward" structure that motivates both parties to work their hardest, post-closing, on the clients' behalf, a concept covered in more depth in Chapter 7. If the buyer claims to have a better idea than that, or has figured out a way around such an approach, run. On that same note, if someone offers a deal that is too good to be true (i.e., a multiple of three or four times trailing 12 months' revenue), investigate, and then run.

Bear in mind this closing thought. It is a lot easier in this industry to find another buyer than it is to find another seller.

WHEN SELLING ISN'T SELLING

Sharon and Matt were equal owners in a successful fee-based advisory practice located near Phoenix, Arizona. Their recent valuation results using the direct market data method came in at just under $6 million. They enjoyed their work and found good synergies in their skill-sets.

Organized as an S corporation, D&H Advisors had a strong and loyal client base, and word of mouth brought in a steady stream of new clients. Top-line growth rates were consistently above 7% annually, and profit distributions were a normal part of the owners' compensation structure. Sharon and Matt consistently performed annual valuations and regular benchmarking reviews and attended to the many operational details of their demanding practice in a proactive manner. They succeeded in almost everything they did. The one area that they struggled with was hiring and retaining high-quality, next-generation advisors—people of their own caliber and work ethic. Over the years, many younger advisors had come and gone and as the founding owners grew into their late 50s, they began to wonder what the future held.

Continuity issues had been attended to. Simply put, if something happened to one of them, the other would step up and take over and ensure that the departing owner was properly and fairly paid for their value. A formal Shareholders' Agreement even provided for life insurance funding and the use of bank financing to "cash out" the first partner to leave on a sudden basis and for some reason other than a well-planned and carefully executed retirement. But neither partner wanted to retire, at least not in the next 5 to 10 years.

Sharon and Matt shared a common goal as they contemplated the future of their practice and their respective equity positions. Both wanted to continue working together, but they also wanted to work fewer hours, take longer vacations, and, somehow, either solve the problem of next-generation talent and the sustainability of their practice model, or contemplate what an exit planning strategy might entail.

Together, Sharon and Matt explored an array of possibilities, considering everything from a formal, long-term succession plan to a complete sale of the practice to merging with a larger firm or even a smaller practice. The solution they figured out and executed was unique. They agreed to "merge" with a much larger business, but the merger allowed Sharon and Matt, working together, to retain control of their practice, continue to operate from the Phoenix location, and have a built-in growth, continuity, succession, and exit plan, depending on the circumstances. They also found a pipeline of proven, qualified, next-generation talent.

The details of the plan provided that their merger partner would acquire a one-third ownership interest in their S corporation. Sharon and Matt would each individually sell an equal interest to the "buyer," for cash now, and then enter into a new Shareholders' Agreement to protect against sudden death or disability or retirement. If something happened suddenly to either Sharon or Matt, the new merger partner would acquire the exiting owner's equity. The plans also called for the parties to meet once a quarter to address and support the practice's needs. Short-term goals included maintaining and supporting Sharon and Matt's success in terms of client satisfaction and retention, steady growth, and good profitability. Longer-term goals included staffing additions and operational support to enable Sharon and Matt to focus on the aspects of the business that they most enjoyed. All parties anticipate that the Phoenix location will be maintained well into the foreseeable future.

Of course, Sharon and Matt now will also have the opportunity to re-sculpt their succession plans and personal retirement plans with the help and support of a larger, stronger, and sustainable financial advisory business.

TEN THINGS BUYERS WILL WANT TO KNOW

. . . plus a few more.

One of the many reasons sellers should perform annual valuations in the years leading up to a sale and transition is that sellers need to know the facts about what they've built. Buyers will perform due diligence and most of the review occurs after a nonbinding letter of intent or term sheet is signed, but the process can move very quickly from beginning to end. Prior to seeking and receiving an offer from one or more interested buyers, sellers need to do their own homework and be ready to answer the following questions in detail:

1. Where exactly is the practice located? Is the lease available, or is it expiring and nonrenewable? Is there room to expand the operations inside the current office format?

2. What is the revenue mix (recurring versus nonrecurring), the average fee charged, and the range of fees? Is the business or client base trending in one direction or another in terms of services or revenue streams?

3. What level of client interaction does the seller maintain? Be specific about the methods, frequency, and depth of client "touches." This is where a great CRM system is helpful.

4. How many clients does the seller personally service? What is the average client tenure? How many clients are out of state? What states are they located in?

5. Are there licensed employees or administrative staff who want to stay on after the sale? Have the licensed employees signed noncompete agreements, or are they free to go after the client base? Is this a practice with a group of book builders, or a single business?

6. What is the seller's AUM? Does the seller have any assets in products subject to a surrender period? In what part of the client base (demographically) is the majority of AUM concentrated?

7. Does the seller want to stay on and work, or sell and leave? Will the seller help transition the clients over? Are there any health reasons, or other reasons (such as regulatory issues) that preclude the seller from supporting the transition for up to one year?
8. What is the average age of the seller's client base? How much of the income is derived from the top 10% of the client base? Top 20% of the client base? Are there any family members in the client base?
9. What is the seller's regulatory structure? Is there any disciplinary history? Are there any current or pending regulatory issues, or any written client complaints received in the past 12 months?
10. Does the seller have any referral pipelines in place? Are they transferable, or tied personally to the seller? Are any referral payments being made, and if so, are they reasonable, transferable, or cancelable?

In the Appendix to this book, buyers and sellers will find a more complete due diligence checklist. The preceding list is intended to help sellers prepare for the event and to understand what a buyer will focus on before any serious discussions begin. Expect that these questions will need to be answered early in the process.

Buyers tend to have a lot more experience in the M&A process than sellers and, as such, often dictate the pace and the direction of the due diligence process. Buyers who have completed one or more acquisitions know exactly what they want to know before deciding whether to proceed further. It is not unusual for a buyer to say, "Just tell me where your practice is located and the AUM, and then I'll decide if I'm interested." Sellers, who have spent a lifetime building and nurturing the practice and the client base, want to talk about the bigger picture, and the special relationships and opportunities at hand.

Part of this process is people, and part of this process is numbers, and time will be made for both in the acquisition process. Sellers usually want to focus on the former, buyers on the latter.

HANDLING KEY EMPLOYEES DURING THE SELLING/LISTING PROCESS

It is hard to keep things secret in a small office. Sellers should assume that staff members will find out eventually, and it is better that the news comes from someone they trust.

Prospective sellers often are reluctant to speak to staff members about their exit plans because they're not sure if the sale will be completed, or if they are even sellable. Why trumpet the news only to fail spectacularly in implementing it? This is where working with an experienced intermediary becomes so important. The pointed advice is this: "If you are not sure that you want to sell, do not list your practice on the open market system, because it will sell." No system is perfect, but about 9 out of 10 serious sellers do find a satisfactory buyer and see their transaction completed. The high buyer-to-seller ratio supports this end result. Depending on value, payment terms, time of the year, location, and even the circumstances of the sale, a good intermediary can provide a prospective seller with more specific and precise guidance as to what to expect, how to succeed, and even where the stumbling points are likely to be found.

Consider the advice and guidance in this book and, when you're ready, when you're sure of your intentions, tell your staff what you're thinking. It is likely that the best match of a buyer will want to retain the key staff members anyway, so this is not bad news, it is simply sharing a plan that is in everyone's best interests. If staff members want to work for the new owner, make that preference a part of the listing and sale process. Buyers will want to know, and this element will need to be addressed during the due diligence phase.

Licensed advisors require more discussion and thought. Depending on their status as a W-2 employee, a shareholder, or a 1099 contractor, and how they are compensated, licensed advisors who work with the seller or *under the seller's roof* may help the cause or they may hinder the cause. This goes back to the "fracture lines" issue covered earlier ("Fixing the Fracture Lines" in Chapter 3). In most cases, a formal valuation and consultation will pick up on this issue. Sellers should be careful not to include any revenue in the valuation or listing/sales process that might be claimed by one of the other advisors. Sorting these issues out in the years before the exit plan is implemented should be the goal.

Obtaining a noncompete, nonsolicitation, no-service agreement from your licensed advisors, or improving the one you have at this juncture may not be possible for a host of reasons. First, in most states, it is against public policy to enforce such an agreement when signed at this stage and for this reason, absent sufficient, perhaps significant, consideration. Restrictive covenants, as they are often called, are a state-specific issue. The employer-employee relationship, or even an independent contractor relationship, can create disparate bargaining positions in the eyes of the court; an arm's-length transaction between a buyer and a seller is usually looked on differently. This is one area where sellers will need the help of a local attorney familiar with this issue. Understand that nonsolicitation issues are different from noncompetition issues, but both can be difficult to address at this late date.

Sometimes sellers want their staff members and licensed associates to participate in the due diligence process, even interviewing the prospective buyer candidate(s). Consider this strategy carefully. The decision on whom to sell to should be a decision reserved to ownership—those who are in the best position to know the facts, assess the opportunities, and weigh the risk factors. Do not give a nonequity owner "veto power" over a prospective buyer. That's too much power without enough information in most cases, and the agenda of one or more staff members is often very different from that of a retiring owner's.

Most transactions at the job/book and practice levels are asset sales (not stock sales), so any employment agreement entered into prior to the sale is probably not going to be transferred or be transferable. Instead, the buyer will negotiate a new employment agreement and compensation formula that fits their model. An important tip is to use accurate benchmarking data to ensure that the compensation paid to a key staff member is reasonable and customary—the seller may decide to overcompensate a special staff member, but the buyer may not.

LETTING GO

It isn't easy to be an independent advisor. It isn't easy to depend on your own abilities to survive and prosper year after year, especially in a one-owner book or practice model. Entrepreneurs are unique and intrepid people. Of course it isn't easy to let go of it all. But being independent means exactly that. Someday, someone is going to have to take over for you. Exit planning, maybe selling what you've built, is the process of taking control over who, when, and how.

For most advisors, their practices are the single largest most valuable asset in their personal portfolios. Yet this asset is closely-held, and illiquid. A practice, by definition, relies almost entirely on one key advisor, and if something happens to that advisor, the value can be lost in a heartbeat. Managing the exit strategy isn't just a goal, it is an absolute necessity. And this perspective doesn't even begin to take the clients' needs and expectations, nor the staff's, into account. Life insurance simply doesn't address all of an owner's responsibilities.

Doing nothing, the attrition route, is indeed one type of exit plan, but it is a self-serving plan. Selling what you've built to a handpicked buyer takes work. Finishing the job is one of the responsibilities of independent ownership. How will your career end? What will your clients say as they look back on this experience? Perhaps there is a better question to consider: What do your clients deserve from you as your career winds down?

Just remember—it is okay to plan your exit and leave. You've earned that right.

CHAPTER 6

The Buyer's Perspective

A NEW DIRECTION

For advisors who are considering an exit plan and selling to a third party, this may be the most important chapter of this book. Smart sellers are well prepared and understand exactly what their counterparts are thinking and doing in preparation for such an event.

The goal of this chapter is to help buyers rethink their approach to the acquisition process, especially for those who have not yet completed an acquisition. This industry needs buyers to succeed in their role. To be clear, FP Transitions' bias is first and foremost toward the advisors' client base being served and transitioned, and second, toward advisors who are or should be selling what they've built rather than letting it die through attrition. To achieve these objectives, though, buyers must be more educated and better prepared to complete successful acquisitions. The end result could well be a doubling of the number of quality sellers on the market in the next 5 to 10 years. It is critical that we succeed as a group. It's a new direction, a better direction, and this chapter should help buyers lead the way.

In that our goal is to help exiting advisors *do a better job* of positioning their practices for sale (by using proper valuation techniques, searching for the best match, and structuring a seamless transition for the client base), buyers need to be equally ready for an operational shift on their part. Buyers need to be prepared for the explosive growth and many additional duties that come with taking on hundreds of new clients and tens or hundreds of millions of dollars in assets and responsibilities. There will also be debt to manage. Growth by acquisition is not, and cannot be, a short-term or impulsive strategy.

As a buyer, if you're reading this book, you've likely already made the decision to expand your practice by acquisition. While referrals and seminars may also be a part of your business model, pursuing an acquisition strategy requires understanding exactly what you expect the net benefit to be. Carefully consider your goals because advisors who are selling will want to know answers to questions like these:

- Is this acquisition primarily about generating more cash flow or more AUM?
- Are you a strategic buyer, or a financial buyer? (Do you know the difference?)
- Are you looking to build capacity, or a team of younger associates?
- Are you looking to acquire a younger client base as a hedge for your aging clients?
- Is your goal to achieve geographic balance and coverage?
- Is your goal to obtain more A list clients? Or to acquire and grow B list clients into A list clients?

Buyers who have a clear direction and a well-considered strategy for their next acquisition can better define their growth trajectory and the infrastructure needed to support it. In addition, buyers will have a much better sense of what they are looking for in an acquisition opportunity and how well the opportunity supports their goals.

In order for any selling practice owner to entrust their client base to a new advisor/owner, buyers will also need to be prepared to show that their own practice or business is capable of growth and sustainability, fiscal stability, creditworthiness, and management expertise (i.e., acknowledging that acquiring and retaining 200 new clients really is feasible). As competition grows for quality acquisition opportunities, buyers need to take the necessary steps, well in advance, to build a base for acquisition(s).

With that, let's reset the table. Here are the basic steps you need to take to succeed as a buyer.

1. Build a base for acquisition now.
2. Understand the M&A process at a master's level.
3. Resolve the valuation issue quickly and efficiently.
4. Learn how the vetting process works between buyers and sellers.
5. Expand the playing field by considering nontraditional acquisition opportunities.

In the following sections, we will address and amplify some of these issues and related topics, relying on previous and subsequent chapters to address the larger and more complicated aspects of valuation, payment terms, tax structures, and the post-closing transition process.

IF AT FIRST YOU DON'T SUCCEED . . .

In 1953, a start-up business called the Rocket Chemical Company and its staff of three set out to create a line of rust-prevention solvents and degreasers. Toiling in a small lab in San Diego, California, they set about to create a "water displacing" formula for use in the aerospace industry. It took 40 attempts to get the formula figured out.

But figure it out they did, and WD-40 was born. The name stands for *water displacement formula perfected on the 40th try*. Imagine what would have happened if the inventors had given up after two dozen or so really solid attempts?!

The story, and the point, of course, is bigger than trying hard and eventually succeeding. WD-40 was initially a product limited to special uses, an example of which was protecting the outer skin of the Atlas missile from rust and corrosion. But that was just for starters. The product actually worked quite well for a variety of other uses—so well that several employees snuck some WD-40 cans out of the plant to use at home on more mundane tasks like squeaky hinges and rusty nuts and bolts. The product eventually became a household staple. By innovating and adapting to the market, this small group of entrepreneurs created something great.

Every day we hear from buyers who have not been successful. In fact, 49 out of every 50 buyers who send in an inquiry to one of our open market or closed market listings won't succeed on that inquiry. That is a statistical certainty. But the problem isn't just numbers and statistics. Most buyers are not prepared to be successful. This is a problem that *can* be solved.

The message here, just to be crystal clear, is that as a buyer prospect in this young and rapidly changing and growing industry, trying hard and trying often is not enough. Innovate. Learn. Improve what you do and how you do it. Think around the problem. Build a practice or a business that is designed for rapid growth, one that has the necessary revenue strength and enterprise strength to accommodate an outright acquisition, a merger, a continuity partnership, a Sell and Stay strategy—whatever makes sense under the right circumstances. Make sure you have a succession plan and a continuity plan—smart sellers are going to ask. Building a base for acquisition is critical, and that is something that starts well in advance of the acquisition opportunity.

Frankly, if advisors follow this logic and build strong, sustainable businesses of their own, they will succeed many times over in terms of cash flow, profitability, equity value, and choices, regardless of whether they acquire another practice or two along the way. In fact, building an enduring business designed for growth by acquisition quite often has the effect of *sellers finding you* instead of the other way around.

BUILD A BASE FOR ACQUISITION

Everything is connected. Sellers quickly learn one thing about the M&A process in this industry: they will not realize full value unless their client base is fully satisfied that their previous advisor has selected a new advisor of equal or greater talent. In other words, clients are generally looking for a value-added situation, not merely an exchange of personalities. Don't overlook this facet, and do not underestimate how hard this is for a selling advisor to actually do. But in fact, as you'll read in the next chapter, the concept of shared-risk/shared-reward that supports most transactions almost demands that the seller find a buyer who is *bigger, better, and faster*. Unless the buyer uses some form of bank financing, sellers tend to risk about two-thirds or more of their value on the clients' satisfaction with their choice of a buyer (the common result of seller financing), so a sale won't happen until and unless the seller is sure of the best possible match.

The result is that sellers who value what they do and have physically valued what they've built will look at the buyer as a bank looks at a borrower. Skeptically. *Prove it to me. Show me that you're prepared. Show me that you can handle all of my clients now and in the years to come. Let me talk to a previous seller with whom you've already done this. Show me your credit score if you expect me to carry the paper on this transaction.* And that's why "best match" matters far more than highest bidder. People who think this is some kind of an auction process simply do not understand how the process actually works.

For all these reasons, it comes down to this, as a general rule: practices buy books. Businesses buy practices. Firms buy businesses. In sum, bigger tends to buy smaller, which eliminates, or at least substantially mitigates, issues of capacity. Serial acquirers in this industry are almost always businesses or firms as defined earlier. By the numbers, here is the data on who sellers have selected as their third-party, or external, buyers in terms of relative size (measured in terms of gross revenue over 1,500 completed transactions):

1. Acquisitions by buyers who are smaller than the seller: 8%
2. Acquisitions by buyers who are about the same size as the seller (+/– 10%): 18%
3. Acquisitions by buyers who were larger than the seller: 74%

In the last category, buyers were typically twice the size of sellers who were listed for sale on the open market or in a closed market setting, again using gross revenue as a reference point. The end result of a high buyer-to-seller ratio is that sellers tend to select buyers who are not only larger, but almost mirror images of themselves in terms of regulatory structure and revenue streams. This, of course, helps to address the issue of culture.

Bigger means more than just gross revenue or GDC from a buyer's perspective. Bigger necessarily implies *stronger* and translates to a sustainable business model. Aim for this defined pattern, and acquisition will be a natural part of your annual growth strategy: *a business must have certain foundational elements in place—an entity structure, a proper equity-centric (or ensemble) organizational structure, and a compensation system that gives it the ability to attract and retain talent while generating a sufficient profit margin (i.e., 30%) to reward and attract a multigenerational ownership structure. The revenue stream may be singular or diversified, but usually about 75% or more is fee-based or recurring. A business is built to be enduring and transferable from one generation to the next. It operates from a bottom-line approach and earnings are used to reward ownership and investment in the business. The ownership-level compensation system shifts to a base salary plus profit distributions and away from production-first oriented compensation.* This is the definition of a financial services or advisory *business.*

The preceding paragraph may contain the definition of your perfect buyer, but buyers don't need to be perfect and they don't have to be at the business level per se. On occasion, banks, credit unions, consolidators, CPA firms, and such can be added to this circle, too. And about one in five transactions are a practice buying a practice, or a book buying another book of the same size or even a bit larger. Issues of location, culture, and fit, even broker-dealer network, matter, too.

The advent of bank financing may well affect the dynamics between buyer and seller size as well. To date, selling advisors tend to prefer larger, stronger buyers because it is the seller who provides the financing (i.e., "seller financing")—a strong buyer with multiple owners is more likely to be a better credit risk. The use of bank financing means that a seller's risk is reduced, sometimes eliminated. It also means that smaller practices and books, owned by younger buyers, may soon be competing with larger, more established businesses in terms of *financial strength* when approaching an acquisition opportunity. Increased financial strength and the higher demand that is likely to result by having more capable buyers in the mix will change the M&A landscape yet again.

The starting point? If you are a prospective buyer, hire a third party to perform a formal valuation on *your* practice or business. You will learn a lot, including how to properly value the next seller who crosses your path (but understand that the valuation approach and method applicable to your ownership structure and purpose may be different than what is required in an acquisition opportunity). Take the time to put an accurate number on what you've spent a career building. Then study not only the answer, but the logic behind the answer. Add to the valuation results a formal benchmarking process, based on valuation inputs and financial statements (not online survey data), and you'll end up with more questions than answers. That's the point. What drives the value you've built? What *have* you built? Where is your model weak and strong? Do you have a balance between revenue strength and enterprise strength? If something happens to you tomorrow, will your enterprise endure, or will it come to a quick end? Asking tough questions and making realistic assessments based on accurate data is the starting point for building a base for acquisition.

The takeaway here is that advisors should build before they buy. We often see buyer prospects who think that the way to build a business is to acquire more books and practices. That approach is just plain wrong. Three books and a practice do not equal a business any more than a pile of bricks and a bag of mortar equals a sturdy wall. Take the time, now, to lay the foundations for a strong, sustainable business, and don't hesitate to ask your IBD or custodian to help and to support your efforts. In short order, turn that business into an acquisition machine and everyone wins. This is a new direction, and a good direction.

WHAT SELLERS WILL WANT TO KNOW

Sellers have many choices when selecting the best buyer from a competitive, open, or closed market process. They're in charge, for the most part. They are also, many times, *the bank* in the transaction, extending seller financing to their buyer for the majority of the purchase price. But there is more to it than that. Selling advisors who take the time and put in the effort to search, perhaps nationwide, for the very best match, care. They care what their clients think. To meet these expectations, sellers shop carefully and tend to look for a value-added transaction.

Due diligence works in both directions and sellers generally get to go first. What follows is a list of questions that sellers commonly ask of buyers who make the group of "finalists" in order to determine the best match.

Practice Information

- What is your fee schedule? What is your pricing model?
- Who is your IBD/custodian? If necessary, do you expect me to change, or will you consider joining my IBD/custodian?

- What is your level of client contact? Where do you meet most of your clients?
- What is your proposal for client retention following this acquisition?
- How do you plan to provide service to clients outside the immediate area?
- What is your current niche market or is it broad based?
- Describe your level of technology and CRM system—do you have a particular program or system that you feel is of great benefit to your current business?
- How do you envision growing the practice you acquire in the years to come?
- What is your current practice's mission statement?
- What do your current clients say about your current practice that makes you most proud? Are there any comments you feel are inaccurate or undeserved (e.g., from a client who left you)? What is true/false about their assessment? How many clients have you lost in the past 36 months? Why?
- Have you acquired another practice before? If so, please describe the experience and what you plan to do differently, if anything, this time.
- What services or benefits do you have to offer to get clients excited about this transition and to make them wish you had been in their life sooner?
- What does a successful post-closing relationship feel like and look like with your predecessor (in this case, the seller)?

Individual Information

- What is your investment expertise?
- Do you have the down payment immediately available, or is it borrowed? Can you provide proof of such financial ability?
- What is your time frame on this purchase, in terms of seller financing needed?
- What is your age? If you have internal successors identified, what are their ages?
- Have you ever faced a conflict of interest in your practice? How was it resolved?
- What is your timeline for retirement? What are the details of your succession plan, continuity plan, and/or exit strategy?
- Why do you want to buy this practice? What are your specific goals?

Staff Information

- Describe your current staff in terms of personnel, titles, responsibilities, tenure, etc.
- Describe your ideal team if it isn't already in place.

- What is your staff support to advisor ratio?
- Explain why the staff of this practice should look forward to joining your practice and become part of your team.

Once the best match has been determined, it is the buyer's turn to perform due diligence. In the appendix to this book, buyers and sellers can each find a more complete due diligence checklist, one from each of their respective positions.

UNDERSTANDING THE AUDITION PROCESS

The Vetting Procedure

Each year, FP Transitions assists a hundred sellers or more who are in search of a buyer who fits their criteria of "best match." Each seller receives about 50 written inquiries from interested and excited buyer prospects in the first 10 to 30 days. This written inquiry, sent to an anonymous advisor who has listed their practice (or book or business) for sale and provided a description about what they've built and what they are looking for in a buyer, is the first communication between the parties. It is important to get it right.

It is humorously ironic then, that one of the most common responses that prospective buyers send to such a seller is along the lines of: "Call me! I have cash!" This is no joke. We see it several times per seller listing, year after year.

This is perhaps the worst opening line a buyer could ever use in front of an educated seller, but still, it is the single most popular approach, give or take a few words. And it never works. In fact, as the Transaction Team and each seller in turn go through the list of interested buyers and their written inquiries, any response along these lines is immediately crossed off the list, no matter who the buyer is or how successful they have been. This type of response is a quick way to move from prospect to casualty.

First, and this is intended more for the advisors thinking about selling, the phrase "I have cash" does not mean "I am willing to pay all cash, up front, no questions asked, no matter what happens or how many clients, if any, stick around a year or two later." It just means that the buyer somehow thinks that this is all a seller cares about. This is one difference between being a buyer and being a prospect.

Many of the seller's clients are their friends, and some are family, or like family. A buyer could offer all cash, *and mean it*, and the seller still wouldn't sell to that buyer if the match wasn't close to perfect. The goal is "best match." If a given buyer is not the best match, in other words, the fit just isn't there, financial terms alone will never overcome this deficiency, no matter how successful their practice or business is, or how much more money they make compared to the seller. Sellers, in this industry at least, don't tend to think that way.

Here are a few excellent inquiries sent to sellers who listed on the open market (or sometimes in a closed market setting) in search of their perfect match. Note that these written inquiries are in the *short to midrange* in terms of length. The only substantive changes made were to the inquiring party's name and city/state or location(s).

> *I am a young(er) CFP with about 20 years of experience in the industry, split mostly between wholesaling (both variable annuities and mutual funds) and my current role as a financial advisor. I am very interested in learning more about your business and client base as it sounds similar to the business that I have built so far. I am located in a very professional office complex in Somewhere, USA, however I am always open to meet with clients at locations convenient to them. This approach tends to be especially helpful with many of my senior clients who don't always like to drive across town if they can avoid it. I am confident that I could help provide advice, guidance, and comfort to your clients through the rest of their retirement and lives. I have a clean U-4 and excellent relationships with all of my clients. I hope to be able to meet and discuss my background and learn more about you and your practice/clients.*

> *We are a three-member, all CFP, family-like business. We have a combined 50+ years of experience and our practice is large enough to comfortably take on and support your clients. We are located in Someplace, USA, and have been with the same broker/dealer since 1985. We successfully acquired a practice through FP Transitions in 2009 and are comfortable and familiar with the M&A process. Our practice focuses on advisory, but we also help clients with variable annuity accounts, alternative investments, insurance, and corporate retirement plans.*
>
> *Our younger two CFPs are in their 40s and have a combined 25 years in business. Those two will be in practice for at least 30 more years, so your clients will be well cared for and will not have to repeat the transition process. Please feel free to contact us at any time.*

> *Our company has been in the industry for many years. We established XYZ Wealth Management over 18 years ago and recently started our own RIA. Our main office is in Someplace, USA. We also*

have offices in San Francisco and Las Vegas. We have successfully acquired and transitioned three different practices with an average 97% retention rate. We are currently looking to expand to the northern part of the state. This seems like the perfect opportunity to do so!

We treat our clients like an extension of our family and never want them to feel like they are an account number. Our firm is on a hybrid platform, which allows us to run our advisory business through our own RIA and commission business through our independent broker-dealer. This also allows us to custody our clients' assets at most custodians. We would appreciate the opportunity to discuss how we can make something greater by putting our two businesses together to help benefit your clients. Please contact me at your earliest convenience. Thank you.

As you can see, it doesn't take a lot of effort to communicate to a listed seller, but it does take some effort and requires the right tone, certainly relevant in a relationship-based industry. In most cases, the buyer understands his or her value proposition and references it in the inquiry. It is worth noting that some buyer prospects also send in lengthy and fact-filled inquiries separately or additionally by email for the Transaction Team to forward to the selling advisor. Some buyers even supplement their online and written communications with an information packet that is gladly submitted to the seller—confidentially—on their behalf.

Here are some less-than-successful inquiries, in their entirety (complete with spelling errors), that did not meet with the listing seller's approval (i.e., the seller wisely chose to proceed with someone else).

- *See our website for more information: www.somethingorother.net.*
- *I am currently on vacation.*
- *Eager to by let's sit down and talk.*
- *Was thinking about building a practice in the area and was intrigued at the timeliness of this sale.*
- *Im willing to pay cash for the whole book if you necessary. I live in Texas, but I am originally from California. Willing to close quickly.*
- *CFP dedicated to relationship based, long-term, family financial planning.*
- *I am only interested in a business within 15 to 20 miles of Sacramento, CA. Please let me know if this does or does not fit my criteria. We can go from there then.*
- *I am trying to get a little more information to see if our practices be a fit.*
- *We have an advisory practice and have a a lot of experience with variable annuities as life insurance agents early in our careers. We think thatr we would be a great match with our high touch sevice model, local*

presence, and many years of industry experience. Please consider us. We also have experience with succession planning for reps, havig purchased four books of similar size to yours in the last four years, Thank you.

First impressions count. No matter how good the acquisition opportunity appears to be, it is never *a race to the altar*! The first buyer to show up on the doorstep is almost never a deciding factor. If you're a buyer, take your time and be professional and respectful throughout the process to all concerned—remember, due diligence starts from the first written or spoken word. Measured and thoughtful steps will go much further than trying to make the "top 10 list" of fastest buyers to respond.

Is It a Good Deal, or Not?

The most difficult acquisitions are those in which a seller refuses to follow any set valuation protocol and simply resorts to a "needs based" approach, as in "This is what I need if I'm going to sell to you" or "This is what I need to retire on." Some advisors who consider selling their book or practice seek out a formal valuation opinion, reluctantly, only as an affirmation of the value they've already decided on. And if there is no such affirmation (i.e., the valuation expert says the seller is wrong), then the expert doesn't understand the potential of the seller's practice. . . . If you are experienced in the M&A process in this or any other industry, this probably isn't news to you.

As we've said from the first chapter, the most contentious issue between a buyer and a seller can be value or valuation—in other words, what is the seller's book, practice, or business worth? In many instances, buyers and sellers can be at polar opposites on this issue. Sellers think their practice is worth more, and buyers think that the practice is worth less. The gap is usually pretty wide, and most of the time it is never fully closed. Disagreements over value kill more transactions than all other issues combined, and often before negotiations even get started.

A valuation result or position that appears to be too high, even *way too high*, however, can be resolved in a number of ways from the buyer's perspective. Consider these steps as a buyer before you walk away and try to find a more cooperative and informed seller:

1. Make sure that you, as a potential buyer, understand the issues of value and valuation in this industry. Obtain a formal valuation on your own practice or business using a standard of *most probable selling price*, and a market-based approach employing the *direct market data method*— the same standard, approach, and method that sellers should use. Once you fully understand how the valuation process works and what drives value in this industry, the seller's position will be easier to deal with.

2. Utilize an authoritative, credentialed, and experienced (in this industry) source to perform a valuation of the seller's book, practice, or business. Offer to split the cost with him or her upon a successful transaction, or even to reimburse the seller in full.
3. Attempt to balance the valuation results or demands with smart and professional payment terms and tax structures. Sometimes it really is as simple as, the seller names the value, and the buyer names the terms. Chapter 7 goes into more detail about the structuring and financing process.
4. Utilize bank financing. Most sellers expect to provide financing and be paid over time, contingently. When bank financing is used to support a transaction, buyers can offer much more aggressive terms, perhaps in exchange for a lower value.

Many of the issues that arise between a buyer and a seller can be resolved if the buyer has a full understanding of how payment terms and financing arrangements and tax strategies actually work. Terms and tax rates can offset a high valuation request in many cases.

The Comprehensive Valuation approach covered in Chapter 3 is inexpensive and remarkably accurate. The purpose of the Comprehensive Valuation Report (CVR) is to take valuation *off the table* as a dividing or contentious issue. This approach is not a compromise. It is a reflection of what is actually happening in the market between informed buyers and sellers, which helps to "center" expectations and goals in the M&A process.

In addition, the CVR provides the valuation opinion *within the context of specified payment terms*. And that is the key factor. Agreeing to a value without all the details is a waste of time. Connect the value and payment/ tax structures and, as a buyer, you've essentially eliminated all of the contentious issues simultaneously. The payment terms referenced in these valuation results are also addressed in the following chapter.

Study and master "Deal Structuring: Payment Terms, Taxes, and Financing" (Chapter 7). Read this chapter a couple of times because this is where a buyer's skill-set needs to be very, very strong. Eliminate from your vocabulary the terms "revenue sharing" or "commission splitting" unless you are buying a very small book. Learn how to use a performance-based promissory note to protect yourself. Learn how to use the acquired cash flows to pay for two-thirds of the purchase price and then to write off every dollar of the purchase price on your tax return over time. When buyers understand how much flexibility and safety they can build into the acquisition process by mastering the payment terms, they will fully appreciate why value and valuation are *not* the issues to focus on.

Here is an example. FP Transitions listed a selling advisor's practice about fifteen years ago who insisted on a three times multiple—not a dime less. This was well before values had climbed to even 60% of that level. Buyer after buyer shunned the seller and walked away. But one young buyer stepped up and completed the acquisition, offering to pay full value if the seller would finance the transaction over eight years with favorable tax consequences for the buyer. The buyer also welcomed the seller's continuing support and referrals and agreed to pay extra for both. The transaction was structured more like a merger (covered further on) and both parties are still cooperating and supporting each other a decade and a half later. And the practice has paid for itself many times over.

Do not get sidetracked by valuation issues. Value or the selling price, alone, does not make a bad deal good, or a good deal bad. Handle value and valuation issues through knowledge and preparation. Remember, sellers get to do this only once. Buyers tend to bring far more experience to the table, so make it count.

Dealing with a Reluctant Seller

One of the most common frustrations that buyers experience is their inability to get enough information from the seller, early in the process, to decide if they want to proceed further. Yes, there may be 50 interested buyers, putting the seller in command and control, but if none of the interested buyers can get enough quality information in a prompt manner, the transaction is destined for failure.

Buyers often communicate to a selling advisor with this refrain: "I don't want to spend a lot of time on this opportunity unless I can be sure this is still something that I am interested in. *I need more information.*" Buyers, start by looking at the Buyer's Due Diligence Checklist included in the Appendix to this book. There is a long list of items that buyers are going to review, and that sellers will need to provide. You are going to get your information, but first things first. Be patient and don't *jump the gun.* Remember that sellers are looking for information on you, too, but their first issue is how best to reduce a large and enthusiastic pool of buyer prospects to a manageable group of finalists, maybe the one best match, in fewer than 30 days, typically. That is *job one.* Work with the seller and follow their lead, focusing on what you can do to convince them that you are or could be their best matching prospect. Cooperation, confidence, and patience are the order of the day. The time will come for you to ask your questions.

If the seller has listed his or her practice on the open market, don't hesitate to call your Transaction Team contact. As a qualified intermediary, this is what they do. As long as you treat all involved with respect and provide clarity as to your needs and goals, you will receive help and support in return. If you're working with a seller on your own, one on one, almost every piece of advice in this section still applies. As a side note, FP Transitions has developed a program that helps a buyer and a seller who have already found each other work through the process of closing a transaction. The Comprehensive Transaction Support (CTS) process guides each party through the necessary steps and helps keep the sale on track. In most cases, the seller has agreed to sell at a certain price with terms "to be hammered out later." So often, this is where a deal can get stalled. In these cases, having a guide, or traffic coordinator, can keep the process moving along.

Another issue that buyers sometimes run into is a seller who always finds one more thing that they don't like, and just can't ever quite commit, or get to, *the finish line.* Sellers get to do this only once, and many advisors— most if you think back to Chapter 1—will never sell. It is hard to let go, and especially hard if the seller is unsure about whether it is the right decision. For most advisors, it *is* personal. Starting and building a successful practice and navigating the currents over several decades makes most owners closer to their work than most members of their family. Advisors may understand the logic for needing to sell and call it a day, but sometimes it is awfully hard to convince their heart.

Follow the advice given earlier. Be patient. But also be clear about your intentions and what you can do to help them on their journey. Sometimes a little space is just what is needed. Rarely does a more aggressive push work, but there is a time and place to do so. The way to do it is to send the prospective seller a written offer, a term sheet laying out the offer and including price, terms, taxes, anticipated closing date, and a 15- to 30-day deadline on acceptance. It may not work, but as an interested buyer, you will know more than you did at the start of the process.

Also consider "tethering" your business to their practice, or your practice to their practice or book with a formal continuity agreement. This strategy, covered in the last section of this chapter, can be an excellent way of being patient, but holding on to the opportunity and solving a major problem for the advisor who is not quite ready to sell.

Consider the possibility that the *correct* value and payment terms and tax structure might also do the job. In a one-on-one transaction (without an intermediary involved), it is still fairly rare for a buyer to present a selling advisor with an offer that is at market rates in terms of value, down payment, and financing structure. Again, a good method of checking your compass, as a buyer, is to go through the same valuation process that a seller goes through (MPSP as the standard of value, DMDM as the approach and method of determining value, as discussed in Chapter 2). You might think your offer is fair, but how does it hold up against what the seller could reasonably expect from the market? You need to know the answer.

Advisors who are considering that an exit plan might be for them often slip into a pattern of procrastination. No disrespect is intended, just an observation that applies to all of us at different times and junctions in our careers. What we hear is something like this: "In five years or so, I'll sell this thing and walk away." But as it turns out, three or four years later, it's the same plan: "In five years or so, I'll sell this thing and walk away, but not quite yet." We call this the "rolling five-year plan." The only thing that consistently changes the course is a serious health issue, which often brings everything to an untimely end, at which point it is often too late to sell what's left of the practice for serious market value.

There is no pithy advice on how to solve this last challenge. Choice is why advisors become independent and exercising that choice is just part of the territory. If you're a buyer pursuing a seller who appears to be on a rolling retirement plan, offer to be their continuity partner. If that doesn't work, move on.

ARE YOU A BUYER OR A PROSPECT?

Let's reexamine the oft-cited 50:1 buyer-to-seller ratio, *from the buyer's perspective*. The ratio is certainly real, but are these "true buyers?" The short answer is "Yes." That only one will purchase a particular practice should not impinge on the other 49 advisors who have at least made an attempt. Even if all 50 were strong, sustainable businesses and ideal cultural fits, still only one suitor can actually complete the acquisition.

This is a good time to discuss the concept of a "qualified buyer," that is, those most likely to succeed on any given opportunity because they are well prepared and, sometimes, even experienced. Qualified buyers are the most likely to be invited to make an offer. If the market demand is high enough, 10 or more qualified buyers is a great result, but not rare. Does that reduce the "real buyer-to-seller ratio" to something closer to 10:1? That's up to the seller. Some sellers insist on talking to, or at least emailing every single prospect, thanking them for their interest. Some sellers prefer to talk only to the two or three best qualified candidates.

The point is, qualified buyers aren't just bigger and stronger businesses. The difference can be found in preparation and experience. Some qualified buyers are book owners or practice owners. Size is not the deciding factor. Qualified buyers have a plan and they've been executing on that plan for a couple of years at least. By contrast, prospects often show up and hope to get lucky. Maybe that's not entirely fair: prospects have a lot to learn, and the best way to learn is to get started and participate in the process. What if you don't succeed on your first try, or even your first 4 tries? However, doing the same thing over and over and expecting a different result, well . . . that's the definition of a "perennial prospect."

The goal of this section is certainly not to admonish anyone, but rather to underscore the need, as an industry, to create more qualified buyers. If we do that, together, there will be more successful acquisitions and more sellers and better value. All of these things need to happen. Quantity is a part of the process, but quality is the key. This is one of the driving forces of the independent financial services industry as it grows and evolves and faces its own M&A issues.

In the preceding chapters, we have challenged the role that independent broker-dealers and custodians have played thus far in the exit planning and succession planning process. Helping to create qualified buyers is an area where these practice management personnel should excel, and advisors, young and old, should be demanding help from their IBDs/custodians in building their own strong, sustainable business models that will, in turn, support a vibrant and well-organized M&A marketplace within their own networks. Instead of supporting predatory buyers (on occasion), IBDs and custodians can and should support legions of qualified buyers who want to build their own base for acquisition.

The competitive open market process is about more than just providing a choice of suitors; it is about seeing the best qualified and best prepared buyers rise to the top. Selling to the best match and to the best qualified buyer means the clients tend to emphatically approve of the value-added transition. This means that the seller obtains best value through the shared-risk/shared-reward payment structure, which, in turn, means that more sellers will come to the market and create great exit plans. All of this is good for the sellers, good for the clients being transferred, good for the industry, and great for advisors interested in growth by acquisition. Call your broker-dealer or custodian today and request their help in building a sustainable and valuable business that is capable of acquiring many books and practices, within the same network, and without.

NONTRADITIONAL ACQUISITION STRATEGIES

The goal of this chapter is to help advisors who are focusing on an acquisition strategy reach their goals. To do so, it is important that advisors understand that there are numerous acquisition strategies and methods that should be considered. Mergers, continuity partners, and continuity agreements, employment opportunities, a Sell and Stay strategy, business building, succession planning—all of these strategies create unique opportunities to bring a practice owner on board during the last three to five years of their career, or sooner, depending on the fact pattern. These strategies can also support bringing a younger book or practice owner on board where they can contribute for decades to come.

Being familiar with *all* the *tools in the toolbox* can often mean the difference not just between success and failure, but spotting an opportunity or missing it completely. The idea that every seller is a 68-year-old book owner waiting for a buyer to knock on their door and take over is a fallacy. Many acquisition opportunities involve advisors who are nowhere near ready to sell and leave, regardless of their age. The nontraditional acquisition strategies covered in this section are intended for this audience of prospective sellers.

Mergers

To determine whether a merger is an appropriate course of action, it is necessary to first understand the wide range of business structuring alternatives that fall under the general category of "mergers." There are a number of related terms that are frequently confused because of their similarity in meaning or their misapplication in the marketplace, so clarifying the terminology is a good place to start.

Legally, a merger is the joining together of two or more previously separate companies into a *single economic entity*, that is, the statutory combination of two or more corporations (or LLCs), in which one of the corporations survives and the other corporation(s) ceases to exist. Statutory mergers are conducted under the rules of Internal Revenue Code (IRC) Section 368, as well as applicable state statutes. In a true merger, most of the owners or leaders of the merged practices or businesses are typically retained for at least several years. The goal of a merger is best expressed by this simple, but challenging equation: $1 + 1 = 3$. Mergers are usually about synergy.

An "acquisition" is taking possession of another practice or business through the purchase of its assets or stock. True acquisitions are also called "takeovers" or "buyouts." All acquisitions involve one practice, business, or firm *purchasing* another. In the financial services industry, the owner of the acquired practice is commonly removed from the equation following a brief post-closing transition period.

A "joint venture" occurs when two or more businesses join to conduct a specific business enterprise with both parties sharing the risks, profits, and losses. A joint venture differs from a merger or acquisition in that both companies typically remain independent during *and after* the joint venture process. The venture is for one specific project only, rather than a continuing business relationship as in a "strategic alliance."

A "strategic alliance" involves a partnership with another business in which the two companies combine efforts to obtain a competitive advantage. This can involve anything from getting a better price for goods by buying in bulk to seeking business opportunities together with each party providing part of the solution or product. The basic idea behind alliances is to mini-mize risk while maximizing leverage. The most common form of strategic alliance is a "nonequity alliance" simply involving a contractual arrange-ment between two firms.

A "partnership" is legally defined as a contractual relationship between two or more persons carrying on a joint business venture with a view toward profit, with each partner incurring liability for losses and the right to share in the profits.

Focusing on mergers and acquisitions, the most commonly pursued ave-nues often revolve around the tax issues. An acquisition is a taxable transac-tion. Following the acquisition of another company's assets, the buyer can often record the acquired assets at their fair market value (usually greater than the seller's tax basis), thereby yielding more depreciation to the buyer. The seller, on the other hand, must pay income taxes on the recaptured differ-ence between the consideration received and the seller's basis in the business.

In a merger, certain exchanges of stock are considered tax-free reorgani-zations, which permit the owners of one company to exchange their shares for the stock of the acquirer without paying taxes (Figure 6.1). In order to qualify as a nontaxable event, the IRC stipulates that the following require-ments be met:

- The transaction must have a bona fide "business purpose" other than tax avoidance.
- There must be a continuity of interest, where the ownership interests of the selling shareholders continue into the acquiring entity.
- There must be a continuity of the business enterprise, where the buyer must either continue the seller's historical business or use a significant proportion of the acquired assets in the business.

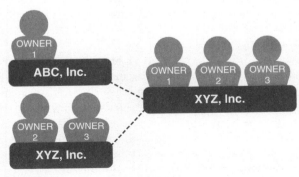

FIGURE 6.1   A Statutory Merger

The IRS has included these basic requirements in four types of legal reorganization, commonly described as type A, B, C, or D reorganizations. The letter designations come from the paragraph letters in the IRC (Section 368) under which they are described.

Aside from the tax consequences, there are several different types of mergers, each distinguished by the relationship between the two financial services or advisory businesses that are merging. A "horizontal merger" occurs when the merged firms are in direct competition in the same markets or provide the same services. A "vertical merger" occurs between a company and one of its suppliers or distribution channels. A "market-extension merger" happens when two firms come together that sell the same services but in different markets.

Mergers tend to work best when the two financial service practices, businesses, or firms are similar in size, but have different skill-sets or market niches. Under such circumstances, a merger can add the strengths of different practitioners together and hopefully eliminate or reduce their respective weaknesses. This sounds great in theory, but it is difficult in execution. Business owners tend to look for people who think like they do, and have similar personalities and skill-sets. If synergies are the goal, merger partners need to look for candidates that enhance existing skills, who offer new and better opportunities for the merged entity than the individuals could find on their own.

Sometimes, though, it really is just a matter of size and scale: $1 + 1 = 2$ is a perfectly acceptable answer, and has been since the second grade. At the very least, it may be a bigger number than either party started with or could achieve on their own. Merging a practice owned by a 40-year-old advisor with a larger practice owned by a 67-year-old advisor who wants to work another five years or so just might make sense, if it is organized correctly, regardless of any synergistic effect.

There are many other ways to achieve a successful merger. Here is a short list of ideas and strategies to complete a merger or acquisition from the buyer's perspective.

- Completing a **partial-book acquisition** of specific clients based on size, geography, or investment portfolio. This allows a seller to continue working with a smaller group of clients and yet monetize part of the value of what he or she has built.
- A "seller" who brings in outside, younger talent to support an **internal succession plan** by acquiring or merging with a book builder, or a smaller but well-staffed practice or business.
- **Acquiring an equity interest** in a larger practice or business. This is a great strategy for a younger owner, whether from the aspect of a current

employee, or an outside book or practice builder—parlay what you've built into a significant equity position as a business owner's successor, or as a member of his or her successor team.

- **Becoming a minority owner** of a practice with an entity structure. This allows an advisor to become the built-in continuity partner, and perhaps exit plan, for the founding advisor.
- Completing a **turnkey acquisition in another state** and keeping almost all of the ownership and staff in place, creating a series of satellite offices.
- **Using the equity or stock in your business** to pay for some or all of an acquired practice or book. This works best with sellers who aren't ready to retire.

There are a hundred iterations of these merger strategies, from merging "up," to a merger of "equals," to merging "down," with every case study requiring or allowing for a unique set of answers and challenges. As a buyer, there is more than one way to grow by acquisition. Learn the rules and find out how everyone else does it, then break it all apart and think for yourself. There is always a way to get things done if you're creative enough and have the tools and theories at your disposal.

Buy-Sell Agreements

Advisors who are interested in acquisition can offer something more than money and a promissory note to a seller who may not be quite ready to leave. For a younger advisor, youth and some experience can translate into a great opportunity. Building on the preceding section, individual advisors might consider "merging" into a larger practice or business and taking an equity position, albeit minority in many cases, in exchange for the opportunity, actually a *contractual right*, to be the eventual successor.

A buy-sell agreement legally specifies how a privately held company or its owners will redistribute ownership in the event that one of the owners dies, becomes disabled, retires, or otherwise leaves the practice or business. (In that a shareholders' agreement refers to a corporation, and an operating agreement refers to an LLC, we are using the more generic term of "buy-sell agreement" to refer to a continuity planning agreement for multiple owners of a corporation, a partnership, or an LLC.) The agreement is a contractual covenant by each owner and the business to redeem the stake of any owner who departs, with the goal of providing payment of value to that individual, or to their estate, and to ensure that the business enterprise survives and continues to provide services to the client base.

Buy-sell agreements allow for the possibility of "merging" the founding generation with the next generation, and then transferring full ownership either suddenly, if necessary, or gradually, if time permits. For businesses or firms set up as an entity (S corporation or LLC, typically) with two or more owners, the choice of continuity partner is clear. A *fellow owner* is the best and obvious choice. If a buy-sell agreement has been entered into, the choice of successor or acquirer is a matter of contract.

Bear in mind that, for purposes of discussing M&A activity, "multiple owners" necessarily implies that a younger advisor has bought into a minority ownership position with an older, founding advisor of a practice or a business for the explicit purpose of continuity initially, and acquisition/succession later. That is what makes this a nontraditional, but effective, acquisition strategy. This approach ties into both the preceding and following sections, "Mergers" and "Continuity Planning." The buy-sell agreement is the device through which ownership is actually transferred in the end.

The buyout process can also be significantly aided by proper funding mechanisms such as life insurance or lump-sum disability insurance. For buyouts triggered by death, a life insurance policy held by the buyer (many times this is the business itself) on each of the owners or the senior owner can be an effective option for funding either a down payment or the entire purchase price. Lump-sum disability insurance is also an option for buyouts triggered by disability, but the policy is generally aimed at providing a significant down payment, relying on the acquired cash flow to pay the rest of the balance. This is a classic example in which some of the new bank financing options work quite well.

Younger advisors who want to buy something "bigger, better, and faster" might consider starting smaller—by acquiring a minority interest in a larger practice or business and *folding their book in*. Taking on a minority interest isn't for everyone. But this is one of the few investment opportunities that, done correctly, comes with ownership, a paycheck, a mentor, and a built-in transfer device.

Continuity Planning

The single biggest threat to an independent book or practice with one owner is not the lack of a succession plan or even an exit plan, it is the lack of a plan to protect the clients and the owner's cash flow and value in the event of sudden death or disability. A continuity agreement is a formal, written contract that assures a seamless transfer of control and responsibility in the event of a sudden departure from the practice or business of any of its owners, young or old. Single owners struggle the most with a solution to this thorny issue.

In the smaller and more common one-owner, one-generational book and practice models, a continuity plan must often look outward for its protection and support, and to realize value—there simply may not be any capable person to stand in who works there. In contrast, an owner in a multigenerational business will benefit from a continuity plan that derives from the company succession plan. An internal ownership track, once implemented and in place, is the single best continuity plan available as clients' needs are addressed by other principals who are invested in the same business. Buyers, this brings us full circle back to the earlier advice: build a base for acquisition—build an enduring business. When you build a strong business model, you can offer a cloak of protection for many smaller book and practice owners. But it works just as well from the opposite direction if you're a buyer.

Advisors who want to grow by acquisition, but who are still young and relatively limited in terms of size, value, and resources, can become the much-needed continuity partner for a larger practice owner with no good internal transition options. By becoming a minority shareholder in the practice owner's entity structure, by either buying in or merging in, both "buyer" and "seller" then enter into a buy-sell agreement that provides contractual certainty as to *what happens next*. This strategy works best when applied to a seller who has about five years left to work, or less, and, interestingly enough, when using bank financing. Perhaps the biggest change to our industry on the M&A front in recent years has been the advent of reliable bank financing, covered in more detail in the following chapter. In this particular example, bank financing can provide the younger, smaller advisor with the necessary capital to make the transaction feasible; the seller isn't *the bank* or lender in the transaction. A buy-in loan typically requires the seller to commit to a five-year plan to sell, but there can be exceptions to this rule. Still, this added push tends to create a *clear glide slope* for all involved, clients included.

Another approach is for the buyer to acquire the seller's assets and then to hire the seller for a period of three to five years, what we call the Sell and Stay strategy, covered in Chapter 4. The payout of the purchase price is adjusted during the seller's employment period, but continuity is "baked in" to the payment structure. In essence, the buyer and seller are "merger partners" by virtue of a continuity plan and the clients have the value-added benefit of working with their former advisor but as part of a larger firm as everyone gets used to the new setting together, gradually and comfortably.

The tools to succeed are simple. Value your business, structure it correctly, and then set up a continuity plan. Once you've figured out how to do these basic things for yourself, do the same for others who are in your area but smaller in terms of value and cash flow. An enduring business model with enterprise strength can become a continuity partner for five or six other smaller practices or books in the same geographic area and within the same broker-dealer or custodial network. Continuity agreements are often structured with little cash exchanged (the bank buy-in format explained earlier being the exception to this rule) and need to be reexecuted or renewed every year or two because circumstances might change.

These standby arrangements provide the owner of the smaller practice with back-up protection, perhaps even a guardian in case of temporary disability, and an obligated buyer, to pay market value with agreed-upon payment terms, at long-term capital gains rates, and even a possible employer for the key staff members. For the owner of the practice, this arrangement is far superior to the popular but questionable revenue sharing approach. Many times, a continuity arrangement will lead into a more formal succession plan or an actual legal merger with the continuity partner.

* * *

The stated goal of this chapter was to help buyers rethink their approach to the acquisition process. The problem in this industry, with respect to the M&A process, isn't that buyers aren't trying hard enough, or aren't showing up. Those are not the problems at all. The problem is that most advisors don't ever sell because, frankly, sellers are not as good at this process as buyers can become. Buyers can and should be the experts in the exit planning process, not in a *predatory sense*, but in a fair and even-handed manner, and in ways not previously anticipated: a business helping a practice owner solve continuity issues and, one day, providing an exit strategy. Two practices merging to solve a host of problems that, alone, are unsolvable. A younger book builder merging into a larger practice, providing solutions never before considered. That's a new direction. That is good for this industry and the clients being served, and, in the end, that will be good for every advisor, from the *buyer's perspective.*

CHAPTER 7

Deal Structuring: Payment Terms, Taxes, and Financing

Value and valuation get all the attention, but the deal structure elements are at least as important and serve to balance the buyer's and seller's risks. Mastering the transaction structure requires developing a working expertise in payment terms, taxes, and both seller and bank financing. This is the area where smart buyers live. Values that seem too high, or even too low, can often be remedied by adjustments to the payment terms and tax structure.

Many advisors assume that once they solve the issue of value (i.e., the selling price), they can simply turn everything over to an attorney and/or CPA and those professionals will finish up the job. However, nothing could be further from reality. In fact, there are many additional steps between valuation and closing, and understanding the ramifications of the terms of a sale can help move the negotiations along much more smoothly.

Setting up and agreeing to proper and reasonable payment terms is an essential part of the selling or acquisition process. Assuming the buyer doesn't pay cash in full, out of pocket, for the acquisition at the time of closing, this chapter will help you answer the following questions: What types of financing are available? How much should the down payment be? Is the down payment refundable if things don't go well? How are payments structured to promote post-closing cooperation and motivation for both parties? Are there contingencies to the payment of the full purchase price? How are such contingencies structured? Does client attrition affect the final purchase price? Does fluctuation in the economy or equity markets affect the final purchase price? What are the tax repercussions to a buyer and a seller? What is seller financing? Is bank financing really a viable option—and if so, how does it work?

Reminder: The terms "job/book," "practice," and "business" as used in this chapter are not used interchangeably—these terms are specifically defined in Chapter 1 and applied accordingly.

SELLER FINANCING

Underlying virtually every acquisition in the independent financial services industry is the assumption that the seller will offer some kind of financing to support the transaction. Up until a couple of years ago, all payment terms and financing arrangements in the M&A space in this industry, at least below about $10 million in value, were strictly between the buyer and the seller, commonly referred to as seller financing. Bank financing, or even private equity, simply was not available to most ownership levels in this industry on a reliable or consistent basis until fairly recently. However, bank financing (SBA and conventional) is rapidly evolving as an acquisition tool, and the M&A landscape in this industry is changing with it. That said, seller financing is still the norm and has significantly shaped the initial M&A processes as we know them today, making this the place to begin the explanation of deal structuring techniques.

There are four primary types of seller financing applicable to the job/ book, practice, or business levels of ownership, the last three of which include contingencies that may alter the final purchase price.

1. A basic promissory note
2. An adjustable or performance-based promissory note
3. An earn-out arrangement
4. A revenue sharing or fee splitting agreement

Seller financing became a necessary structuring component in this industry because very few buyers could or would write a check to the seller for the full purchase price at closing. This fact is less attributable to the sufficiency of a buyer's cash reserves and more to the basic payment structuring technique that recognizes the importance of keeping the seller motivated to help with post-closing client retention. Post-closing seller motivation and support is critical in a relationship-based industry. At the same time, relatively few sales of any size ($250,000 and up, for example) are struck with no cash down at closing—predatory buyers of jobs/books or small practices, and internal succession plans at the business and firm levels being the exceptions.

The most common structure for the sale or acquisition of a financial services practice or business (an exit plan) includes three distinct elements: (1) an asset-based transaction (as opposed to buying or selling stock); (2) a nonrefundable cash down payment; and (3) seller financing of the balance for two to five years. It is not unusual to employ both seller financing and bank financing in the same transaction. Bank financing can usually be amortized for up to 10 years, which makes it a powerful tool from the buyer's perspective, potentially creating a better post-acquisition cash flow model without the requirement of long-term seller financing. Even so, bank financing is commonly used *in conjunction with* seller financing to ensure adequate post-closing motivation and to balance the risks. After all, if the clients don't transfer and stay, the buyer has bought "a bag of air." Smart payment structuring is intended to prevent this from occurring.

As a general rule, the more recurring revenue there is, the larger the down payment and the shorter the seller financing terms—results that might have something to do with the much higher demand level for such practices and businesses. Seller financing usually contains some type of contingency to ensure that assets and cash flow actually transfer and can be retained for a period of time in the years after the transaction has been closed. Contingent seller financing is appropriate for most third-party transactions. However, contingent seller financing is not used for internal sales or formal succession plans because transition risk is typically mitigated by client familiarity and a seller/business partner who continues to work alongside the advisor/investor.

Contingent seller financing for third-party transactions at the practice or business levels is often structured as a performance-based note, and more rarely these days as an earn-out arrangement. For tax reasons, among others, revenue sharing or fee splitting arrangements should be limited to acquisitions of a job or a book. Payment structures to sell or acquire at the job/book level have historically been 100% seller financed with the entire purchase price paid on a contingent basis using an earn-out or revenue sharing arrangement (they are not the same things, as you'll read). There are better and more appropriate financing methods, at least if you're a seller, but this is how it has been done in the past.

The four primary types of seller financing are each examined and explained in more detail later.

THE SHARED-RISK/SHARED-REWARD CONCEPT

The element of seller financing within a typical payment structure has had a very positive effect on practice transitions in this industry—consistent, post-closing, 95%+ client transition and retention rate, remarkable when you consider that most exit plans are external, not internal. In other words, the buyer is often a complete stranger to the client base before being introduced by the seller. A high post-closing client transition rate doesn't happen automatically or by accident; everything from the initial valuation to the deal structure to the transition plan affects the final result.

By utilizing contingent seller financing for the majority of the purchase price and a significant, nonrefundable down payment from the buyer, most successful third-party transactions have been created using a shared-risk/

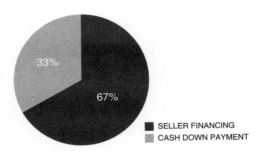

FIGURE 7.1   Seller-Financed Payment Structure

shared-reward format. Post-closing, buyer and seller need to work together to monetize the transaction. This financing arrangement, born of necessity, effectively creates an "economic marriage" between buyer and seller (Figure 7.1).

For sellers, this isn't a "hand over the keys" process where they wish the buyer good luck and say good-bye. Buyer and seller must work together after closing until the client base is informed and settled in. That's more than just a contractual requirement—if the "economic marriage" doesn't work well, the payment structuring contingencies will kick in and significantly affect the final purchase price or value. As a result, sellers look at buyers not only as their replacement, but as a creditor would look at a borrower. This is why this has never been, and likely never will be, an auction process that is won by the high bidder, at least in the world of seller financing.

In order to balance the risks between a buyer and a seller, financing tools must be carefully considered and applied correctly. Many private attorneys who aren't familiar with our industry often use terms like "earn-outs," "revenue sharing," and "contingent seller financing" interchangeably. Worse, some of the practice management personnel at the IBDs and custodians do the same, or limit their solution set to one primary financing method. The intricacies involved in the financing approach and the choice of contingencies affects every aspect of the sale or acquisition process. Failure in the M&A process is no accident. Avoidance of problems and mistakes is mostly a matter of knowledge and application.

Carefully consider the *shared-risk/shared-reward* concept when creating your own payment structure, especially if you elect to utilize some type of external or bank financing that substantially cashes out the seller of a book, practice, or business at the time of closing. The same is true in reverse if you're selling on a revenue sharing basis with no down payment, the way many broker-dealers encourage or at least support. If a buyer has no "skin in the game," how hard are they going to work to keep the bottom half of the newly acquired client base? Wouldn't a buyer work harder if they paid a significant down payment and had to at least recapture that investment from a new group of clients? Wouldn't that be better for the client base as a whole, and the seller, and the broker-dealer/custodian? There are many more such questions, but what is really needed are answers. The answers lie in the proven systems and processes derived from competitive open market transactions and payment structures, including the contingent seller financing tools examined next.

PERFORMANCE-BASED PROMISSORY NOTES

The most commonly used contingent financing method at the practice or business levels over the past 10 years has been a performance-based promissory note (also called an adjustable note). Basic, fixed notes can also be used, but tend to be limited to internal exit plans and advanced succession plans where client transition risk can be more easily anticipated and reduced or eliminated. Performance-based notes are a powerful payment structuring technique with a proven track record in this industry—an integral part of a shared-risk/shared-reward strategy. This is a specific, viable alternative to the use of a revenue sharing arrangement.

A properly constructed performance-based note includes a one-time "look back," usually on the one-year anniversary of closing, but the timing is flexible depending on the circumstances. From the seller's point of view, performance-based notes are predictable and carry an interest rate on the balance and a "lock-in" at the end of the seller's post-closing consulting duties (read on for more on the structure and importance of consulting agreements). From the buyer's point of view, downside protection is provided should the anticipated cash flow not materialize after the sale closes. Once the clients have been delivered and introduced, the risk is gradually shifted to the buyer and away from the seller, which is a powerful motivational aspect of this shared-risk/shared-reward financing technique. This approach underscores the economic marriage aspect of the process. This is the role that earn-out arrangements used to play in payment structuring.

Performance-based promissory notes can be set up in a variety of ways, but in most cases have a buffer built in that contemplates the effect of market fluctuations. Losses of 5% to 7% of the cash flow post-closing are often not enough to trigger an adjustment to the note value, whereas the loss of 15% of the clients and/or assets, for whatever reason, would almost certainly cause an adjustment to the final value, but only if something occurred in the first year after closing. After that, client satisfaction and retention rests squarely on the buyer's shoulders.

When contingent financing of any kind is utilized, the seller's goal isn't to find the buyer with the most money; it is to find the buyer who can retain the most clients one year or so after the sale. Otherwise, the seller will never realize the full value of the sale. We learned long ago from watching buyers and sellers during the post-closing period that choosing *best price* often backfires in a contingently financed, shared-risk/shared-reward transaction.

Those who sell their jobs/books could also use a performance-based note, but rarely do, a fact that needs to change. Buyers dominate the job/book ownership level of the M&A spectrum and dictate value and terms. Sellers at this level tend to feel glad that they are getting any value at all, having invested little into infrastructure and nothing into durability—and they're not completely wrong. Still, on behalf of their clients, book builders could easily do better when executing their exit plan along the lines of a practice owner without much effort. Sellers usually can enjoy better tax treatment, better realized value, and greater client satisfaction with a performance-based note versus a revenue sharing arrangement even if *it's just a job/book* or a small practice.

EARN-OUT ARRANGEMENTS

An earn-out arrangement is a seller financing method that is often used in conjunction with a significant down payment and a formal asset purchase agreement. In an earn-out arrangement, the buyer pays a percentage of future practice revenues from all of the acquired clients and assets to the seller for an agreed-upon period of time, or up to a set amount. Earn-outs have been a common part of many payment structures at the practice level, less so at the business level, and never at the firm level. In the past, earn-outs served to balance the risks between a buyer and a seller when a transaction or commission-based practice was being sold. Over the past 5 to 10 years, earn-outs have been increasingly viewed with disfavor by sellers who have been selling more valuable practices and enjoying much higher demand for their fee-based models.

Buyers and sellers can structure an earn-out arrangement in many different ways, depending on the circumstances of the sale and the licensing status of the parties. Earn-out payments can be made monthly, quarterly, or annually, and the percentage rate can increase or decrease from the first payment to the last, or remain level throughout the seller-financed period. Given the variable nature of the payments, every check the buyer writes out and that the seller receives will likely be for a different amount since payment reflects actual receipt of cash flow from the acquired clients for the prior month or quarter. It is strongly recommended that the seller remain licensed for the duration of the earn-out period at least if FINRA regulated. This is the position of most IBDs and it limits the use and length of the earn-out period for a FINRA-regulated advisor. The process is easier, of course, for fee-only models, but the demand for such seller listings is high enough that smart buyers don't even attempt to offer an earn-out arrangement, at least if they expect to make the list of finalists.

Earn-out arrangements are based on gross revenues or GDC from the acquired client base. The most common method is to create an earn-out for a fixed period of time, typically one to three years, depending on licensing considerations. Earn-outs, by their nature, are always paid in arrears based on the actual cash flow received from the acquired client base. To calculate an earn-out, it is necessary to know the purchase price, the gross revenues derived from the acquired client base for the 12 months preceding closing, the amount of the cash down payment, the amount of any promissory note or notes, and the length of financing the seller is willing to extend. Earn-out arrangements should never be the sole payment method in any given payment structure as might be the case with a revenue sharing approach.

Most earn-out arrangements are not "capped" or limited in the amount to be paid. If the gross revenue from the acquired client base grows rapidly in the buyer's hands, the earn-out payments will also increase at the same pace. The opposite is true as well. Tables 7.1 through 7.3 represent examples of how earn-out payment arrangements might be structured to supplement a nonrefundable cash down payment in an acquisition of clients and assets that produced $500,000 in the trailing 12-month period prior to the closing of the transaction.

TABLE 7.1   Example 1: Total Payments for Two-Year Period = $321,750

Projected Period	Gross Revenue Received	% Agreed to Be Paid Out	Actual Payment
Year 1	$500,000	33%	$165,000
Year 2	$475,000	33%	$156,750

TABLE 7.2   Example 2: Total Payments for Three-Year Period = $297,000

Projected Period	Gross Revenue Received	% Agreed to Be Paid Out	Actual Payment
Year 1	$500,000	20%	$100,000
Year 2	$475,000	20%	$ 95,000
Year 3	$510,000	20%	$102,000

TABLE 7.3 Example 3: Total Payments for Five-Year Period = $691,750

Projected Period	Gross Revenue Received	% Agreed to Be Paid Out	Actual Payment
Year 1	$500,000	33%	$165,000
Year 2	$475,000	33%	$156,750
Year 3	$510,000	25%	$127,500
Year 4	$530,000	25%	$132,500
Year 5	$550,000	20%	$110,000

It is important to understand that the use of an earn-out arrangement will ultimately increase or decrease the final purchase price, depending on the retained assets and clients and new business referrals—even economic conditions such as a recession or a booming economy will impact the final value paid under an earn-out arrangement. Even regulatory changes could impact the final result. Every payment is contingent in some respect.

Earn-out arrangements typically do not carry a stated rate of interest on the unpaid balance. Instead, sellers will report interest on an installment sale basis (more information on this topic is presented further on) as ordinary income in the same manner as any other interest income. If the installment sales contract does not provide a stated interest rate, or if it is insufficient for tax purposes as is frequently the case when using an earn-out arrangement, part of the stated principal may be *recharacterized* as "imputed" interest. Sellers, with the help of their CPA, should use the applicable federal rate (AFR) to figure the unstated interest on the sale.

Payments received by a seller under an earn-out arrangement usually require the seller to be licensed in states where the transitioned clients are located for the duration of the payments, which also means that the seller should maintain errors and omissions insurance coverage for the duration of the earn-out arrangement—steps many retiring sellers are not willing to take. If not, an earn-out should not be used, at least beyond a one- or two-year post-closing period. For all these reasons, a performance-based promissory note is the better and more commonly used payment structuring device.

An earn-out arrangement, used properly, can create flexibility in the payment structure that will reward and motivate the seller to deliver and help the buyer retain the clients and assets. Conversely, if a seller does not assist in the transition, is not effective in that support role, or does not choose a buyer or successor who is a good match for the practice, then the earn-out arrangement may result in the seller receiving final payments that are less, perhaps much less, than the agreed-upon purchase price (i.e., the shared-risk/shared-reward concept). The result can also be that the buyer ends up paying much more than the agreed-upon or anticipated purchase price. Of course, this only happens if the buyer receives far more revenue than was originally bargained for.

REVENUE SHARING OR FEE SPLITTING ARRANGEMENTS

An earn-out arrangement is not the same thing as a revenue sharing or fee splitting arrangement. It is different in at least three key respects: (1) earn-outs are a part of a complete, balanced financing package, not the entire payment, documentation, and valuation plan as is the case with a revenue sharing arrangement; (2) earn-out arrangements usually result in the payments to the seller being taxed at long-term capital gains rates, as opposed to ordinary income rates under a revenue sharing arrangement; and (3) an earn-out arrangement is usually preceded by a fairly significant down payment, which tends to create motivation for both parties to retain all or most of the clients and to attain a high level of client satisfaction post-closing.

A revenue sharing or fee splitting arrangement (essentially the same thing) is usually accomplished by utilizing a free form or template provided by an independent broker-dealer (IBD) or custodian. IBDs and custodians routinely hand out short-form contracts (two or three pages in length is typical, but some are a little longer) to their advisors at no charge as a *substitute* for a formal or more comprehensive document set, and often as a base-level continuity plan. These basic agreements allow a seller and a buyer/continuity partner to agree on terms of a sale in the event of an advisor's death, permanent disability, *or retirement*.

The typical structure of a revenue sharing arrangement is for a buyer to agree to pay a seller some percentage of every dollar they receive (30% to 50% is the common range) from all of the seller's former clients—a list of those specific clients is, or should be, attached to the assignment form. The payments often continue for two to five years, depending on the estimated and agreed value, and payment is usually sent to the seller on a monthly or quarterly basis with a copy of the calculations either by the IBD, the custodian, or the buyer. As with an earn-out arrangement, every payment is variable. To reframe one of the key differences, in the absence of a down payment, the *entire purchase price* is a variable when using a revenue sharing arrangement.

In fairness, a revenue sharing arrangement can be a great financing tool from the buyer's perspective. It is simple, requires little professional input or guidance, and is almost risk free. There is typically no down payment, nor any guarantee of final performance, nor any requirement to even attempt to service all the acquired clients. The buyer is not obligated to make any payments on client accounts they don't service, can't service, or prefer not to service after the transaction is closed. Most revenue sharing transactions result in *ordinary income tax rates* to the seller on the entire sale proceeds.

It is also very interesting to see how this financing method has been made to work on occasion to the advantage of a seller during a gradual retirement process. Some sellers who "sell" using this financing technique for some reason other than death or disability, don't actually leave or retire. Why would they? There is no set of formal, legal contracts that requires them to stop working and, after all, they're still being paid for the work they do, albeit on a reduced level as the "buyer" is factored into the equation. It can be more like *two partners* than a buyer and a seller. Understand that revenue sharing arrangements transfer a cash flow stream. Rarely is there a clear transfer of all of the assets that typically comprise such a model, nor even a separation of responsibilities and liabilities. That's part of the problem caused when these simple, do-it-yourself forms stray beyond a continuity plan (death or disability) and venture into the territory of an exit plan.

A handful of intrepid sellers have actually turned this whole situation around and become "predatory sellers," entering into a revenue sharing arrangement in one case for 20 years at 33% of revenue from their former client base and all new referrals! The young buyer thought he had an easy and risk-free transaction with nothing down. The arbitrator of the case felt otherwise and sided with the seller.

It is important to note that this payment structuring technique and the related contracts stem from NASD Rule IM-2420-2, the Continuing Commissions Policy, now newly codified as FINRA Rule 2040. Under this policy/ rule, continuing commissions must be paid according to a bona fide contract entered into by the buyer and seller *at a time when the seller is still registered or licensed and in good standing.* Be certain to read *all* the requirements of this rule and consult with qualified legal counsel and/or your compliance officer before implementing a transaction based on this rule. It is more difficult to transfer a FINRA-regulated model than an RIA model, so buyers and sellers need to be extra vigilant when working and exiting under the FINRA umbrella.

EARNEST-MONEY DEPOSITS

In a competitive acquisition environment, sellers need to know that the buyer they select is serious and committed to completing the transaction. Payment of an earnest money deposit helps to confirm that the buyer is serious. If not, it is still beneficial to know early in the process so a seller can consider a better qualified and more serious buyer prospect and further refine the list of finalists.

Many third-party buyers and sellers in the FP Transitions system utilize a "term sheet" or a letter of intent (there is actually a difference) that calls for an earnest-money deposit of at least 1% of the purchase price. This deposit is typically placed into an escrow account and is credited toward the down payment when the transaction is completed.

Similar to a real estate transaction, the earnest-money deposit is closely tied to an agreed-upon due diligence schedule that helps to establish a clear time frame for the transaction. A third-party buyer is usually entitled to a refund of the earnest-money deposit in the event that he or she decides not to proceed with the purchase after completing due diligence but within the allotted time frame. Requiring an earnest-money deposit is a great way to help determine which buyers are really serious and which are not early in the process, and quickly—an important issue with a 50-to-1 buyer-to-seller ratio and other finalists impatiently waiting in the wings.

Use a neutral and professional escrow process for the receipt, retention, and eventual payment of the earnest-money deposit. Once the required sums are paid in, the documents are signed, submitted, and accounted for, and the closing date arrives, the transaction is closed and the down payment (which now includes the earnest-money deposit) is wire transferred from escrow to the seller's bank account. This is a common structure for any sale in excess of $500,000, and it doesn't hurt to do the job right on smaller deals.

On this note, many sellers at the job/book or practice levels still jump at the first offer they receive, sometimes initiated by receiving an unsolicited letter in the mail. It is flattering to be sought after and to feel valuable and wanted. In a one-to-one transaction, an earnest-money deposit may not be necessary, but never dispense with a significant down payment and proper payment terms whether you're selling a book, a practice, or certainly a business; post-closing motivations are intricately wound into the deal structure and financing choices and will define your ultimate success, or failure. Remember Rule No. 1.

DOWN PAYMENTS

A nonrefundable down payment, in some amount, should be part of every payment structure across the board. Typical down payments for financial service/advisory practices range from 10% to 40%, depending on the size, value, amount of recurring revenue, and enterprise strength of the practice or business in transition—factors that may help explain and partly justify the lack of a down payment when jobs/books are acquired. Businesses tend to command a much higher down payment, often in the 35% to 75% range (of the total purchase price).

The down payment helps to define the buyer's risk in the transaction and is usually paid to the seller at the time of closing and should always be nonrefundable. Down payments tend to be higher in instances where there is more recurring revenue, where the sale is of a business rather than a practice, or where the risk of client attrition post-closing is minimal. Other factors that affect the size of the down payment include profitability, growth rates, post-closing support by the seller and the seller's key staff members, the absence of book builders *under the seller's roof*, the buyer's size relative to the seller's, and the tax structure of the transaction, among other things.

Bank financing provides buyers with the opportunity to pay up to about 75% of the purchase price as a down payment. Aggressive and experienced buyers can use this financing tool to "step in front of" the many buyer prospects produced by the ultracompetitive open market listing process and capture a seller's attention. Coupled with being a "best match" for the seller's client base, this financing strategy demands consideration and is covered in detail later in this chapter.

It is interesting to note that, historically, the acquisition of a job/book tends to employ a basic revenue-sharing arrangement with no down payment. The average one-third (33%) down payment sellers of a practice enjoy is often absent. We've talked to thousands of buyers and sellers involved in these "nothing down" transactions over the years and this is what we commonly hear: one-year post-closing, that 33% down payment element that was missing tends to mirror the lost (sometimes *discarded* is a more appropriate term) clients and cash flow in a revenue-sharing transaction. Too many sellers who use a revenue-sharing arrangement end up monetizing about 66 to 75 cents on the dollar. It isn't what the buyer and seller valued the book at; it is what the buyer actually pays based on the clients and cash flow the buyer chooses or can effectively retain. Think about that. Employing basic but formal payment structuring techniques, as well as a competitive search process to ensure *best match*, methods such as those used by a practice could improve many aspects of the process for a job/book owner and the clients they serve. Broker-dealers and custodians—these last few sentences apply to you as well.

BASIC TAX STRATEGIES

The tax treatment to a buyer and to a seller changes the realized value, perhaps significantly. Many advisors assume that they have little control or choice when it comes to taxes on what they ultimately realize in value from selling their job, practice, or business, and that is incorrect. Buyers also have some good choices to make, and important ones at that. Let's begin with an overview of the basic tax strategies applicable to each level of owner-ship and from the separate vantage points of seller and buyer, with more advanced strategies covered later in this chapter under asset and stock sales.

Tax Strategy (101) for Jobs/Books

For almost all job/book owners, long-term capital gains tax treatment on the sale proceeds is a possibility, but practically, it is overlooked and not always considered a necessity. In fact, most of the simple two- to three-page revenue sharing agreements handed out by IBDs and custodians are silent on the tax issue, which will usually result in ordinary income tax treatment to the seller on the entire sale proceeds (it doesn't have to be that way, but it usually is). Buyers dictate the terms and tax results with the support of their IBD/custodial network, and sellers either don't realize or don't care that they have some say in the process.

The sale of assets, including *just a cash flow stream*, can actually result in long-term capital gains treatment *if the seller is aware of the issue*, cares, and builds it into the documentation process. It is usually a matter of information and guidance. Book builders who want to learn more about how to achieve a better tax result should keep reading. At this ownership level, buyers have it pretty much figured out. But book owners can absolutely have everything that practice owners expect, if they know what to ask for and have a basic plan.

Tax Strategy (201) for Practice Owners

Sellers at this level should, and do, receive the majority of their sale proceeds at long-term capital gains tax rates, while buyers can enjoy the ability to write off or depreciate the entire purchase price, the best of both worlds. These tax benefits, at least in part, tend to support an aggressive group of competitive and informed buyers, hence the 50:1 buyer-to-seller ratio. In addition, smart buyers tend to place a higher value on what they're buying when they can also receive a favorable tax result, one of the few times the tax code works for both sides simultaneously.

From the seller's perspective, the sale of "capital assets," a term that gen-erally describes what an independent advisor is selling in his or her practice, results in a favorable tax result if the valuation method, payment structure, and documentation approaches are well coordinated and thought out. About 70% to 85% of practice value can usually be received at long-term capital gains tax rates, with the balance at ordinary income rates commensurate with the post-closing consulting and noncompete/nonsolicitation elements.

Do not assume that a favorable tax result for both parties is the goal or the automatic result, especially if the seller's IBD/custodian is involved and supplying the documents and/or the valuation opinion. That's not their job or their expertise. The documentation process and the payment structuring elements need to explicitly spell out the tax allocation structure and the expectations of both buyer and seller to make this aspect work properly. In other words, it takes some know-how and a little work and an impartial guide to do this right and benefit both sides of the transaction.

Tax Treatment (301) for Business Owners

Sellers of businesses should receive all or most of their value at long-term capital gains tax rates regardless of whether they are selling stock or assets. Sellers should expect and demand this result. Buyers should plan for this element and make that result a part of their offer. Sellers, at this level, if you receive an offer or a term sheet that is silent on this issue, or that has a poor tax result for you, renegotiate or immediately set out to find another buyer.

Buyers, depending on the payment structure and transfer mechanism, should have the tax benefit of basis in the investment or a long-term depreciable asset. Buyers often argue that being able to deduct or depreciate the asset is more valuable than basis, but that is just an argument dependent on what the seller chooses to sell. Sellers, if the buyer's debt ratio is so tight that the tax results make or break the transition, you've likely got the wrong buyer no matter how good the match is. In the future, basis will likely be very valuable to a buyer as taxes continue to escalate, but by no means is the tax benefit lost because it isn't expensed or depreciated.

At the business level, it is no longer a seller's market dominated by buyers. This is a true seller's market with commensurate value, payment terms, and tax structures. This is what, and why, larger practice owners should aspire to. Selling at this level is fun. Buying at this level is lucrative.

INSTALLMENT SALES

The installment method of accounting provides an exception to the general principles of income recognition, allowing a seller to defer income, for tax purposes, until payment is actually received. This is relevant because of the preceding discussions centered on the use of seller financing—these are transactions not typically paid for in full, in cash, at the time of closing.

Under an installment sale, the seller receives at least one payment *after* the tax year in which the sale occurs. Examples of installment sales include use of a basic promissory note, an adjustable or performance-based note, or an earn-out arrangement—basically any approach that involves payments in more than one tax year. Although installment sales are quite common in the buying or selling of a financial services or advisory practice or business, the use of *contingent payments* under an installment sales method is an additional tax aspect to be carefully considered.

The benefits of an installment sale are easiest to understand when comparing both the cash and accrual methods of accounting. Under the cash method, a taxpayer recognizes income *when it is physically received*. This is how most books, practices, and businesses are set up—if you're not sure if this method applies to you, ask your CPA or accountant. Sellers who use an accrual method of accounting must recognize income as soon as he or she *has a right to the income*. Relatively few independent advisors fall under this category, but make sure you know the difference and which method you have selected, especially if you are engaged, or expect to be engaged in, M&A activity.

On this point, also be aware that a handful of states are adjusting their tax codes to address the use of installment sales and improve the state's ability to collect taxes on such a sale sooner, rather than upon the seller's actual receipt of the proceeds. The takeaway from all of these issues is simply this— as you consider your future and the use of either a succession plan or an exit plan, talk to your accountant and an experienced intermediary about these issues well in advance of developing and implementing your plans. Taxes, as you well know, play a central role in the planning and execution phases.

As a seller, you will likely be required to report gain under the installment method. Sellers, however, can "elect out" on or before the due date for filing their tax return for the year of the sale. Sellers may elect out by reporting *all* of their gain as income in the year of the sale on Internal Revenue Service Form 4797, Sales of Business Property. Some sellers make such an election if they anticipate significant increases in tax rates in the years to come, but the issues go beyond this level of thinking, especially when contingent payments are involved.

Final thought: for additional information and self-education, refer to IRS Publication 537, Installment Sales. For the record, Publication 537 is about 17,000 words long, not including the supporting forms—cumulatively, about one-fourth the length of this book! And this is only one aspect of the tax code that applies to your transaction. The takeaway? Don't do this alone or on a two- or three-page form.

ASSET-BASED SALES/ACQUISITIONS

There are two basic avenues to consider when selling your book, practice, or business to a third party—the sale of assets or the sale of stock. The ability to sell stock assumes that the seller is organized as a corporation or an LLC.

A sole proprietorship can sell only assets. At least 9 out of 10 transactions between buyers and sellers of independently owned books or practices are consummated as asset sales. (A revenue sharing arrangement, as might be used by a book owner or acquirer, is technically an asset-based transaction, but it focuses on sharing a cash flow stream rather than clearly transferring ownership of a client base, as is the case with an asset purchase and sale agreement.) If in doubt, consider an asset-based sale or acquisition to be the default.

A transfer of assets between advisors of two different practices or businesses is generally simpler, safer, and easier when compared to a stock sale. An asset-based acquisition allows a buyer to purchase what they see, or at least what they want to purchase. Stock purchases, in contrast, include known and unknown liabilities. That's usually bad, but most stock sales are internal such as through a succession plan and the buyer is often an employee who already works there. External sales, or those that involve a third party, tend to lean heavily toward the asset sale approach.

If you take the time to lay out a professional plan and assemble your documentation correctly (it's not that hard to do), you should enjoy these results every time in an asset-based transaction:

- The sale of assets will predominantly be taxed at long-term capital gains rates.
- The acquisition of those assets will result in the buyer's ability to write off or depreciate the entire purchase price.

These results are even obtainable by buyers and sellers of a job/book, but usually not within a two- or three-page basic broker-dealer agreement—it takes a little more work and professional input to achieve good results. Obtaining long-term capital gains tax treatment on the sale of assets sometimes surprises both buyers and sellers, but the primary assets being sold are categorized as "capital assets" and enjoy beneficial tax treatment in most cases.

Typically, the assets to be sold by an independent financial advisor include:

- Seller's goodwill
- Client list and files and associated revenues (recurring and nonrecurring)
- An agreement(s) not to compete or solicit the clients after closing by each licensed/registered advisor
- Furniture, fixtures, and equipment
- A personal services contract obligating the seller to assist in the transition process post-closing
- Occasionally, real property or intellectual property

The valuation process puts a single number on these cumulative "assets." The amount paid for each one of these assets varies and is negotiable, within reason. The tax consequences to the seller of an asset sale depend entirely upon the tax classification and treatment of the individual assets that comprise the job/book, practice, or business, and the arm's-length agreement of the parties to the transaction.

FP Transitions' Comprehensive Valuation Report considers and presents the current tax structure (an example of which is shown in Figure 7.2), within the context of the valuation opinion. The most recent data at the time of this publication supports a tax structure of 81% of the purchase price allocated to capital assets such as seller's goodwill, client files, and associated revenues, 14% of the purchase price allocated to the seller's post-closing consulting duties, and the remainder to the noncompetition/nonsolicitation agreement(s). These tax allocations change almost every year based on what buyers actually negotiate and pay to sellers—a reflection of the payment structuring dynamics and competitive forces in the open marketplace. The Comprehensive Valuation Report considers the most recent tax allocation elements in its value calculation.

To support this tax allocation strategy, the documentation needs to be well thought out and properly drafted. The post-closing consulting agreement, for example, needs to clearly set forth specific duties that the seller will provide to the buyer as well as licensing/registration obligations, even E&O insurance costs and responsibilities, issues that vary from one type of practice or business to another. The consulting agreement also needs to set up a coordinated hand-off from seller to buyer and must work in conjunction with the restrictive covenants in the noncompete/nonsolicitation/nonservice agreement(s) that prohibit any unwanted contact by the seller, from the buyer's perspective.

One common misconception is that the tax allocation or tax rates are somehow affected by the method of payment. *How* that amount is paid,

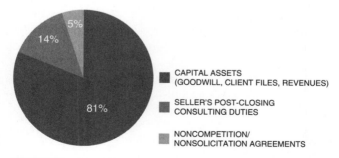

FIGURE 7.2　Tax Allocation—Average Payment Structure

such as in cash, through a basic note, a performance-based note, or an earn-out arrangement is largely irrelevant (this statement intentionally omits revenue sharing/revenue splitting arrangements, and assumes you've read and understood the impact of the installment sales treatment discussed earlier).

Ultimately, a buyer and seller must coordinate their respective tax treatment of the assets being sold or acquired and that is why the documentation must be professionally drafted and clear. Table 7.4 is a basic chart, in *simple English*, of how various asset classes are treated by the buyer and the seller.

The best way to address taxes and their impact on the transaction is to build them into the M&A process, starting at the very beginning with the valuation results—again, taking this issue off the table almost immediately. From there, with both buyer and seller understanding the clear expectations from the outset, the asset purchase agreement can easily and clearly memorialize the contractual elements. To this end, IRC Form 8594 is used

TABLE 7.4   Asset Classes and Their Treatment by Buyers and Sellers

Type of Asset	Life of Asset on Buyer's Tax Return	Reported on Seller's Tax Return
Client List	15 Years	Capital Gains
Seller's Name and Goodwill	15 Years	Capital Gains
Noncompete Agreement	15 Years	Ordinary Income
Seller's Post-Closing Assistance	Expensed as Paid	Ordinary Income Subject to FICA
Computers/Electronic Equipment	5 Years with Option to Expense in Year 1	Capital Gains (with Recapture of Depreciation of Ordinary Income)
Furniture and Fixtures	7 Years with Option to Expense in Year 1	Capital Gains (with Recapture of Depreciation of Ordinary Income)
Inventories of Office Supplies	Expensed as Paid	Ordinary Income
Leasehold Improvements	39 Years or Expensed when Abandoned	Capital Gains (with Recapture of Depreciation at 25%)
Real Estate	39 Years	Capital Gains (with Recapture of Depreciation at 25%)

to report the sale and purchase of a group of assets that constitute a practice or a business (and for a job or book as well). Both the purchaser and seller must file Form 8594 with their own individual income tax return.

STOCK-BASED SALES/ACQUISITIONS

Stock sales are used in a limited number of circumstances, but they certainly are not rare, even at the practice level. Businesses and firms are more likely to use stock sales for two reasons. First, businesses and firms are more likely to sell internally, and usually not all at once, but gradually over time, which entails the use of an entity structure. For example, a key employee or a son or a daughter might buy a 20% interest in the S corporation where they work and pay it off over five or six years, and then buy another 10% to 20%, and so on. Second, in the case of a stand-alone RIA, which is a common structure at these ownership levels, buying stock can actually be easier than buying assets, even though liabilities are included in the purchase. In this section, we'll examine these concepts in more depth with an emphasis on the tax strategies employed in a sale or an acquisition.

From the seller's perspective, there often isn't much difference between selling stock and selling assets. In most cases, the sale of stock will result in long-term capital gains treatment less any basis the seller might have in their investment (usually not much except in the case of a prior acquisition). Sellers typically don't receive all of their proceeds at these preferential tax rates because some of the purchase price is still allocated to the seller's post-closing support (through a consulting agreement) and the seller's post-closing restrictive covenants (noncompete, nonsolicitation, no-service), just as with an asset sale. Practice owners, as compared to business or firm owners, typically receive less of their proceeds at long-term capital gains tax rates than do business owners because of the higher transition risk with a one-owner practice model, which suggests a larger allocation of value to the seller's post-closing consulting services. In addition, if a business or firm owner is executing a succession plan, the initial and partial sales of stock or ownership do not involve the use of a post-closing consulting agreement or restrictive covenants because the selling shareholder is still involved in the operations.

From the buyer's point of view, the difference between buying assets and buying stock is more significant. First, buyers who acquire and pay for the stock of a practice or business may not have the ability to write off the purchase price over time as with an asset-based acquisition, but they do receive basis for use later in their careers. If recent trends in tax rates are any indication, such basis may be worth a lot 20 years from now because when today's buyer becomes tomorrow's seller, the basis (in this example, the principal amount the buyer paid to the seller) is subtracted from the sales proceeds and is not taxed. In other words, if a practice is acquired today for $500,000 and 20 years from now it is sold for $2 million, the seller is taxed on only $1.5 million of the proceeds. Second, buyers of stock buy the history of the practice or business they acquire, including existing or potential liabilities and even future litigation. The very thought of doing this tends to make most buyers recoil a bit, but such issues can be mitigated using hold-harmless provisions and indemnification language, even offset rights in the ongoing payments post-closing.

The preceding comments in this section apply to S corporations and LLCs that have elected to be taxed as disregarded entities and S corporations. C corporations are an entirely different matter.

While fairly rare at the practice and business levels, C corporations add a level of complexity and perhaps cost upon sale. If assets are sold, a C corporation pays taxes on the proceeds and then the shareholders who receive those monies are taxed again. This is the well-known issue of "double taxation," though most practice and business owners spend their careers successfully avoiding this issue with help from their tax counselor by diverting almost all money to compensation as opposed to paying dividends. This solution does not work upon the sale of assets in an exit plan. Some sellers attempt to ignore the C corporation during the M&A process, selling the assets personally and pursuing a tax allocation strategy similar to that laid out earlier. This maneuver, however, is suspect and may or may not pass an audit, so check with your CPA.

The better strategy is to talk to your CPA and/or a qualified intermediary about 10 years before you're thinking of selling and find out exactly *why* you're a C corporation. Most advisors we talk to elect S corporation tax treatment after further consultation with their CPA and are armed with a clear plan for the future. Even then, there may be a built-in gains tax (the *big* tax) for 5 to 10 years after the election, depending on current tax law. Make the decision to change early, but make it based on a formal and professional plan, not reflexively based on what might happen to you or in your life. Most practices and businesses in this industry would be better structured as some type of a pass-through tax conduit (S corporation, LLC taxed as a disregarded entity, or partnership), whether as part of an exit plan or a succession plan.

Note that some M&A transactions, especially in the case where C corporations are involved, are bifurcated, and may include both a stock sale and an asset sale. In these cases, the overall value is split (not necessarily 50/50) and paid in part for the stock and in part for the assets. This particular approach is aggressive and requires a high level of professional guidance every time, but it should be in the realm of consideration as you lay out your exit and tax strategies.

LLCs taxed as partnerships are yet another matter. In our experience, many advisors who have selected this particular entity and tax approach have not been well coached by their own legal team. The problem is that while lawyers will answer the questions put to them, most LLC owners don't know what questions they need to ask. The attractive element about this entity type is reflected by the common use of the terms "fluid and flexible" to describe its structure and format. Who doesn't want an entity structure that can easily adapt to almost anything you want to build? Hence, many, if not most, recently formed entities in this profession are LLCs taxed as partnerships. Utilizing a partnership structure within an LLC is a powerful tool, to be sure, but it can also be like driving your Ferrari to the grocery store—best be careful. Sometimes a more suitable vehicle is better, depending on your needs and goals.

What isn't made clear to many advisors is that an LLC taxed as a partnership is a most complicated body of tax law, and every significant step you want to make in the future needs to be cross-checked with your CPA and/or tax attorney (the difference between an attorney and a tax attorney is about $500/hour). Don't believe me on the complexity issue? Read your operating agreement and see how much of it you actually understand. As an owner of an LLC taxed as a partnership for the past 20 years, I've learned something new about my own entity structure almost every year—and I knew a fair amount to begin with. This can be really complicated stuff.

LLCs taxed as partnerships require professional assistance through the M&A process 100% of the time. This is the downside of a *fluid and flexible* structure. You will need assistance from an experienced M&A intermediary, a CPA, and a tax attorney who can work together to guide you safely through the maze of tax laws and industry regulations. Depending on how your LLC is set up and operates (the form and functionality derived from your operating agreement), the tax results can be the same as if you were in an S corporation, or something very different, and unexpected. In fact, for tax purposes, it even makes a difference who the buyer is—the entity by redemption, the individual members or partners by direct sale/acquisition, or a third party.

If you expect to receive long-term capital gains tax treatment upon the sale of your interests, make sure that is what your attorney set forth in your operating agreement. The sale of an ownership interest in an LLC taxed as a partnership can result in long-term capital gains *or* ordinary income (the results of a concept commonly known as "guaranteed payments")—you generally get to decide, as the owner, if you think far enough ahead and know enough to ask. If you're late to address this issue and you have partners who will survive you and might outflank you, they may become the decision makers and may prefer a different tax strategy that favors them and the survivability of the business they're taking over.

As if it couldn't get more complicated, let's consider one more possibility. Under IRC Section 338, it may be possible for a buyer to get the tax advantages of an asset purchase with the legal advantages of a stock purchase. This can be the result, in certain instances, when buyer and seller join in making an election to treat the stock purchase/sale transaction as an asset purchase and sale for federal income tax purposes. If this is of interest, talk to your CPA or a qualified intermediary. Sometimes it is important just to know enough to ask the questions, and that is the goal here.

Incidentally, issues such as these are part of any well-thought-out and executed exit or succession plan, one more reason why planning early and in a formal, written, and professional manner is so important. Working through such details and esoteric issues almost obscures the real point behind all this thinking and planning: the clients and their families are the main point of such exercises. That's why we're going to remind you frequently and never lose sight of the real purpose of good M&A work in a relationship-based model.

Additional non-tax-oriented information on the use of asset-based or stock-based transactions is provided at the start of Chapter 8 as well.

BANK FINANCING

Bank financing looks to be the single most important advancement in the M&A space for independent advisors in the past 10 years. FP Transitions handled one of the first bank-financed transactions in the industry at the practice level in 2002, a $1 million SBA-guaranteed loan. Honestly, at that time, the process was arduous, painfully slow, and the results uncertain right up until the night before closing. But things have changed, dramatically, and for the better.

Today, bank financing, when used correctly and coupled with a skilled lender and deal-structuring expert, is a powerful tool that can reshape your plan or accelerate your current path. So why, then, is this subject being written about at the end of Chapter 7? The answer is that bank financing doesn't replace all the supporting elements covered to this point. Whether as buyer or seller, you still need to use the proper approach and method to accurately determine value and set up the correct tax results. You still need basic payment structuring elements to create a shared-risk/shared-reward format intended to transition an intangible, professional services model. You still need some level of seller financing to achieve maximum client transition rates and realize full value. Bank financing, whether SBA or conventional, is a tool that must be used in conjunction with all the other moving pieces.

One more important aspect of this process that you need to consider is this—the very high buyer-to-seller ratio mostly reflects a pool of larger, stronger buyers who have the financial strength to complete the transaction on their own. What will the buyer-to-seller ratio be if smaller, financially weaker but now equally capable buyers can also step into the circle supported by bank financing? It could make smaller practices the financial equal of larger practices and businesses, at least in terms of the offer sheet. This could result in even greater demand for sellers. We'll see. Bank financing certainly creates some interesting dynamics and choices.

Generally, lending to the investment advisory space requires lending against goodwill and cash flow, a loan type that has long carried a strong negative bias in the banking profession. So what changed? Three things have reshaped the landscape. First, a strong and defined history of value and transferability has been established for this industry, augmented by a competitive open marketplace, with thousands of valuations supported by successful M&A activity. Second, the SBA lending process has been greatly improved through technology and skilled lenders. In addition, conventional financing can be used in certain situations where SBA financing may not be a good fit. Third, financial services and advisory practices and businesses have turned out to be great borrowers, with a low default rate and strong growth rates, low overhead, and predictable revenue streams—in other words, high "cash flow quality," underscoring the need for a valuation system that can measure and reward these unique intangibles.

Available external financing for this industry can be a strategic lever at many different levels, positioning an advisory practice to:

- Pursue growth opportunities more aggressively within an industry with high, long-term growth rates.
- Accelerate a current internal succession plan.
- Create a more attractive and powerful buyer in a competitive M&A market where buyers significantly outnumber sellers.
- Provide working capital to build enterprise strength and support organic growth—collectively, a platform for acquisitions, succession planning, and/or continuity planning.

Not every bank does this kind of work or makes these loans. In fact, very few banks are qualified or capable of handling this highly regulated space properly or efficiently. This is not the domain of your neighborhood bank or SBA lender, even if (especially if) they can print out a preapproval letter in five minutes. We've learned that the "work out process" requires that our team integrate seamlessly with the lending team to navigate all the potential pitfalls in the combined lending and M&A process and to do so within a reasonable period of time. Our choice of lending SBA partner in this space is Live Oak Bank.

THE MECHANICS OF THE PROCESS

Bank financing in this industry is an SBA (Small Business Administration) guaranteed loan process. As you might expect, there are more than a few rules. Bank financing under SBA guidelines will generally fall within these boundaries:

- Loan amounts typically between $250,000 to $5 million.
- Interest rates at prime plus 2% to 2.75%.
- 25% "equity infusion" is often required, whether from a cash down payment, seller subordinated note, or both.
- Minimum 1.75% × debt service ratio.
- Borrower credit score(s) of 680 or better.
- Up to 10-year repayment terms.

It is possible to structure loans for more than $5 million, so don't think of that as a "hard cap." It depends more on the situation and the lending and planning expertise. All of these parameters are subject to change. One of the most important elements for planning and evaluation purposes, as either a buyer or a seller, is the requirement of a 25% equity infusion. This element supports the shared-risk/shared-reward concept in the M&A process and deserves singular attention and explanation.

In the advisory space, banks must lend against goodwill and cash flow rather than tangible assets (Figure 7.3). As a result, the lending process will generally only cover 75% of the value of a given practice, business, or firm. The other 25% can be handled in a number of ways. The most direct avenue is for a buyer/borrower to pay 25% of the purchase price as a nonrefundable down payment, with the bank financing the balance. If the buyer cannot or does not want to pay that much down, it is possible to work around this issue. One common solution is that the seller could agree to carry a note subordinate to the bank's interest. Another possibility is that, for internal exit plans, the buyer acquires about 25% of the company gradually, over time, and then uses bank financing to acquire the remaining, un-owned 75% portion, or value, when the seller is ready to fully retire and cash out. Regardless of the solution, it is important that the seller have an ongoing financial interest and incentive to support the transition for a period of time post-closing.

KEY ASSUMPTIONS

$1.5M Purchase
$1M Bank Financing; $.5M Seller Note (5 years; 6%)

| $1M Bank Loan | **+** | $.5M Seller Note | **➡** | $1.75 × Min. Required Business DSC |
| ~ $135K Annual Debt Service | | ~ $115K Annual Debt Service | | $437K Firm Cash Flow Required |

FIGURE 7.3 An Example of the Structure of Bank Financing

The 1.75% × minimum debt service ratio is another important element to understand and plan for. Free cash flow, which is available to service debt, is a critical element in assessing a borrower's creditworthiness. At the end of the day, a practice or business must have enough cash flow to repay the debt, plus have a *cushion*. Lenders look for a minimum 1.75% × debt service ratio, meaning a practice or business (or firm) must produce a 75% cash cushion *after* paying its debt. This ratio indicates the number of times the financial obligations of the subject practice or business are covered by its earnings. A ratio of 1.75% × means that the borrower is in good financial health and can meet its financial obligations through the cash generated by normal operations. The basic formula is expressed as:

Cash Flow Coverage Ratio = Operating Cash Flows
(before owners' compensation) / Total Debt Payment

From the bank's perspective, a borrower must further demonstrate the capacity to transform a book into a practice or a business, revenue into profitability, and clients into strategic and profitable assets, if they haven't done so already. In short, effective portfolio/book management is a necessary, but not solely sufficient element for building a practice or business that can consistently support bank financing. All the elements that go into building a successful and profitable advisory practice or business—organic growth, client composition, retention, scale, technology, and the investment management process—are key elements in projecting as a strong borrower. This is best summarized as follows: as a buyer, *you need to prepare ahead of time*. Start with a formal valuation and related set of benchmarks and then start asking a lot of questions. As a seller, work only with buyers who are qualified and prepared.

There are five distinct stages of the loan application process:

1. **Qualification:** Initial information is exchanged to see if the acquisition opportunity meets the bank's general parameters.
2. **Proposal:** A proposal is issued by the bank after the borrower has been qualified. If the proposal is accepted by the borrower, the process moves to underwriting.
3. **Underwriting:** This stage is characterized by a detailed analysis with a lot of information exchanged, resulting in formal approval or decline.
4. **Commitment:** After underwriting, a commitment letter is issued, which removes the uncertainty of a financing contingency from the process. As long as closing conditions are met and there is no material adverse change in the practice or business prior to close, financing is firm.
5. **Closing:** Time frame is determined by payment complexity and buyer preparedness.

The common reasons for rejecting a loan application for an SBA loan aren't that much different in most cases from a non-SBA or conventional loan—lack of cash flow sufficient to pay the debt, poor personal credit, an unreliable valuation result, declining trends in terms of profitability, growth rates, client-demographics, and so on, with no explanation for how they will be reversed. It is pretty much as simple as that.

Bank financing does make the overall process (when considering the post-closing financing period) move faster and with more certainty, especially from a seller's vantage point. But also understand that bank financing, whether conventional or SBA-backed, will take additional time (as in a month or two) to close or complete the transaction, highly relevant when there is a back-up offer and/or when the first-place buyer isn't prequalified and well prepared. At the same time, while the closing timeline may be extended by bank financing, the commitment letter is generally provided within two weeks of application, essentially eliminating the financing contingency provided that closing conditions are met. This can mitigate the risk that if the financing fails for some reason, the back-up offer will likely have expired, leaving the seller to restart the entire process. Accordingly, work with buyers who are ready to go (i.e., are preapproved by a reputable and experienced lender in this industry) and adjust your term sheet or LOI to accommodate the realities and complexities of the bank financing process.

A final note: In case you skipped ahead, go back and reread the section in Chapter 2 on valuations for bank financing. This is a special process. Ultimately, every fact pattern in this industry presents a minimal hard asset model that relies on cash flows. The debt level inserted as the result of an acquisition must be accommodated by the combined cash flows. Everything is connected and must be *in balance*.

BLENDING SELLER AND BANK FINANCING TOGETHER

Seller financing has certainly proven its value in terms of supporting "best match" and high client-retention rates, but the benefits have also had a cost. Seller financing places about two-thirds of the risk of every transaction on the shoulders of the seller, while immediately transferring full control of the cash flow to the buyer. In addition, sellers have had to play the role of banker and patiently wait to realize the value they'd built over a lifetime. Occasionally, the financing effort is interrupted or altered by events beyond anyone's control—think recession, market fluctuations, tax rate increases, regulatory issues and changes, and the like.

The challenge in working with bank financing is that it does not (and should not) completely eliminate the use of seller financing. The two financing elements need to complement each other. Used in this manner, bank financing can provide substantially more cash at the time of closing, greatly reducing the seller's risk in the transaction. At the same time, bank financing provides the buyer with a "longer runway" with which to work in terms of cash flow and ROI (return on investment) issues. An SBA loan can provide a buyer more than twice the amortization period a seller can or will reasonably support.

Buyers who choose to pay all cash (a combination perhaps of bank financing and a significant down payment out of cash reserves) will certainly find many ready and willing sellers, but there is a consistent problem that comes up. Buyers are now assuming all the transition risk, at least in the case of an external, third-party buyer, and will often require discounting of the fair market value in exchange. In other words, there is a cost that the seller must be willing to incur—it may be a little, or it may be a lot. On the other hand, a transaction structured with a 10% down payment, 70% bank financing, and 20% seller-financed carry-back note can deliver full value in a very reasonable time frame, with 80% paid up front, as shown in Figure 7.4.

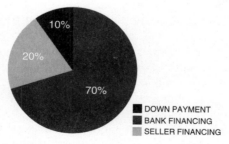

FIGURE 7.4   Payment Structure with 70% Bank Financing

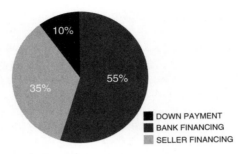

■ DOWN PAYMENT
■ BANK FINANCING
▨ SELLER FINANCING

FIGURE 7.5   Payment Structure with
55% Bank Financing

Every deal structure is unique and must reflect the transition risk and cash flow quality of the acquisition opportunity. If there is a concentration risk (10% of the clients are responsible for 50% of the assets and cash flow, for example) or other issue, the transaction might be structured with a larger seller-financed element, such as 30% or more (see Figure 7.5). In contrast, if the exit plan involves a son, a daughter, or one or more key employees who have already established themselves as owners/shareholders in the seller's business, a 100%, nondiscounted, bank-financed transaction to buy out the remaining interest by a retiring owner might well make sense.

ACCELERATION OPTIONS

This section is included in this book because this information was not available for publication in our first book and because it is relevant to independent advisors who are focused on an internal exit plan or succession plan.

Acceleration refers to an existing plan or buyout structure that has already been implemented and is likely relying on seller financing over a period of five years or more. In such circumstances, the founder or controlling shareholder is playing the role of banker. A third-party lender can provide the ability to accelerate the existing plan and to cash out the seller at current tax rates while providing the buyer with additional years over which to amortize the debt.

Every plan and situation is unique and requires further analysis, but bank financing provides options that simply didn't exist even a few years ago. Acceleration can provide important benefits to both buyer and seller. A staged succession plan supported by bank financing can empower both sellers (our term is "G-1," for Generation One) and buyers (our term is "G-2," for Generation Two). Think of staged succession in terms of traveling on an interstate highway. Available financing provides seller and buyer(s) with a series of "off-" or "on-ramps," depending on the route. As long as the business or firm has adequate cash flow and debt service capacity to support financing to take out G-1's remaining ownership interest, available bank financing provides G-1 with a series of choices, "off-ramps" if you will, where G-1 can deviate from the original plan and thinking and bring the trip to an end (with check in hand!).

The flip side is that financing provides G-2 with a series of on-ramps where they can acquire complete ownership of the business or firm. FP Transitions has worked with Live Oak Bank to create a unique loan process for use by G-2s (or even G-3s) to acquire up to 40% of the business or firm in instances where G-1 intends to exit sometime within five years. The SBA loan process does not typically accommodate this strategy.

Utilizing a partial buy-in loan to start the process and help G-1 take some money off the table immediately, the bank can subsequently provide financing to the business or firm to acquire G-1's remaining ownership interest upon full retirement. For G-2, financing for staged buy-ins overcomes the historical personal liquidity challenge for G-2/G-3 to buy into the business and it shifts the role of banker from G-1 to an actual bank—as it should be.

WORKING CAPITAL LOANS

Obtaining a basic, simple working capital loan could be, ironically, the most important next step you take to facilitating your exit plan or succession plan, and this discussion applies as much to prospective buyers as to sellers and business builders. This type of loan should be considered the initial point of entry into the bank financing system. As a buyer, if you are in the process of building out or improving your systems and processes, expanding operations, and generally preparing for an acquisition or other means of rapid growth, these loans are an excellent tool.

Unlike a line of credit (LOC), a working capital loan is fully amortized (up to 10 years). The underlying idea is that with an amortized payment embedded in the cash flow, the advisory practice can demonstrate its capacity for regular debt service. This contrasts with paying off an LOC with varying payments depending on whether you had a good or mediocre quarter or year. Although some practice owners counter that they'd simply be happy with a small LOC, don't want a loan or debt *on the books*, or don't really need a full working capital loan, there are solid rationales to reconsider the proper use of debt in your growing business structure:

- There is a famous adage in the banking world: always borrow money when you don't need it.

- If the opportunity to purchase a small book or practice appears, the cash is readily available.
- Prospective buyers often cite the need to grow as the primary reason for acquisition, but it is more important to first grow in terms of both revenue strength and enterprise strength to support a successful and aggressive acquisition strategy in the future. A working capital loan can be used to help grow a practice into a business (in terms of staffing, technology, floor space, etc.) before ever approaching a seller.
- If the preference centers on an internal exit plan or succession plan, a working capital loan demonstrates to next-generation advisors that the business is committed to growth by using a working capital facility to drive growth opportunities.
- This loan format adds a measure of certainty to the future needs of the business. Unlike an LOC, which is short term and usually subject to annual renewal, with a fully amortized loan, the loan is only callable in the event of payment default.

A working capital loan can also provide an advisor with knowledge of the loan process and proper use of debt, while familiarizing the lender with the advisor's practice, business, or firm (everything from cash flow to the valuation results), enabling all parties to be more responsive when the larger succession (or acquisition need) moves front and center. While it is certainly possible to "jump right in" during an acquisition or sale, a small initial working capital loan makes for an excellent, and practical, "trial run." This aspect underscores the previous point about working with buyers who are prepared and prequalified.

The size of a working capital loan is situational. In most instances, these loans will be less than $350,000, an amount that can usually be expedited by our lender's "small loan desk," with underwriting requirements further streamlined for loans of less than $150,000.

Apart from positioning an acquisitive practice, or one focused on succession planning, to assess bank financing more quickly and more adequately, the initial working capital loan enables a borrowing practice, business, or firm to address cash timing needs associated with its quarterly billing cycle. In the context of internal succession, it sends a positive initial message to next-generation advisors buying in that the business is committed to growth by adding a working capital facility to enable it to be more responsive to organic growth opportunities—and that the owner, or future owners, don't have to also be the financing source.

*   *   *

As we noted at the beginning of this chapter, bank financing has come a long way in a very short time. It is a good tool. So what's the catch? Why doesn't everybody use bank financing for their transactions? First and foremost, it is more challenging than just having solid credit scores and a cash flow structure that underwriters will look upon favorably. Generally, even after the bank approves a loan, underwriting will still require substantially more documentation than in a seller-financed transaction. Therefore, both buyer and seller need to be completely on board with the idea of adding a layer of complexity and the extra time that is part of the bank financing process.

Still, this is a major shift in our industry based primarily on a solid history of existing loans and on a deep database that underscores the special nature and value of an independent financial services or advisory practice or business. While it can take some work and a fair degree of expertise to make sure the loan succeeds and acquisition goals are met, ultimately this added feature provides benefits to both parties long after the initial motivations for a purchase and sale are satisfied.

CHAPTER 8

Due Diligence and Documentation

As a brief refresher, the term "exit plan" describes a transaction with either an external buyer or an internal buyer in which the transaction is completed in one step—not suddenly as with a continuity plan, just completely. External buyers usually have a very similar regulatory structure and revenue model, but are complete strangers to the client base, while an internal buyer is someone you hired and trained, know, and trust.

An external sale to a third party usually requires that buyer and seller follow the formalities of the M&A due diligence and documentation process to the letter—steps outlined in this chapter. Selling to an employee or group of employees, perhaps even a son or a daughter, is a different challenge. Selling internally assumes that the buyer already has access to much of the information they'll need, and sometimes the parties believe this supports a more relaxed approach to documenting the transaction. Regardless of the level of familiarity between a buyer and a seller, it is wise to always take a formal stance when it comes to due diligence and documentation. The goal isn't to discover and write down *all the things that can go right*, but to prepare and prevent against *all the things that might go wrong*, and the list can be long. Solid preparation and paperwork tends to alleviate most of the potential issues.

While most advisors may intuitively understand the progression of a sale or acquisition, it is important to remember that both buyer and seller need to be on the same page with similar expectations and a sense of pace during this stage of the transaction. Buyers often make a quick decision to pursue a practice and want to start negotiating right away. The seller, however, may still be coming to grips with the onslaught of buyer interest and inquiries received through an open market or even a closed market listing, if that is how they started the process. Sometimes, sellers may even be second-guessing their decision to sell. With all this in mind, one of the goals of this chapter is to encourage agreement on the progression of due diligence and the timeline for documenting the transaction and bringing it to a successful conclusion. Adhering to a formal structure will allow all parties to operate at approximately the same pace, with similar expectations, which, in turn, will allow for thoughtful negotiations and resolution of the contract details.

The best advice is this—whether selling externally to a complete stranger or internally to a key staff member, carefully follow the formalities outlined in this chapter. Buyers, whether you know the seller well or not, perform due diligence as though your career rests on this acquisition decision and its success. Sellers, take the time to observe the formalities and do the work it takes. The steps and the documentation outlined further on are part of a professionally executed exit plan for this unique and highly regulated industry.

CONDUCTING DUE DILIGENCE

The Beaufort scale is an empirical measure that relates wind speed to observed conditions at sea or on land. This scale was originally designed to allow sailors to estimate wind speed by observing the surface of the sea. Its full name is the Beaufort wind force scale.

The scale was finalized in 1805 by Francis Beaufort, later to earn the rank of Rear Admiral in the Royal Navy. The scale that carries Beaufort's name had a long and complex evolution and was first used officially during the voyage of the HMS *Beagle* (the ship made famous by young naturalist Charles Darwin during a survey voyage) many years later. Simply put, naval officers needed a standard scale in order to remove subjectivity from weather observations and record keeping. Beaufort succeeded in standardizing the scale that is still used today.

The modern-day Beaufort scale consists of 13 numbers ranging from 0 to 12. A Beaufort force of 0 is assigned to calm winds and a smooth water surface. A Beaufort force of 12 is assigned when waves are greater in height than 46 feet and the sea is completely white with foam and spray with almost no visibility, usually associated with hurricane-force winds of greater than 74 mph. The initial scale of 13 classes related qualitative wind conditions to the more practical effects on the sails of a frigate, then the main ship of the Royal Navy, from "just sufficient to give steerage" to "that which no canvas sails could withstand."

Fast forward to the modern day and the small town where I spend part of my time, the metropolis of Depoe Bay. As visitors drive into this small town, they are greeted by a flagpole (Figure 8.1), maintained by the harbor master, that often flies one red pennant (even on a *nice day* on the Oregon coast). One red pennant indicates the presence, or anticipation, of something more than a strong breeze and something less than a gale, based on specific, observable conditions (levels 6 to 7 on the Beaufort scale). One pennant is often related to a "small craft advisory." Two red pennants, as you might guess, signal a spectacular weekend of storm watching!

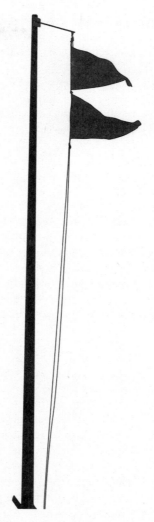

FIGURE 8.1   The Harbor Master's Flag with Two Red Flags, Letting People Know That Severe Storms Are on the Way

Due diligence is often spoken of as the search for red flags, that is, problems or deficiencies or differences in the seller's practice or business from what was promised or expected. Finding red flags during the due diligence process is normal. The bigger question is, one red flag or two? No red flags means the buyer probably hasn't looked thoroughly enough. The practice or business to be acquired might be perfect, but probably not. Buyers should expect to discover undisclosed facts—no one can ever think to present everything the other side will want to know. Sellers, do your level best. Buyers, recognize that just like a windy day, a red flag is merely a cautionary sign, not a signal to retreat.

The term "due diligence," applicable to the M&A process, refers to the investigation, analysis, and review of an acquisition opportunity. Due diligence should start with a "30,000 foot view" as the potential buyer begins to form a broad picture of the practice and its operations. As a buyer reviews more and more information, and in greater detail, this picture should narrow into sharp focus. Be aware that due diligence continues right up until the moment of closing, and in this industry, it works in both directions—buyer of seller, and seller of buyer.

During the due diligence process, physical access to the clients by the buyer is typically not permitted. Sellers should carefully check their IBD's or custodian's privacy policy statements and any confidentiality restrictions that may be in place if the goal is otherwise. Not all transactions close, or are completed, and for this reason, meeting the client base is almost never allowed prior to the formal closing. The rare exception to this rule might include a very large client whose post-closing approval and support could *make or break* the deal. Still, such a situation can be accommodated by an appropriate deal structure.

Although the concept of due diligence has been around for eons, the term first came into common use through the Securities Act of 1933 (the "Act"), making it at least an interesting coincidence for the M&A process in the independent financial services industry. The Act included a "Due Diligence" defense that could be relied upon by broker-dealers in the event they were accused of inadequate disclosure to investors of material information with respect to the purchase of securities. Provided that broker-dealers performed adequate and professional due diligence into a given company whose equity interests they were selling, and such findings were disclosed to the investors, the broker-dealer would not be held liable or responsible for nondisclosure of material facts later discovered.

Due diligence was quickly adopted by the broker-dealer community as a standard practice, and investigations were carried out on any stock offerings in which the broker-dealer involved itself. Originally the term was limited to public offerings of equity investments, but over time it came to be associated with investigations of private mergers and acquisitions as well.

Do not depend on practice management personnel at your broker-dealer or custodian for this type of work or support, no matter what they say or what documentation they provide. This is not what they do. Having access to practice data, client reports, historical revenue information, and such makes them very helpful, but performing due diligence is the buyer's and seller's individual responsibilities. No one can "think like an owner," like an owner. To this end, each side of the transaction should assign a primary contact or designee to facilitate rapid and clear communications and to maintain a clear channel for delivery and responsibility in terms of responses and/or documentation. All communications, however delivered, should be marked CONFIDENTIAL.

A sample due diligence checklist is included in the Appendix to this book, one for buyers, and a separate checklist for sellers. Every acquisition has its own due diligence issues and buyers and sellers must adapt to the fact pattern at issue. The primary areas to consider from a **buyer's** perspective include:

- Organizational structure (books versus a single enterprise)
- Entity structure/regulatory structure/licensing
- Information systems/CRM system
- Client profile/transferability issues/concentration risks
- Regulatory issues/compliance issues
- Financial and tax information/accounting practices/liabilities or debts
- Purchase/negotiation issues
- Employment and labor matters/current staffing
- Compensation structure (relevant if any employees or advisors are to be retained)
- Personal property
- Material contracts/referral agreements (including transferability)
- Turnkey asset management platforms/outsourced money managers

The payment terms will also impact the due diligence process. Buyers who acquire a very small book with no down payment, with the balance entirely seller financed on a revenue sharing arrangement, will not need to do much due diligence. There's little to no risk, at least in terms of realizable cash flow. On the other hand, a buyer who is acquiring the stock of a business valued at $6.75 million that is organized as an S corporation, using bank financing to cover 60% of the purchase price after a 15% nonrefundable down payment, will need to be razor-sharp in the due diligence process. Most due diligence efforts fall somewhere in between.

The primary issues to consider from a **seller's** perspective (depending on the amount and extent of seller financing) include:

- Buyer's credit score
- Buyer's financial commitments and debts

- Buyer's previous acquisition history (previous seller references are important)
- Buyer's regulatory structure, licensing, and disciplinary history (if any)
- Buyer's continuity plan and succession plan
- Buyer's recent valuation results (relevant to collateral/security issues if seller financing is involved)
- Buyer's organizational structure (books versus a single enterprise) and entity structure
- Buyer's ownership structure

As with buyers, the payment terms will determine the impact of due diligence on a seller. If a seller receives 35% of the purchase price as a non-refundable down payment and another 50% of the purchase price through a bank-financed loan, due diligence is primarily focused on the balance. Still, sellers should always conduct due diligence as the buyer's character and creditworthiness are always an issue until the transaction has closed *and* until the clients have given their approval (figuratively speaking, perhaps).

What if, prior to closing, the buyer finds issues that are material and that weren't fully disclosed? Depending on the severity and relevancy, the buyer has several choices. First, they could allow the shared-risk/shared-reward payment structure to alleviate the issues post-closing (the more flexibility built into the payment structure, the lower the pressure on due diligence). Alternatively, the buyer can ask for an adjustment to the purchase price and to the payment terms as well. Or, the buyer could walk away. Having a well-structured LOI or term sheet helps to create a clear set of "next steps," including obligations, time frame, and repercussions. Remember, material omissions are not always intentional or malicious. A situation may crop up that the buyer finds substantive, but the seller has lived with for many years and has never worried about or even thought about.

Sometimes there are details that simply didn't arise during the due diligence review and that suddenly appear in the days before closing. For example, sometimes a seller has one or more undisclosed liens against the practice itself. That sounds bad, but many times such liens are the result of leasing a copier, or obtaining a line of credit or a bank loan. It is also not unusual that the lienholder neglects to remove a lien after the obligation has passed. Practice owners (sellers) rarely check for such issues absent an event such as a sale of the practice. It is important to check, and to deal with such issues in a professional manner during the M&A process. Another example is that one of the seller's larger clients decides to change advisors, or withdraw most of their assets, or dies, substantially changing the cash flow dynamics and arguably the valuation result. For any and all of these reasons, always start with the "best match" between buyer and seller and a fair and balanced deal structure; resolution of any such due diligence issues is always possible if the parties work well together and depend on each other to succeed.

FP Transitions performs a lien search on every seller's practice or business prior to closing on the buyer's behalf, just in case. It's amazing what can surface after 20 to 30 years in business, and though even the seller is often surprised at the results, the findings are usually easily dealt with and resolved. The goal is to be thorough.

Due diligence on the seller is often primarily performed by the buyer or the buyer's key personnel, but in some instances, outside counsel may be brought in for assistance. For example, the buyer's CPA or accountant can be helpful in spotting issues with the seller's financial statements or tax information—especially if they have some knowledge of the financial services or advisory profession. The buyer's legal counsel should review the seller's corporate documentation (very thoroughly if a stock sale is involved), relevant contracts and, if the attorney is qualified, the seller's regulatory and licensing information. How much outside help a buyer retains to support the due diligence review depends on the risk structured into the transaction and the team the buyer has assembled.

Due diligence is an interesting and unpredictable process. Expect that going in. But take control of the process, both as a buyer and as a seller, through proper documentation. Creating clear, written expectations, a set time frame, a protocol for success, and resolution mechanisms from day one helps to ensure that all parties achieve their goals. Putting these pieces in place properly almost always requires a team of qualified professionals.

ASSEMBLING AND MANAGING YOUR TEAM

Advisors who want to buy or sell a practice or a business will need some help to do the job right. A typical team for this purpose will include:

- A qualified valuation analyst
- A tax professional
- A lawyer
- Someone familiar with your regulatory structure and your IBD or custodian's rules and procedures
- A qualified intermediary

To be clear, this list applies to both buyers and sellers. Both parties typically need their own team, with some slight overlap as will be explained further on, and in the next section.

In our experience, one of the most valuable members of the team is going to be each party's CPA, or accountant; that's because properly managing cash flow and helping advisors realize value on a tax-efficient basis is part of what this group does for a living. FP Transitions works comfortably with several hundred CPAs and accountants every year to assist independent advisors who are designing and implementing their exit plans and, alternatively, their succession plans. Nothing in the processes discussed to this point, with the exception of performing a formal valuation, should be unfamiliar to an experienced tax professional.

Having a good lawyer on the team is part of the process, too. It is not always necessary to have an attorney with a high degree of securities law knowledge or expertise, but at the very least, they need to know what FINRA stands for and/or the basics of the Investment Advisers Act. For the most part, find an experienced attorney for the team who practices business law and knows a thing or two about M&A work. Don't overlook the important role that your attorney will perform in this process—their job is to be an advocate for you, and only you. Their job is to help you steer clear of unnecessary risks, or at least to help you understand where problems might be encountered, even how you can better structure the deal to your advantage. Of course, the other side's attorney is tasked with the same mission. Neither side should allow their attorney to negotiate the economic aspects of the transaction—that is not their skill-set and is mostly the job of the buyer and seller, maybe with help from their CPAs and accountants, valuation personnel, or the intermediary.

A qualified intermediary is descriptive of a company like FP Transitions, and others in this field who assist buyers, or sellers, or both in their quest to *do the job right*, not unlike a general contractor in the building of a home. Advisors interested in buying or selling an independent financial services or advisory practice or business find that the process takes a lot of time, and often over a very short window. In addition, practice and business owners do not go through this process very often and usually don't have much experience, at least as sellers. Many advisors do not always negotiate well on their own behalf, and are not familiar with the legalities, taxes, rules, and regulations surrounding a merger, sale, or acquisition. Most sellers, and first-time buyers, aren't even sure what questions to ask.

The role of an experienced intermediary is to bring industry-specific knowledge and expertise to bear for the client during the M&A process. As a qualified intermediary, FP Transitions works with both buyers and sellers, and their respective legal counsel and tax professionals, and their IBDs and custodians, to achieve success. In addition to working with both sides in a nonadvocacy format (more information is provided on this unique but important aspect in the following section of this chapter), FP Transitions also provides valuation support, deal structuring expertise, documentation, analysis of seller or bank financing, general guidance, tax strategies, post-closing transition planning, and even post-closing mediation if needed.

Attorneys and CPAs or accountants are not qualified intermediaries—they have an important, but very different and more narrowly focused job. Business brokers, if their only function is to introduce a seller to a potential buyer, would not be considered a qualified intermediary. Under no circumstances is a practice management staff person at a buyer's and/or seller's IBD/custodian a qualified intermediary—they are well intentioned and knowledgeable, but their job is to make sure the clients and assets don't leave their network.

Consider including your spouse or significant other in the M&A process as well, maybe not as a part of the team but certainly within the information loop. Buying or selling a business is a major process and knowing how the details and documents interact can help take some of the mystery out of it.

Missing from this list thus far is the investment banker. Do you need one? Most advisors would say no; but it depends on how you view this team member and the size of the transaction. Investment bankers tend to work with firms and larger businesses almost exclusively, thereby applying to about 2% of the independent industry. Typically, an investment banker will act as some kind of intermediary with multiple functions. Their role ranges from search coordination to deal negotiation to finance structuring. Depending on the investment banker and the transaction size, only one of these services may be offered. Ultimately, however, both buyer and seller can profit from using some kind of intermediary. This full range of services allows the more complex businesses to explore a wider range of options while smaller and mid-sized practices can benefit from a la carte services. Either way, buying or selling is often made much easier by including the use of a qualified intermediary. The fees for such services vary, but are often seen in the savings generated by having a knowledgeable and coordinated team craft and guide the transaction. In other words, a good intermediary will often pay for themselves.

Buyers may also need to add one more professional to this list, a banker, depending on financing choices. Sellers can drive this choice by knowing when and how to utilize bank financing and reduce their transaction risk—a good idea for every business and many larger practice models. These details are addressed in Chapter 7.

ADVOCACY VERSUS NONADVOCACY APPROACH

Both buyer and seller need to give some thought to directing their team members and articulating each role in the due diligence and negotiation process. At FP Transitions, we don't believe in "fighting to the finish" in order to close a transaction. Although M&A closings in other industries may see combative attorneys "duking it out" over a bloodied closing table, in this industry, the closing merely represents the first day in an important transition process centered on client satisfaction with the exit plan.

Successfully transferring the most valuable asset of an advisory practice, the client base, requires that both buyer and seller leave the closing table as *cordial business partners*. Only on the day after the closing do both parties begin the introduction process with the clients. That transfer process ultimately determines the success of the sale and the value of the practice or business. With this goal in mind, a truly successful deal is one in which the transaction's momentum, and trust, continues well after the closing date. This industry is unique in this aspect. We often say that our approach is one of *advocating for the deal*. Also referred to as a nonadvocacy position, this approach can often be counterintuitive to many attorneys.

FP Transitions' nonadvocacy approach does not by any means replace the use of attorneys. Before anything is signed, each side confers with their individual legal and tax counsel, and we subsequently discuss and include requested suggestions or modifications in the deal structure and documentation. An experienced intermediary operates on the premise that input from all of the team members is vital and will help coordinate the many roles and responsibilities. The point is to ensure that everyone works together with the same goal in mind. The end result is that 90% of our transactions are completed and usually with a very high post-closing client retention rate measured in the years after the closing. In hindsight, the post-closing default rate is nominal, so something about this process works quite well, and has for almost 20 years. Nonadvocacy is an approach that has worked well for thousands of buyers and sellers who made the choice to get along and work together for the good of the clients they serve.

In fairness, there are other ways to get things done. We do not have the market cornered on all the best ideas in the world. This is simply our way of doing things for the advisors we serve and the clients they serve.

DOCUMENTING THE TRANSACTION

The methods used to sell or transition a job, practice, or business often reflect the methods used to build each ownership level. The typical documentation package commonly used to sell or to acquire *a job or a book* is fairly simple, often reflecting a sole proprietorship and limited to no infrastructure.

- Basic revenue sharing arrangement (as a general rule, the payment plan should not exceed five years in length)
- Valuation is essentially "baked-in" (final value will be determined by adding up the payments)

- Taxes are typically ordinary income to the seller, expensed by the buyer if revenue is shared at this level (i.e., sometimes the revenue is split by the IBD or custodian)

Caution: Do not confuse *simple* with effective or lucrative, at least from the seller's point of view. If a seller of a book expects market value and expects to *actually realize* most of that value at optimal tax rates, the documentation package should include all or most of the elements appropriate to the *practice level* of ownership. These include:

- Market-based valuation
- Nondisclosure/confidentiality agreement(s)
- Letter of intent
- Asset purchase and sale agreement
- Post-closing consulting agreement
- Noncompetition/nonsolicitation/no-service agreements
- Performance-based promissory note (seller financing)
- Security and collateralization
- Bill of sale

Book owners often conclude that the costs, in terms of dollars, time, and trouble, will offset any benefits to be derived. Perhaps, but another way to say it is that the cost of correct and professional documentation pays for itself, sometimes substantially more.

The documentation package to support the sale or acquisition of a *business* includes all of the items listed in this section under sale of a practice plus these possible additions or substitutions:

- Earnings-based valuation
- Stock purchase and sale agreement
- Bank financing agreements
- Employment agreements for the seller's key staff members
- Post-closing employment agreement for the seller

A further explanation of some of the primary documents in this inventory list is provided further on, excluding documents addressed in previous chapters or sections of this book.

Nondisclosure Agreement/Confidentiality

The place to start in every transaction is to focus on confidentiality. If you're the buyer, you will need to know just about everything with regard to the acquisition opportunity. If you're the seller, this may be the person or company you will one day introduce your clients to. And the reality is that not all transactions are completed—sometimes the parties consistently find multiple red flags instead of one. Safeguarding personal and client information is just smart business.

Just as due diligence works both ways, so does the need to keep everything confidential. Start with a reciprocal nondisclosure agreement (NDA). A sample is provided in the Appendix that can be edited to fit your own situation. An NDA, also called a confidentiality agreement, is a legally enforceable contract that creates a confidential relationship, in this case, between a prospective buyer and a prospective seller. NDAs aren't used because one side doesn't trust the other party—if the parties didn't trust each other, there wouldn't be any discussion at all. Trust is the prerequisite to an NDA.

The type of information covered by an NDA is virtually unlimited. In fact, any knowledge exchanged between those involved can be considered and defined as confidential. In this industry, examples of confidential information include client lists, client information, master account numbers, financial information (P&Ls, balance sheets, cash flow statements, etc.), software, marketing materials, intake forms, passwords, regulatory disclosures, arbitration matters, complaint files, or regulatory records. While this list isn't exhaustive, it is designed to help advisors think of other instances of information that should be protected. Also be sure to review any and all applicable IBD or custodian privacy policy statements when considering how much information to release and when.

Regardless of its function or the information it protects, an NDA generally addresses these specific issues:

- Definitions of exactly what is considered "confidential information"
- Exclusions from what is considered "confidential information"
- Specific obligations from all involved people or parties
- Time periods that apply to the obligations

When should a buyer and seller enter into a written NDA? At FP Transitions, we implement this process *before* the parties even start talking directly (assuming the seller has listed on the open market or even in a closed market setting), but certainly after enough basic information has been shared that there is strong and mutual interest in further discussion and exploration. In a nonadvocacy setting, this is a requisite step in the M&A process.

Nondisclosure agreements often exclude some information from protection. Exclusions might comprise information already considered common or public knowledge (such as regulatory findings published by a governmental agency). Additionally, NDAs explicitly spell out that the person receiving the information is to keep it secret and limit its use. This means an advisor cannot breach the agreement, encourage others to breach it, or allow others to access the confidential information through improper or unconventional methods. Also see Chapter 10 regarding NDAs and additional confidentiality requirements if the buyer and seller are with different IBDs.

Letters of Intent/Term Sheets

At the practice and business levels, it is not uncommon for a buyer to present a seller with an offer in the form of a letter of intent (LOI), or a term sheet. An LOI helps to frame the main issues and creates a time frame for due diligence and the completion or closing of the transaction. Typically, at least some due diligence has been completed in order to support the offer, which necessitates the previous execution of an NDA. In a highly regulated industry such as financial services and advisory, and when buyers "buy what they know," most of the due diligence takes place *after* the LOI has been submitted and accepted.

Technically, a letter of intent is a letter from buyer to seller in which the buyer states his or her intent to reach a definitive agreement for the acquisition of the seller's practice or business. The letter typically sets forth certain material terms and conditions of the acquisition such as price, payment details and time frame, a purchase of assets or stock, and represents the initial understanding of the parties. An LOI is usually signed by both buyer and seller. The letter is not a substitute for the purchase agreement and, accordingly, usually does not contain all of the material terms of the transaction. The stated goal of the parties is to reach a definitive written agreement within a specified time frame that encompasses the terms set forth in the LOI.

A term sheet is slightly different in that it sets forth the most important terms and conditions of the proposed acquisition, but is in the form of a list (i.e., the payment terms, the closing date, the deal structure, etc.) rather than a formal letter. In addition, unlike letters of intent that are signed by both the buyer and the seller, term sheets are not necessarily signed by the parties, or at least not by both parties. Practically, there is little difference between the two forms, as most buyers will expect the seller to acknowledge the offer in one way or another. It is the buyer's prerogative to deliver to the seller the LOI or term sheet, since the buyer is the one making the offer. Experienced buyers will prefer one format over another and will gradually develop a style that works well for them.

Typically, LOIs and term sheets are nonbinding but there is a presumption under the law that both parties will work in good faith to reach a definitive agreement once they've committed to each other. The parties may choose to make certain provisions of their LOI or term sheet binding (for example, confidentiality, return of documents, dispute resolution mechanisms, and payment of attorney fees or expenses in the case of a material breach or bad faith by one side). The LOI/term sheet should reference whether the buyer intends to assume the seller's office lease, or otherwise continue in the same office space (often requiring landlord approval) or, conversely, relocate the entire operation. The terms of an LOI may prevent a seller from negotiating with other potential buyers—a smart requirement from a buyer, maybe not for a seller. Accordingly, it is important to clearly state which provisions of the document are binding on the parties, and which are not.

In FP Transitions' open market system (and closed market systems with larger IBDs or custodians), it is common for a seller to receive multiple offers. Though it is the buyer's prerogative to make an offer, in a competitive selling situation, sellers typically first invite a select group of buyers to do so. Practically, this is the process of a seller selecting who he or she feels is the best match out of the pool of prospects. In an effort to streamline the process and make it easier for the seller to effectively compare one offer to another, FP Transitions usually requests that all qualified buyers utilize a uniform LOI format and submit all offers during a specific "window," such as "over the next 10 days starting on X date." Using this approach, a seller can more easily compare the multiple offers side by side and focus only on the price and payment terms from the best qualified, best matched buyers.

Buyers often don't like the idea of "competing" with other offers. However, in many cases, this is for the best. Without a formal, simultaneous review of the multiple offers, a seller can easily confuse the advantages of one offer compared to another. The open market listing and offer process is structured to support a seller's need to find the best match through a competitive, organized setting.

In a professionally structured transaction, it is also customary for an earnest money deposit to be placed into an escrow account to ensure the buyer's commitment. This is more likely if there are multiple qualified buyers in a competitive buying situation. The earnest money deposit is usually about 1% of the purchase price and is refundable up until a certain date agreed to by both buyer and seller. Once the "go/no go" date has passed, the deposit is nonrefundable. The mechanics of this process tend to create a brisk pace for due diligence and an early "final commitment" from the buyer. If the first buyer elects not to proceed early in the process, his or her earnest money deposit is returned and the next buyer can still be easily approached given that a very limited amount of time has passed since their offer was submitted and placed in the queue.

The value of an LOI or term sheet must be weighed against the time spent negotiating it, as opposed to just starting with the actual purchase agreement.

Private transactions, in which the buyer and seller already know each other and there are no other offers pending, often dispense with the formality of an LOI and proceed directly to the purchase agreements. Internal transactions, common at the business and firm levels of ownership, also tend not to use an LOI or term sheet, at least in furtherance of a succession plan with multiple, incremental stock purchases. A complete buyout by one or more key employees as with an exit plan is a different matter. Acquisitions at the job/book level also typically dispense with this formality, but that's not always a good idea. Ignoring such formalities can be expensive, as evidenced in part by this level's general acceptance of the worst payment structure and tax rates of all the ownership levels—observing formalities can only improve this situation.

LOIs can be very formal or very simple. Either way, it never hurts to use them to shape the transaction structure and to memorialize both parties' understanding of the deal. A sample LOI is included in the Appendix of this book, in which buyers and sellers can observe the commonly addressed issues and topics.

The Purchase and Sale Agreement

Once due diligence is substantially completed, the parties move forward with drafting a definitive purchase agreement. Purchase and sale agreements at the job/book, practice, or business ownership levels will typically fall into one of three categories:

1. An asset purchase and sale agreement
2. A stock purchase and sale agreement
3. An LLC membership/unit purchase and sale agreement

These agreements tend to follow the outline provided by the letter of intent (LOI) or term sheet, usually with a few modifications. The LOI serves as the blueprint for the purchase and sale agreement, but sometimes the plans change or require adjustment as a result of the due diligence process. In addition, the purchase and sale agreement contains many more details than can or should be addressed in the LOI or term sheet. The purchase and sale agreement, unlike the LOI or term sheet, is intended to be fully and legally enforceable once agreed to.

The party responsible for drafting the purchase and sale agreement, usually the buyer, has a distinct advantage over the receiving party. While that may be the norm and works for many transactions and in other industries, this industry is unique. In that the clients *get the final vote*, sometimes years later, the FP Transitions approach and that of this M&A guide is to provide a neutral, "level playing field" documentation process that adheres to the shared-risk/shared-reward concept. In our experience, this is how to obtain the highest level of client satisfaction, which ensures that the seller realizes best match and highest value, which means that the buyer has transitioned and will likely retain 95% to 100% of the client relationships and thus the cash flow they sought to acquire. Everything is connected.

In that more than 90% of all exit plans are documented using an asset purchase and sale agreement, most of this section focuses on that document, noting any important differences for the other two types of purchase agreements. The FP Transitions asset purchase and sale agreement, as an example, contains these principal sections:

- A preamble (naming the specific parties, their addresses, and their contact information)
- A list of assets being purchased, as well as any assets being excluded
- A list of liabilities being assumed (if any—an office lease is the most common example)
- A tax allocation structure to coordinate each party's tax filings
- Payment structure including down payment, use of a promissory note, contingencies, and so forth
- Security and collateralization, including restrictions on the buyer as to dispensation of the acquired clients/assets
- New client referrals (post-closing)
- Agreement of the parties as to post-closing seller licensing or registration requirements, and payment of E&O insurance
- Seller's representations and warranties
- Buyer's representations and warranties
- Covenants of seller
- Covenants of buyer
- Conditions precedent to buyer's and seller's obligations
- Indemnification provisions
- Default and acceleration provisions
- Closing date and procedures
- Rights and obligations subsequent to closing
- Confidentiality
- Miscellaneous provisions including jurisdiction, venue, attorney fees, dispute resolution mechanism, etc.

Typically attached as schedules or exhibits to the asset purchase and sale agreement (depending on the payment structure and transaction details) are the following:

- List of client accounts
- Post-closing consulting agreement

- Noncompetition/nonsolicitation agreement
- Security/collateralization agreement
- Performance-based promissory note
- Bill of sale
- Personal guaranty
- Financial statements of the seller
- UCC search results

The first four schedules or exhibits listed here, the list of client accounts, the consulting agreement, the noncompetition/nonsolicitation agreement, and the security or collateralization agreement, are explained in more detail further on (with the performance-based promissory note explained in Chapter 7). These *primary support agreements* are the most important in the exhibit list in terms of buyers and sellers needing to understand and appreciate what these agreements do and how they affect the final results.

In addition, one or more schedules or addenda may be attached to the purchase and sale agreement in which material details of the transaction not already captured in the base agreement are memorialized and agreed to. Addenda also provide for any last-minute adjustments without having to alter the entire purchase and sale agreement document, especially if it has already been signed by the parties. FP Transitions attorneys start with a comprehensive base document, like all attorneys do, and then tailor it to the terms and specifics of the transaction. While most transactions utilize common structuring elements and documents such as those listed earlier, no two transactions are exactly the same.

It's probably obvious by now that a lot goes into the documentation process. The preceding list must be tailored in many respects to the rules and regulations that accompany most advisors to work every day. The preceding list should also help buyers and sellers better understand why a letter of intent or term sheet is used to frame the primary issues only, and not to provide all of the details. The details are better addressed in the purchase and sale agreement and attachments. The goal, of course, isn't to draft "the perfect agreement" or to generate a pound of paperwork for every million dollars of value—the goal is to transfer and retain 100% of the trusting client relationships.

In many ways, a stock purchase agreement is simpler—the buyer purchases an established entity and everything comes with it. In other ways, it can be more complex. The key differences are that a stock purchase agreement has a different tax outcome (possibly for both parties), and "everything" also includes liabilities of the selling entity, known and unknown. The tax difference usually does not affect the valuation result or purchase price; the liability issue might. Sometimes the liability issues are easily mitigated with an indemnification and hold-harmless clause, and sometimes it takes a lot more. As lawyers will frequently tell you, "It depends."

Acquirers of RIAs may sometimes prefer the stock route. Since an RIA practice or business is almost always set up as an entity (S corporation or LLC's are the predominant choices), the investment advisory agreements they enter into with a client are usually between the entity and the client, not the individual advisor and the client. Selling stock means that the buyer acquires an ongoing practice or business *and* retains the existing contracts that are in place and producing revenue. Rules and regulations still likely trigger a notice to the clients of a change of control even under these circumstances. Still, many RIAs prefer a stock sale because giving notice (or even obtaining written permission if called for by a contract) is often easier than quickly trying to execute new contracts with the entire client base shortly after closing.

Stock purchase and sale agreements are also commonly used at the business and firm levels of ownership. However, at these levels, most of the transactions are not exit plans but true succession plans in which the stock is sold incrementally to key employees. Businesses and firms, including practice owners currently building toward these models, however, comprise only 5% to 8% of the independent space. Regardless, the primary support agreements explained further on are equally applicable to an asset purchase and sale agreement, a stock purchase and sale agreement, or an LLC membership/unit purchase and sale agreement.

List of Clients / Accounts   Attached to the purchase and sale agreement, as a schedule or an exhibit, is a complete list of client accounts. This list is an integral part of the transaction and touches on many of the agreement's functions. For example, the client list is a major part of the "assets being purchased." It is also tied to the confidentiality provisions, as well as the agreement not to compete or solicit. The referral agreement section centers on new clients referred after closing by the seller who are not already on the client list or a family member of anyone on that list.

The list of client accounts serves many purposes, but is especially relevant given the highly regulated environment the transaction takes place within. If the regulatory structure involves FINRA regulations, a different set of rules applies to the revenues derived from that client list than if, for example, a fee-only RIA practice is being transitioned. The specific clients being transitioned and the cash flows they represent are also often tied to the post-closing payment contingencies such as a performance-based promissory note, or sometimes an earn-out arrangement, as well as the restrictive covenants (i.e., the noncompete agreement(s)). These competing aspects tend to help balance the process and ensure that all of the clients are listed, and subsequently included as part of the post-closing contract process.

Consulting Agreement

In most transactions that involve books or practices, the seller does not stay on post-closing as an employee—mergers and the Sell and Stay strategy being the exceptions to the rule. Continued employment is sometimes an option, but the "bandwidth" the seller eats up in terms of cash flow (i.e., salary or compensation) tends to reduce the likelihood of the seller's long-term post-closing involvement, at least at the book or smaller practice ownership levels. Instead, it is far more likely that the seller or sellers offer post-closing support for 6 to 12 months to transition the client relationships to the buyer, and then gradually step back from the forefront. This overall process is memorialized in a consulting agreement.

The post-closing consulting agreement is typically a personal services contract between each selling owner/advisor and the buyer (often a corporation or an LLC) and is a very important component in the M&A process. The services covered by this agreement include the seller's post-closing assistance and support in delivering and helping the buyer to get to know the clients, their goals and needs, and subsequently helping to retain those clients and assets. The consulting agreement is *not* an employment agreement—they are very different documents and contracts, with unique employment law and tax consequences. In most cases, the seller does not, and should not, receive additional compensation for working to transition already promised deliverables, that is, the relationships and assets that support the entire value proposition. The purpose of the consulting agreement is to memorialize the seller's post-closing support and transition duties, in detail, and to ensure that, together, the buyer and seller can exert sufficient and professional control over the transition process to achieve success.

The duty of transitioning the clients and assets is structured as an integral part of the value proposition for the assets purchased. In other words, the consulting support function should be a part of the valuation assumptions— without the post-closing consulting element, it really is *just a list of clients*. This is yet another reason that an M&A, industry-specific valuation, is essential. The consulting agreement clarifies the roles and duties of the parties as to who is in charge, what will be done, who will do it, how will the work be performed, and the value to be paid for this crucial client transition element. Consider this simple question: How much less would a buyer pay for just a list of intangible, relationship-based assets without the former and primary advisor's support and cooperation? In the answer lies the value of this agreement, literally.

The consulting agreement is typically the shortest agreement in terms of duration. The seller's post-closing transition support usually lasts from 6 to 12 months, assuming the best match has been selected as a buyer. This is relevant to the tax issues in that the tax allocation assigned to this portion (ordinary income tax rates to the seller) is often written off first and almost completely during the first year or two of the transaction. See also Table 7.4, "Asset Classes and Their Treatment by Buyers and Sellers," in Chapter 7.

Noncompete/Nonsolicitation Agreement

Every transaction, whether for the acquisition or sale of a book, a practice, or a business, and whether in the form of an asset purchase and sale agreement or a stock purchase and sale agreement or an LLC purchase and sale agreement, should include the seller's formal, written agreement not to compete with, or solicit, or serve, the client base being transferred. The average length of a noncompetition agreement is three to five years. Regardless, it tends to last at least until the purchase price is paid in full through seller financing, but three to five years is usually reasonable even in the case of bank financing.

Noncompetition agreements must be reasonable in time, scope, and geography, and specific in terms of the business activity addressed. The laws vary from state to state on these issues, but do not confuse the enforceability of a noncompete/nonsolicitation agreement in this setting with one between an employer and an employee—these are different arenas with different levels of enforceability. The disparate bargaining positions of an employer and an employee are not the same as between a buyer and a seller; the latter tends to be fully enforceable if drafted properly.

There are several methods of strengthening a buyer's hand when considering noncompetition/nonsolicitation issues. For example, in addition to having the seller sign a well-drafted agreement, buyers should also consider acquiring the seller's trade name, office phone numbers (even if these items may not be used in the future), key staff members, software, and marketing systems, if possible. Structuring the financing to include a contingency effectively penalizes a seller who breaches or encroaches on the noncompetition/nonsolicitation agreement by immediately or quickly and permanently reducing the amount of money paid to the seller if any of the clients or cash flow is diverted. Finally, buyers who have similar revenue models but are larger and stronger than the seller (i.e., a business buying a practice, or a practice buying a book) are in a better position to offer the clients a value-added opportunity from which they are less likely to turn away. These steps cumulatively make it much harder for a seller to unfairly compete in violation of a formal agreement.

Collateralization and Security

Seller financing is involved in almost every payment structure, even when bank financing is used, as explained in Chapter 7. The amount and type(s) of financing, as well as the amount paid in a nonrefundable down payment, often determine the level and amount of security and collateral required of a buyer or successor.

At a minimum, when an asset purchase and sale agreement format is being used, the balance owed (subject to any contingencies) in a third-party transaction or exit plan should be personally guaranteed by the buyer. Life insurance is also a consideration, on both parties, to address unpaid obligations by individuals post-closing. This is more important when the buyer is a sole proprietor or a single-owner corporation or LLC, less important when the buyer is a business or firm with multiple owners and multiple generations of ownership. To this end, sellers, too, have an obligation to support the transaction, and their sudden death or disability immediately after closing may have a significant negative impact on the results of the transaction. Life insurance can help to mitigate the damages. Policies for this purpose are often collaterally assigned.

FP Transitions typically recommends that the parties include a security agreement in their transaction documents and that the seller file a Uniform Commercial Code lien notice, called a UCC-1 financing statement, against at least the assets being sold, if not more, until the deferred portion of the purchase price is paid in full. This step provides limited recourse and is no substitute for the cumulative effect and benefits of all the other shared-risk/shared-reward aspects of the process (a market based valuation, a buyer's substantial and nonrefundable down payment, limited length of seller financing, one year post-closing support by the seller, a competitive search for the best-matching buyer, etc.). The goal of collateralization and security is *not* repossession of the assets—that is not a good idea in most cases. The goal is to provide the seller with sufficient recourse to realize the value of the transaction.

It is also easier to secure and collateralize a balance owed when the debt is in the form of a promissory note for a sum certain. Most promissory notes are personally guaranteed and backed with a lien on the acquired assets. However, earn-out arrangements can also be secured and guaranteed if structured properly.

Financial professionals understand the importance of *following the rules*. The M&A process has its own set of rules, but with an added level of complexity: two parties, perhaps complete strangers to each other, must work together to follow the rules and achieve success, in a highly regulated industry. Though the client base being transitioned will likely never read the transaction documents, nor see any part of the due diligence review, they ultimately serve as the judge and jury over the entire process. In the end, all of the work, the decisions, and the paperwork—it all comes down to the clients and their decision on whether or not to accept the new advisor.

Buyers and sellers are often inundated with information, tips, and strategies for how to achieve their respective goals. Be sure to understand the steps needed to achieve a long-lasting, well-coordinated transaction that works for everyone involved. No amount of paperwork will change or fix a poor transaction or an acrimonious relationship with the other party. The most important lesson to be imparted from this chapter is the need to carefully assemble and professionally manage your M&A team. This group of professionals, and their ability to follow your directions and work well with the other side, will ultimately decide your success or failure.

CHAPTER 9

Key Legal Issues in the M&A Process

It all seems so clear. After several involved discussions, a 63-year-old gentleman shakes hands with a 45-year-old woman. He is going to sell his practice to her and the business she has built. Due diligence is under way and proceeding smoothly and the transaction is to be closed in about 30 days.

He has spent the last 30 years building a very nice fee-based practice outside of Sacramento, California. Organized as a single shareholder S corporation, Anthony, the seller, is 75% fee-based, but has no stand-alone RIA. Instead, he works under a hybrid system with a major independent broker-dealer. Years ago, Anthony was more commission-based but, over time, that has changed. Though his practice now strongly trends toward the fee-based side, he couldn't bring himself to completely give up his broker-dealer relationship or income.

Madison, the buyer, is an SEC-level, stand-alone RIA located in Chicago. Her company wants to establish a West Coast presence and decided that acquiring a turnkey practice would be faster and more efficient than starting from scratch. Madison founded her practice after leaving a wirehouse, later joined an independent broker-dealer, and then evolved into a predominantly fee-based business model. She also has some insurance income in order to better support her larger and more sophisticated business clients. Organized as an LLC and taxed as a partnership, Madison's firm has $4 billion in assets under management (AUM) and five owners; she is the CEO. This will be the firm's third acquisition, but its first out of state.

Several weeks later, after completing due diligence for this asset-based transaction, Anthony and Madison headed into the final stages of their transaction. Now, sitting in front of each of them in their respective offices, is a stack of documents. Both parties need to read through the purchase and sale agreement, and all of the supporting agreements, schedules, and exhibits. This is it.

Often, even the smartest advisors will scan over a legal document with the assumption that "I'm a smart person. I've done this before, or something similar, and it seems pretty clear. I know what sections really matter—the rest is boilerplate." In an hour or two, they finish the read through with but a handful of questions for their attorneys.

The purpose of this chapter is to help buyers and sellers better understand what to look for and how to identify some of the key legal issues in the M&A process. The purchase and sale agreement governs virtually the entire transaction and it is often *the little things* that matter—the sections that are often overlooked or misunderstood. Buyers and sellers need to understand the nuance in some of the "boilerplate" verbiage, including when changes are needed and what can be safely left alone. In many ways, the strength of the purchase agreement determines how well everyone sleeps after the sale closes.

WHAT EXACTLY IS "BOILERPLATE"?

And why should you care?

In the world of law, the term "boilerplate" describes those parts of a contract that are considered "standard language." The term refers to *reusable text* that does not change very much, if at all, from one contract to the next. For lawyers, it is often considered the easy part of the drafting process. For advisors who are buying or selling a highly regulated practice or business largely comprised of intangible assets, it is anything but.

The term "boilerplate" originates from the printing industry and from newspapers in particular and begins back in the 1890s or so. Steam boilers of that era were built from very heavy and tough sheets of steel. Boiler plate originally referred to the sheet steel used to make boilers. But similar sheets of steel were used by printers for engraving copy that was intended for widespread reproduction in multiple issues of newspapers—in other words, ads and syndicated columns that were to be printed over and over again. Copy that was used only once was set in much softer, durable metal such as lead. Accordingly, the print that was supplied to printers and newspapers in ready-to-use, steel prefabricated printing plates that could not be modified before printing, came to be known as boilerplate. Eventually, any part of the newspaper or print that rarely changed, such as the masthead, was called boilerplate.

In a purchase and sale agreement, boilerplate, at least from *the layman's perspective*, includes all of the end matter in a contract. Specifically, the miscellaneous clauses regarding venue, jurisdiction, attorney fees, integration, notices, amendments, confidentiality, and the like. But the boilerplate sections usually include much more. Falling under this heading in a general sense are the following sections of a purchase and sale agreement:

- Seller's representations and warranties
- Buyer's representations and warranties
- Seller's covenants and conditions
- Buyer's covenants and conditions
- Indemnification and hold harmless clauses
- Resolution of conflicts

Though the legal profession will quickly and correctly point out that all of these sections are carefully reviewed and adjusted as needed for the intricacies of any particular deal, they all look the same from the layman's perspective from one contract to the next. Worse, and maybe more important, these sections are not easily or fully understood by most advisors, so the functionality and application is left to the drafting party. Lawyers are trained draftsmen, but the buying and selling advisors have a much better understanding of the facts and of how their unique practices actually function.

So what do you need to know as a buying or selling party about these sections? The answer is, at least enough to read these sections with clarity of purpose; enough to spot inaccuracies in what *the lawyers say you are saying* to the other side, and to ask good questions of your counsel before you sign the agreement. To help you do this, we are going to start at the top of the preceding list and work through each area in the following sections, and then proceed to address some of the basic but important issues that many buyers and sellers face within the "four corners" of the purchase and sale agreement, and a few issues that come out of that document and arise after closing.

To be clear, the best set of transaction documents is the one that you sign and then put in your bottom desk drawer and never look at again until years later. That doesn't happen simply because the documents are so well drafted, but clear and complete drafting is a part of it. Documents are great when they accurately memorialize all the elements of a transaction correctly assembled from day one, and both sides have a clear understanding of their rights, duties, and obligations. Let's begin with reps and warranties.

REPS AND WARRANTIES

In the M&A process, the parties must make statements of fact to each other and be able to rely on them. "Reps and Warranties" and "Covenants and Conditions" are terms commonly used in a purchase and sale agreement to describe the assertions that a buyer makes to a seller and that a seller makes to a buyer. The goal is "full disclosure," a concept well understood by financial advisors. In the absence of full disclosure, almost always viewed with the clarity of hindsight, the issue shifts to allocation of risk—who, then, shall be responsible for any losses or damages if the statements were incorrect or if material omissions occurred?

Almost all buyers and sellers, and even some lawyers, fail to understand the difference between representations and warranties that are standard in purchase agreements. Many think the terms are synonymous and thus use them interchangeably. The distinctions can be subtle, however, and tend to lie in the domain of legal draftsmanship. In application, the terms so often overlap each other that instead of one section of the purchase agreement titled "Representations" and another titled "Warranties," one section is usually titled "Representations and Warranties." A buyer will make their own representations and warranties in one section, and the seller will make their own representations and warranties in a separate section. Here is a walk-through of what you need to know as a buyer or a seller.

A *representation* is a statement of fact about the past and/or the present. A *warranty* is an assurance and generally moves from the present to the future. A *covenant*, by comparison, is a promise by a party in which it pledges that something is either done, will be done, or will not be done—covenants and conditions are covered in the following section. When a purchase agreement uses the terms "representations" and "warranties" together, such as "Seller's Representations and Warranties," it is blending the past, present, and future within the terms of that section of the contract. Every contract and transaction is different, but the language in this section is basically the same for most practices and businesses in this industry, hence the term "boilerplate." But these are very important statements and they must be accurate.

No one is in a better position to judge the accuracy of such statements and assurances than the individual buying and selling advisors, which is why it is so important to actually read and understand *what you're saying to the other party* in this text. An asset purchase and sale agreement commonly addresses at least these basic facts under the seller's representations and warranties.

- Seller's form of business (sole proprietorship, partnership, C corp, S corp, or limited liability company)
- Seller's business structure and state of organization
- Seller's authorization to sell and deliver the assets
- Delivery and accuracy of seller's current financial statements
- Status of any labor issues or disputes
- Payment of all past taxes when due

- Status of any noncancelable contracts
- Requirement of any third-party approvals needed or encumbrances held
- Seller's compliance with licensure/registration, permits, laws, codes, rules, and regulations
- Status of current client list (i.e., has any client notified seller that they intend to end the relationship)
- Status of any past, pending, or anticipated litigation
- Accuracy of the representations and warranties

These seller's representations to the buyer usually also relate to the information that the buyer is relying on to value and pay for the book, practice, or business. Accordingly, the seller not only states that all financial information provided is true and correct, the seller also should deliver information to support this statement such as current financial statements, client lists, copies of any noncancelable contracts such as an office lease, vendor agreements, and such. The following are four examples of representations and warranties on these issues.

- **Example 1:** Seller represents and warrants that he/she/it has all requisite power and authority to own, transfer, and assign the assets that are the subject of this purchase agreement. . . .
- **Example 2:** Seller has delivered to buyer year-end financial statements for seller's business for the years 20_____, 20_____, and 20_____. Such financial statements are attached to this agreement as Exhibit #_____ and are incorporated herein by reference. The financial statements that have been delivered are correct, complete, and fairly present the financial condition of seller as of the dates of such financial statements. . . .
- **Example 3:** Seller represents and warrants that Exhibit One, attached hereto, lists all of the present clients and client accounts of the business, except for those clients and client accounts expressly excluded in writing herein. . . .
- **Example 4:** Seller represents and warrants that, at the time of closing, there will be no material leases, employment contracts, contracts for services or maintenance, or other similar contracts existing or related to or connected with the operation of seller's business. . . .

A seller's representations and warranties are usually considerably longer and more detailed than a buyer's representations and warranties. This is because the buyer is depending on facts that the seller is in the best position, perhaps the only position, to know and is paying value for what they are buying. Exceptions to this general rule of more extensive sellers' representations and warranties than buyers include instances where the buyer is paying the seller with its own stock in whole or in part, or when the buyer's ability to pay is in doubt (as might be the case when a practice attempts to acquire a business or a firm), in which case the seller needs to fully understand and be able to rely on the buyer's stated financial position.

From a buyer's perspective, the seller's reps and warranties support the due diligence process. Essentially, they provide an opportunity, and the incentive, for the seller to disclose any and all potential issues prior to completing the transaction that may not have been uncovered by the buyer. From a seller's perspective, the buyer's reps and warranties will touch on the soundness of a buyer's existing operations, particularly when a seller is accepting a note from a buyer for part of the purchase price. Full disclosure is a common element for independent financial advisors and it continues right through the M&A process. Putting the buyer on notice of any and all material issues with the selling book, practice, or business, for example, shifts the responsibility away from the seller post-closing toward the buyer.

Why does all this matter to advisors engaged in a transaction? Damages and liability, in short. This is the world of the contract litigator and that's a place buyers and sellers probably should avoid. The means to do so lies in full disclosure and clear documentation. As mentioned in the previous chapter, finding red flags in the process of reviewing someone else's practice or business is normal—there is no such thing as the perfect practice. As a seller, do not try to *paint the picture of perfection* in the transaction documents, no matter how tempting that may be. Imperfections are covered by the payment terms, which are, or should be, taken into account in the valuation process (covered in Chapter 3).

COVENANTS AND CONDITIONS

Like representations and warranties, the terms "covenants" and "conditions" are closely related in functionality. However, it is usually easier to work with these concepts separately, or at least as set forth in separate, often consecutive sections of the agreement. "Covenants" and "conditions" are a standard part of every professionally drafted purchase and sale agreement.

Covenants are ongoing promises by one party to take or not take certain actions. The term "conditions" appears to be self-explanatory, but more explanation is warranted to understand how they function alongside of covenants. In some sense, covenants and conditions result from an issue of "timing." Remember that up until the point where the parties sign the purchase and sale agreement, the "controlling document" has been the letter of intent or term sheet. However, signing the purchase and sale agreement does not necessarily mean that the transaction has been completed or closed.

A signed agreement is evidence that the parties have reached an accord on all material points in the transaction. Closing is the point at which funds are paid and *ownership* of the assets is officially transferred from seller to buyer. Sometimes documents are signed in full and the transaction is never closed. And that is why *covenants and conditions* are a necessary part of the documentation process.

Most transactions between a buyer and a seller of an independent advisory practice or business have a *semiformal* closing procedure. Sometimes the parties will all gather at one of the attorneys' offices and have a signing ceremony. Occasionally, in more contentious transactions (very uncommon in this industry), the parties will come in and sign separately. Most of the time, documents are signed and scanned and emailed to the respective attorneys. The point is, most transactions are signed *and closed later.* Sometimes a couple of days go by between signing and closing, and sometimes it is a couple of months.

This interim period is usually necessary for the parties to finalize certain issues, to gather all the necessary supporting documents, and, on occasion, to allow the buyer to complete the financing effort (wire transfers, down payment, bank financing, etc.). In addition, if a formal escrow process is utilized, escrow will require at least a brief period to gather and inventory all of the documents from both sides, obtain third-party consents, perform lien checks on the seller and/or seller's business (also allowing time to resolve any liens), and verify compliance with all contract terms. In addition, it is not unusual for a buyer and a seller to be in different states, separated by hundreds or thousands of miles, making a formal closing at one attorney's offices more difficult.

This post-signing/pre-closing time period must be handled in a precise and legal manner and this is often the primary function of covenants and conditions. From the buyers' and sellers' perspectives, each party has a "signed deal" but not a closed or completed deal. Minimizing risks and clarifying who is responsible for what in the meantime is the goal of these sections of a purchase and sale agreement.

Here is an example of a **seller's covenants** that cover the period of time *between signing and closing*.

Seller agrees that between the date of this agreement and the closing date, seller will:
1. Use commercially reasonable best efforts to continue to operate the business in the usual and ordinary course and in conformity with all applicable laws, ordinances, regulations, rules, or orders....
2. Not assign, sell, lease, or otherwise transfer or dispose of any of the client accounts or assets used in the performance of its

business and transferred under this agreement, whether now owned or hereafter acquired. . . .

3. Maintain all its assets other than inventories in their present condition, reasonable wear and tear and ordinary usage excepted, and maintain the inventories at levels normally maintained. . . .

4. At reasonable times and upon reasonable notice before the closing date, seller will provide buyer or its representatives with reasonable access during business hours to the assets, titles, contracts, or other financial and business records of seller and furnish such additional information as buyer from time to time may reasonably request. . . .

Here is an example of the **seller's covenants** that cover the period of time *after closing and during the consulting period.*

Seller agrees that between the date of this agreement and the termination of the consulting agreement (attached as Exhibit #___), seller will:

1. Use commercially reasonable efforts to give effect to the transactions contemplated by this agreement and to fulfill all the conditions and obligations of seller under this agreement, and to transition the client accounts to buyer and to otherwise consummate and fulfill the terms of this agreement. . . .

2. Fulfill all other obligations set forth in the consulting agreement. . . .

The buyer's covenants are usually fewer in number and focus on the buyer using commercially reasonable efforts to give effect to the transactions contemplated by the agreement, performing all actions reasonably required to carry out his or her (or, if an entity is the formal buyer, "its") obligations. A buyer should also covenant that, if for any reason the sale is not closed, all confidential information the buyer received from the seller in the course of investigating, negotiating, and performing the transactions contemplated by the purchase and sale agreement will be returned, safeguarded, and/or destroyed. In addition, a buyer should provide the seller a covenant not to solicit or serve any of the clients or client accounts of the seller in the event the transaction fails to be completed.

Covenants, in a general sense, may be either affirmative or negative. Examples of affirmative covenants by the seller include:

- Operating the business in the usual and ordinary course
- Using commercially reasonable efforts to give effect to the transaction

- Maintaining business relationships (with employees, clients, broker-dealers/custodians, vendors, etc.)
- Complying with all laws, rules, and regulations (state and federal)
- Maintaining all insurance in force and effect (property and casualty, errors and omissions, etc.)

Examples of negative covenants by the seller include:

- Not increasing the pay of employees, advisors, representatives, or entering into severance agreements
- Not making any significant capital expenditures or acquisitions
- Not terminating customer, vendor, or broker-dealer, or third-party money management agreements
- Not negotiating with any other party concerning the sale of the business
- Not pledging or transferring any company assets outside of the ordinary course of business

Though the seller tends to provide the buyer with more, and more extensive, reps and warranties and covenants, the buyer tends to focus on the conditions to its performance. Conditions can provide a buyer an "escape hatch," allowing them to walk away from the deal if certain conditions are not met. Each party, for their own reasons, should pay careful attention to the stated conditions. Examples of conditions that a buyer might request of a seller include:

- All material representations and warranties shall be true as of the closing date as fully as though such representations and warranties had been made on and as of the closing date
- Seller shall not have violated or failed to materially perform in accordance with any covenant contained in the agreement
- The buyer shall be satisfied with his/her/its due diligence investigation at its sole discretion
- There shall have been no adverse change or development in the seller's business
- The buyer shall have obtained financing to fund the purchase price (a financing contingency)
- The seller shall have obtained all necessary authorizations and consents

As explained in Chapter 7, most transactions have historically been completed utilizing some form of seller financing. It is becoming more commonplace for buyers, especially in a highly competitive acquisition market, to rely on bank financing. Traditionally, few banks have had the expertise, experience, and willingness to lend on an acquisition in this industry and as a result, many traditional bank loan applications fail in underwriting. This is usually more a consequence of unfamiliarity with this unique profession than of the buyer's creditworthiness. (As certain banks become more familiar with the financial advisory arena, this is less of a problem. An experienced intermediary can help identify which banks are knowledgeable and experienced in this industry.) Regardless, in the case of a financing contingency, a seller could expend significant time and expense in interviewing and selecting a buyer, dismissing all the other candidates, only to see the deal fall through at the last minute because the buyer failed to obtain a loan. If one of the conditions included a financing contingency, there may be no consequence for a buyer who acted in good faith and did the best they could. The seller, however, is left to restart the entire process. The takeaway: Sellers should work only with buyers who are preapproved by a bank that has a history of successfully lending to buyers in this industry.

Here are some tips and strategies for handling covenants and conditions in the purchase and sale agreement.

- Introduce "materiality" into the closing conditions. In other words, a client who files an arbitration claim against the seller in the days before closing should provide the buyer with the right to walk away from the deal only if that event could materially impact the seller's business. In most cases, it should not be sufficient that certain events merely happen or don't happen. Those events need to be material.
- Sellers should execute a formal back-up offer, just in case.
- Buyers and sellers should attempt to keep the post-signing, pre-closing period short, even addressing this timing issue in the letter of intent.
- Sellers should identify any financing contingencies at the letter of intent stage. In addition, a qualified intermediary can provide information on which banks are likely to approve a loan given the specifics of the acquisition opportunity and guide the parties through this often complex maze.
- Eliminate as conditions, issues or items that are within that party's control (i.e., "The buyer must be satisfied with its due diligence review in its sole discretion"). This gives the buyer too much power and too much leeway to walk away.

Covenants and conditions are critically important to both a buyer and a seller. They might look and read like boilerplate, but they are not. Read these sections carefully, every time, and ask the hard questions. The goal in providing this information isn't to turn advisors into lawyers (or to make advisors glad that they aren't!), but rather to help buyers and sellers better understand what to look for and how to identify some of the key legal issues that might directly affect their position.

INDEMNIFICATION AND HOLD HARMLESS CLAUSES

To further mitigate the risk of financial loss from a party that hasn't represented something that is material, or has depended on a statement that turns out to be false, a purchase agreement should contain an indemnification clause. This clause protects the other party from an omitted and material issue or misrepresentation that may lead to a financial loss *after the closing*—and further incentivizes each side to make full and complete disclosure ahead of time. Everything is connected.

In short, indemnification is a contractual obligation by one party to compensate another party for damages, losses, or liabilities they may have incurred. Essentially, indemnification and hold harmless clauses in a purchase and sale agreement are a means of shifting risk between the buyer and seller. One of the most common causes for indemnification by a selling advisor who is part of a sale or merger are a breach of the seller's representations and warranties, as well as covenants. In other words, if a seller breaches a representation or warranty, or material covenant, and that causes losses, damages, or liability, then the seller must indemnify the buyer. Indemnification typically addresses any liabilities arising out of the ownership or operation of the practice or business before closing, as well as all liabilities specifically retained by the seller after closing.

In legal circles, the term "hold harmless" tends to be construed more broadly than "indemnification" but, practically, the definition of the latter term can easily be broadened to accomplish the same goals. Effectively, the terms are synonymous. And even without indemnification provisions, one party can always file a lawsuit for breach of contract if the other party breaches the purchase and sale agreement. Adding in specific indemnification provisions serves to broaden (or reduce) the scope of such potential claims.

Here is an example of an indemnification clause that might be used in a purchase and sale agreement **from a seller to a buyer**—note the clear connection to representations and warranties and covenants.

> Seller shall indemnify, defend, and hold buyer, its directors, officers, employees, shareholders, and agents, harmless from and against damages of any kind or character, incurred or suffered by any such indemnified party arising out of or in any manner incident, relating or attributable to: (1) any misrepresentation, breach of warranty, covenant or agreement made or to be performed by seller under this

agreement or any agreement which is an exhibit to this agreement, (2) excluded liabilities, (3) any federal, state, or local taxes payable by seller of any type or description, attributable to periods prior to closing, (4) any third party claim, demand, suits, or actions in any way solely arising out of or relating to the seller's operation of the business or other conduct prior to or after the closing, or (5) any legal fees and expenses to successfully enforce the indemnification obligations for assumed liabilities under this paragraph.

Here is an example of an indemnification clause that might be used in a purchase and sale agreement **from a buyer to a seller**—again, note the connection to representations and warranties and covenants.

Buyer shall indemnify, defend, and hold seller, its directors, officers, employees, shareholders, and agents, harmless from and against loss, costs, claims, liability, and damages and attorney fees and expenses of any kind or character, incurred or suffered by any such indemnified party arising out of or in any manner incident, relating or attributable to: (1) any misrepresentation, breach of warranty, covenant, or agreement made or to be performed by buyer under this agreement or any agreement which is an exhibit to this agreement, (2) any federal, state, or local taxes payable by buyer of any type or description, attributable to periods after the closing, (3) any third party claim, demand, suits, or actions in any way solely arising out of or relating to the buyer's operation of the business or other conduct after the closing, or (4) any legal fees and expenses to successfully enforce the indemnification obligations under this paragraph.

Consider this basic example of a problem that can arise post-closing, triggering the indemnity clause. Instead of using an informed and professional valuation, a buyer and seller simply agree that a book is worth a multiple of 2.0 times trailing 12 months' recurring revenue. In the months after closing, the buyer discovers that the seller has overstated the revenue in total as well as the amount that is recurring versus transactional. Because the purchase and sale agreement contains a representation and warranty from the seller that "The financial statements that have been delivered are correct, complete, and fairly present the financial condition of seller as of the dates of such financial statements . . . ," the buyer could have cause to make an indemnity claim based on the allegation that he or she overpaid for the book based on the seller's misrepresentations. The use of such a simple rule of thumb valuation limits other aspects of value normally considered in a more sophisticated approach and method, making the argument that much easier for the buyer's litigation attorney. If successful, the buyer may be able to reduce the purchase price previously agreed to.

Here are some tips and strategies for negotiating the indemnification provisions in the purchase and sale agreement.

- Read and review this section carefully, and talk to your lawyer and qualified intermediary to help you think through all aspects.
- Carefully consider the reps and warranties—having read that section once, read it a second time considering the statements and assurances from the indemnification angle. This is a common trigger for the use of an indemnification right.
- Place a time limit on the post-closing period during which the buyer should be "made whole" by the seller. For example, consider a statement along the lines of "All representations and warranties shall survive the closing of this agreement for three years." A dollar limit should also be considered.
- Review errors and omissions coverage on this issue. Since most transactions are asset sales, this means that sellers remain liable for activities prior to closing and, to a lesser degree, some liabilities immediately after closing prior to the buyer being formally introduced and taking over full responsibility.

Buyers should also consider including the right to offset damages against future payments due to the seller under a promissory note or earn-out arrangement to satisfy any outstanding indemnification obligation of the seller. Damages for this purpose, however, should be strictly limited to an award or determination by an arbitrator or a court, or by a settlement agreement between buyer and seller. A seller should never allow a buyer to unilaterally offset any amount due and owing on their own volition, no matter how egregious the buyer thinks the transgression is or may be. Clear legal text to this effect is a must and this leads the discussion directly into the realm of protections, default provisions, and dispute resolution mechanisms.

PROTECTIONS AGAINST DEATH OR DISABILITY

The use of seller financing means that the seller acts as "the bank" or the lender in the transaction, often for a period of several years. If the buyer is a sole proprietorship, or a single-owner entity, it is common for the seller to request that the buyer collaterally assign sufficient life insurance to the seller to address any unpaid balance in the event of the buyer's untimely demise. Buyers who are larger and have multiple owners tend not to have this issue, or have other ways of dealing with such protection measures, specifically an internal continuity plan and agreement. Sellers should include this element in their due diligence review process.

The same post-closing protection issue occurs in the other direction as well. Sellers often promise to assist in the transition of the client base to the buyer under the terms of a consulting agreement (detailed in Chapter 8), or a similar personal obligation. This agreement, or duty, supports the value proposition in that the seller must deliver the clients to the buyer and support their retention. In most cases, the seller's support is limited to 6 to 12 months of post-closing support, but this is a critical time period and the seller's duties are not easily delegated to a subordinate. If something were to happen to the seller in the first month after closing, before the seller introduced the new owner, the buyer would be deprived of a critical ally and advantage in executing the client transition plan.

To protect against this possibility, it is common for the seller to collaterally assign sufficient life insurance to the buyer until the client transition plan has been substantially accomplished. While it logically makes sense to consider a lump sum disability policy as well, practically, the cost and the seller's age often eliminates the possibility. Still, it should at least be a consideration and factored into the post-closing considerations. Experienced buyers will often address issues like this in the letter of intent or term sheet.

Remember that in a properly structured and valued transaction, the payment terms tend to contain a contingency (i.e., a performance-based promissory note) to further protect against the seller's ability, or availability, to deliver the clients, assets, and related cash flow. This is an important consideration in every instance, but even more so when the seller is uninsurable. The buyer's risk is largely attributable to the nonrefundable down payment and the time and energy expended to complete the transaction. The use of bank financing, however, can greatly increase the buyer's risk if a larger, nonrefundable cash payment is made at the time of closing, making the post-closing transition period, and the seller's obligations thereunder, a risk in need of adequate protection.

DEFAULT PROVISIONS

If the word "default" comes up post-closing, something has likely gone wrong. The question is, what happens next? The answer depends on who caused the default, and why. Let's begin with the buyer. Most of the previous sections (reps and warranties, covenants and conditions, indemnification) tended to assume that the seller is the one most likely to cause or contribute to a problem or a misunderstanding because the buyer is largely relying on the seller up until the moment, post-closing, where the clients, assets, and cash flow are physically delivered. But here, the tables are often turned. In a majority of cases, it is the buyer who is the alleged defaulting party.

The general fact pattern in most transactions is that the seller's role in the process is largely *over and done with* 6 to 12 months after the closing. Buyers, especially if seller financing is utilized, will have an ongoing, perhaps monthly payment obligation to the seller for three to five years, or more in some cases. There is simply more opportunity and a higher likelihood of a buyer default over time, at least when compared to the seller—in fact, defaults are not common primarily due to the payment contingencies in place in most deal structures. The typical causes of a buyer being in default of the purchase and sale agreement are these:

- Failure to make, within a reasonable time, any payment of principal or interest.
- Termination of buyer's business, loss or suspension of buyer's (or buyer's principal's) state or federal securities licenses, registrations, or appointments for ninety (90) days or more.
- Commencement of any insolvency proceedings by or against the buyer.
- A sale or transfer of buyer's practice or business or the sale or intentional transfer of any of the acquired client accounts prior to seller being paid in full and without the seller's written approval.
- The death or permanent disability of buyer or, if buyer is a corporation or limited liability company, then the death or permanent disability of the principal who, as a shareholder or a member, owns a majority of the outstanding shares or membership interests of buyer.

The typical causes of a seller being in default of the purchase and sale agreement are these:

- Seller's material breach of the noncompetition/nonsolicitation agreement.
- Seller's material breach of the consulting agreement (which includes failure to deliver the clients, assets, and related cash flows).

All of the preceding default events, for both buyer and seller, are subject to a written notice by the party intending to declare a default and the failure of the other party to remedy the default event within a reasonable time, usually 10 to 15 days. The purchase and sale agreement should provide that the seller is required to give only one such notice in a 12-month period—after one notice, default may occur immediately upon the next late payment of principal or interest. Another common solution is to make every overdue payment or installment subject to a minimum charge of $250 or so, regardless of how late it is—enough to make sure it doesn't happen more than once, if at all.

The concept of "acceleration" is important to understand as well. Many purchase and sale agreements provide that, if the buyer is found to be in default, the entire unpaid balance and any accrued interest shall be immediately due and payable. This should be harmonized with the default provisions in the promissory note that is the actual debt instrument. The point isn't for the seller to be paid more quickly, but for the buyer to avoid a default at all costs, and for a seller to have effective remedies if the buyer has indeed failed. In the event that an earn-out arrangement is utilized as part of the seller financing, the agreement should specify how the accelerated balance is to be calculated.

Practically speaking, a default tends to fall into one of two categories:

1. **Clerical or administrative:** For example, a securities license or registration, or a business license was flagged to renew on the wrong date, but no one caught it until after the fact. The life insurance policy lapsed due to an oversight. The S corporation or LLC renewal form and payment were not submitted on time and the entity was administratively dissolved.

2. **Material or financial:** For example, the buyer did not or could not make a payment when due. Or, the seller "changed his or her mind" a week after closing and decided to continue working with the clients and retain all fees or commissions, ignoring the buyer's position in the matter. In either case, there is likely to be some extenuating circumstance or reason for the action, or inaction, but the default is a matter of fact.

Issues that arise under the clerical or administrative category are why purchase and sale agreements have a "cure phase," but such issues should also raise a red flag to both buyer and seller to stay on top of critical items that are key to the practice's or business's long-term success. This is why a properly drafted agreement provides some latitude, but not enough to encourage or permit continuing miscues. Material or financial issues are an entirely different matter. When faced with an issue of materiality, the aggrieved party needs to consider all the facts and make a decision as to whether to trigger a default, proceed to arbitration and begin working on collection, or to request mediation and try to work it out. These solutions are addressed in the following section.

RESOLUTION OF CONFLICTS

Some kind of disagreement, or conflict, is almost inevitable in the transitioning of hundreds of relationship-based accounts, so it is best to work out the issues in advance. A multilayered approach is best in our experience. The starting point is finding the "best match" between seller and buyer—two people or two teams that work well together in solving the problems of business and life. This element dovetails into a shared-risk/shared-reward concept that financially motivates buyer and seller to cooperate post-closing. In addition, a well-drafted document set that supports these two foundational elements and memorializes the parties' intentions and obligations is essential. To this end, another important section of the purchase and sale agreement contains the dispute resolution mechanisms.

The primary issues to consider on this avenue are these:

- The use of arbitration, mediation, or a judge/jury to address a party's grievances.
- The venue and jurisdiction of the court, arbitration, or mediation setting.
- The payment of attorney fees and costs of resolution.

Here is an example of how these issues might be addressed and resolved in the purchase and sale agreement:

> **Arbitration.** Any dispute, controversy, or claim arising out of or relating to this agreement will be settled by binding arbitration. There will be one arbitrator who will be a retired federal or state judge within a minimum of 10 years of judicial experience or will have such alternate qualifications that are mutually agreeable to the parties. Any arbitration will be conducted in _____ (city), _____ (state). The arbitrator will have authority to issue preliminary and other equitable relief. The arbitrator will have the discretion to order a pre-hearing exchange of information by the parties and an exchange of summaries of testimony of proposed witnesses. The arbitrator will have the authority to order such summary procedures and proceedings as will quickly and efficiently attain a just result.
>
> **Governing Law.** This agreement will be governed by and construed in accordance with the laws of the state of_____, without regard to conflict-of-laws principles.
>
> **Attorney Fees.** If any arbitration, suit, or action is instituted to interpret or enforce the provisions of this agreement, to rescind this

agreement, or otherwise with respect to the subject matter of this agreement, the party prevailing on an issue will be entitled to recover with respect to such issue, in addition to costs, reasonable attorney fees incurred in the preparation, prosecution, or defense of such arbitration, suit, or action as determined by the arbitrator or trial court, and, if any appeal is taken from such decision, reasonable attorney fees as determined on appeal.

The goal of every buyer and seller should be to resolve conflict quickly and as easily as possible, and, if not, then efficiently and clearly. The use of alternative dispute resolution measures should at least be considered by every advisor as a tool for solving problems. Alternative dispute resolution ("ADR"), meaning mediation and arbitration, became trendy in the early 1990s. At the time, many state court systems were taking three to five years to get civil cases to trial. ADR was perceived to be a faster and less expensive path to an end point. Experience shows that *unrestrained ADR* is often no quicker and no less expensive than civil litigation. Most private arbitration services have rules that provide for pre-hearing proceedings that mirror local civil proceedings, so the time and expense of getting to the hearing date—motions and discovery practice—can mirror those of civil court cases. When the expense of paying the daily rate for three arbitrators is added in ($10,000 a day for a panel of arbitrators is not unheard of), paying a $150 daily court fee for a judge, a jury, two bailiffs, and a large room starts to look like a bargain. Further, absent a clear case of fraud within the arbitration, the outcome is irreversible.

Of course, ADR does have its adherents and for good reason. Generally, court proceedings are public. Some confidential information in court pleadings, exhibits, and testimony can be sealed but the outcome will be public. If keeping the dispute or controversy off the *small town social radar* is important, a closed-door arbitration may be clearly preferable. However, disregarding what gets passed through the gossip tree, experience teaches us that arbitration awards eventually become court judgments, so the word gets out eventually.

The ability to choose the arbitrator may also make ADR desirable. Because 95% or more of a court's cases fall within the purview of criminal law and family law, judges tend to be former criminal law or family law lawyers with little or no civil law experience, let alone securities or regulatory expertise. If the parties can choose the arbitrator, they can look for technical expertise where technical matters will be at issue.

FP Transitions provides post-closing mediation services at no additional cost if both sides choose to use this approach (a service reserved to sellers who list on its open market system or in one of its organized IBD closed market settings and their buyers). It is fairly rare to need such support, but mediation can often solve many issues that surface and is certainly a preferable *first step* to arbitration or litigation.

Why should anyone mediate? Several reasons. It imposes a cooling-off period. Presumably, by the time the mediation conference has occurred, the first bills from one's lawyers have been paid. The cost of litigation has become palpable. And, it brings another voice to the discussion. Clearly, the reason mediation is even necessary is that the other side cannot see *the rightness of your position.* Whether their blindness is attributable to the party, or to the party's lawyer, who sees a big fee in stretching this out, the mediator can preach reason to the decision maker when you've lost his or her ear. Or so you hope. Of course, they might be thinking the same of you.

Over the past 10 years, the post-closing default rate FP Transitions has experienced in the closings it has supervised is about 2%. That, of course, makes no difference at all if you're in that 2% group—but it does underscore one important point. The best way to avoid being placed in a default situation is to closely follow the advice on these pages and select the best match, take valuation off the table by using the proper standard, approach, and method, create a shared-risk/shared-reward transaction, perform due diligence in a professional manner, and then document it all properly.

It is also interesting to note that transactions completed using the strategies in this book in the year or two *prior* to the Great Recession, specifically those with seller financing that extended into years 2008 through 2010, did not experience higher default rates than the norm. The use of contingent seller financing helped to resolve issues surrounding value and valuation, and post-closing cash flow, automatically.

BASIC (BUT NOT TRIVIAL) LEGAL ISSUES

The Effective Closing Date

The closing date of a transaction is usually marked by the moment when ownership changes hands. It is the point when the transaction is completed. As explained earlier in this chapter, this date may be different from the date the agreements are signed, but there may also be a *third date* that controls the entire process, often referred to as "the effective date." The effective date is the date the parties deem the transaction to have occurred. In a contract, this date is often established with the simple statement, "Dated effective the first day of January, 20__ (the "Effective Date")."

Consider this example: a transaction valued at $895,000 may have the buyer and seller sign the asset purchase agreement on November 22, 2016, with a closing date of January 1, 2017. However, due to bad weather or a travel issue or some other delay, the parties do not formally close the transaction until January 9. The document can still provide for an "effective closing date" of January 1, 2017. The effective date is the date when the transaction is deemed to have occurred and it is mostly a matter of agreement between the parties. Most of the time, the closing and effective date of a transaction are the same day. When there is a discrepancy, it is usually for a matter of convenience.

The effective closing date can be any date that the parties agree to, within reason, but it is often the first day of any given month. Legally, the effective date signals the beginning of the buyer's ownership and responsibility. On and after the effective date, the cash flows of the acquired book, practice, or business legally belong to the buyer even though the seller may still physically receive those funds. It is essential that the "line of demarcation" is clear and that is why the purchase and sale agreement should spell out both the closing date and "the effective date," with the latter controlling most of the decisions.

Special adjustments need to be made for RIAs or IARs who bill in advance or in arrears, with an agreement that memorializes *what fees belong to whom.* While the effective date may be clear as a matter of contract, it is still necessary to state *who receives a fee* versus *who earned the fee* versus *who gets to keep the fee.* Commission revenue has similar challenges depending on the point of view (buyer or seller). Details like these are why everything needs to be well planned, agreed to in advance, and committed to writing. Most of these issues are challenging only for the first 90 days or so, and tools such as *the closing date* and *the effective date* are valuable implements in constructing a solid transaction.

One final point that arises in this area is that sellers who enter into a transaction during the latter part of a calendar year (i.e., November or December) prefer to close on January 1 to defer any tax obligations into a new year as opposed to the current year. This is common, though the concept of "constructive receipt" will determine when taxes are due and owing. Receiving money in one year, which includes having it paid into escrow, and not taking possession until the next year may not effectively or legally *retime* the tax obligation. Buyers and sellers should address this issue at the letter of intent stage. These timing issues come up frequently, and are rarely an impediment. A qualified intermediary can guide the parties through a range of palatable solutions, avoiding any last-minute changes to the purchase and sale agreement.

Last-Minute Changes before Closing

It is not uncommon that one or both parties to the purchase and sale agreement need to make a small, last-minute change. In fact, it happens all the time. The question is whether the changes are to be made *before* or *after* both parties have signed the agreement.

In the case where the purchase agreement has not been signed, it is best to prepare and send out a new agreement—yes, even if just one word has changed. Start fresh, track the change(s), notify the other side, and if acceptable, execute (sign) the newest, latest version. Another way to handle the issue, however, is to go back to that good old-fashioned pen and cross out the error, legibly write in the correction, and have *both parties* initial the change when signing the final draft. Either approach works.

Last-Minute Changes after Closing

Contracts haven't been carved into stone in a long, long time, and contrary to my grandchildren's thinking, I wasn't there when it last happened. Things change. Stuff gets overlooked. This is one of the benefits of having a seller find their best match, someone with whom they work well and easily. If a purchase agreement has only two signatories, a buyer and a seller, it takes only the agreement of those two parties to change the contract terms, *even after closing*.

However, unlike the method used to make minor corrections or changes before closing, this process definitely requires more formality. Every change needs to be in writing. The proper way to change a contract or purchase agreement after closing is to execute an addendum or an amendment to permanently memorialize the change and have both parties sign off. It sounds simple, but sometimes it isn't. As you've read before, "everything is connected" in this process and changing one thing can impact other things. It takes a bit of study, just to be sure moving one item doesn't create unintended consequences, but it can be done. Consider issues like this when assembling and managing your support team.

Signatures on a Purchase Agreement

Signing a purchase and sale agreement seems like a simple task, but it can involve some important legal issues. Because financial advisory practices and businesses sometimes fall under the purview of multiple regulatory structures, and because a license is often tied to an individual rather than an entity (such as an S corporation or LLC), it is critical to understand exactly who is selling and who is buying, and who has the authority to sign the agreement. Many of these issues can be addressed during the due diligence review, which should include discovery as to all owners, advisors, and producers, as well as basic corporate records and stock ledgers.

In most cases, the controlling and authorized parties are clear by the time the closing date arrives. But buyers and sellers must be cognizant of these issues and know enough to ask good questions and to "look around the corner" just to be sure. Since most transactions are structured as asset sales, we'll start with this group of mostly books and practices.

Asset Sales   The process of deciding who needs to sign the transaction documents is usually quite simple when jobs/books are being sold or acquired. Many times the parties, as buyer and seller, enter into a basic revenue sharing agreement and the transaction is a transfer of cash flow from one individual to another individual. If the parties elect a more formal process, such as using an asset-based purchase and sale agreement and both are sole proprietorships, it is still as simple as just stating the names of the participating individuals.

Sometimes a trade name or an assumed business name (ABN) is filed by a sole proprietor, whether as a buyer or a seller. The term "DBA" for "doing business as" is also commonly used. An ABN, or DBA, is not an entity, but simply a name other than the proprietor's name. An entity can also file for and hold its own ABN. It is a good practice to list any and all such trade names for the sake of clarity, but the buyer's legal, individual name and the seller's legal, individual name normally suffice when both operate as sole proprietorships.

The process is slightly more complicated if the buyer or seller is an entity. In this industry, in the case of a seller, *both* the entity and the individual are usually named as "Sellers" on the purchase and sale agreement to eliminate any issues as to who owns what. If the seller is organized as an S corporation, for example, and is selling "everything," including client relationships, goodwill, desks and chairs and file cabinets, there actually are *two* sellers involved in the sale of the assets. The goodwill tends to be personal, as is the obligation to provide post-closing consulting support and the restrictive covenants (agreement not to compete or solicit), while the corporation will likely have paid for and depreciated the furniture and fixtures. A buyer should expect that the agreement will be signed by the person or people who have the authority to bind the entity—the president, for example. To be on the safe side, a buyer should require all of the partners, shareholders, or LLC members to sign the purchase and sale agreement.

If the buyer is an entity (corporation or LLC), the entity may well be listed as "the Buyer" on the purchase and sale agreement. This is quite common, though in many cases the significant owners (usually anyone with

20% or more of the stock or ownership interests) will sign as guarantors on any seller financing that is provided. An advisor who is selling the assets of his or her practice or business to a corporation or LLC will want to have the agreement signed by the people with the authority to bind the buying entity. To be on the safe side, a seller should also request all of the partners, shareholders, or LLC members to sign the purchase and sale agreement.

The alternative to having all owners sign the purchase and sale agreement is to determine who is authorized to sign on behalf of the entity. In a corporation, for instance, officers usually have authority to sign agreements on behalf of the business, with such authority granted through the bylaws in most cases. A buyer can perform due diligence on these issues as one solution. Another is to require a representation and warranty by the signer that he or she has all requisite power and authority to sign the agreement on behalf of the business. Yet another solution is to request a formal, signed resolution by the corporation authorizing the transaction. Depending on the circumstances, all three steps might make sense. Coming full circle, the easiest and safest approach is to require that all owners sign the agreement.

Stock Sales   If an advisor (or group of advisors) is selling all of their stock in a corporation or membership interest in an LLC, each shareholder must sign a stock purchase and sale agreement, which is different from the more basic asset-based purchase and sale agreement. No one will sign on behalf of the entity, such as the president, since the entity is not the seller. If the purchasers of the stock are individuals, each individual buyer should sign the agreement. If the buyer is another entity, the person or people with legal authority to bind the buying entity will need to sign and, as a general rule, it is best to have all owners of the buying entity sign the agreement.

Spouses' Signatures   There are a few situations in which it may be prudent to include the signature of a buyer's or seller's spouse on the purchase and sale agreement. Under the heading of *General Advice*, for advisors who are married and live in a community property state and who are selling the assets of a sole proprietorship, the buyer (or buyer's attorney) may request that the seller's spouse co-sign the agreement. Otherwise, the spouse might later claim an interest in the practice assets under community property law. Legally, in a community property state, if a buyer pays a fair and reasonable price to purchase assets from a sole proprietorship whose spouse played no role in the operations, the law does not require that the buyer obtain consent from the owner's spouse. The problem is, "fair and reasonable" are judged in hindsight. Again, the best general rule is, when in doubt, have everyone with an interest sign the agreement.

Most buyers utilize seller financing to some degree (via a promissory note, or a performance-based note), which means that the seller is going to look at the buyer as a bank looks at a borrower. Banks don't hesitate to require spouses to co-sign unsecured debts. But practically, it works a little differently between individual buyers and sellers. In such instances, most buyers balk at such a requirement and often will walk away from the deal before agreeing to have their spouses co-sign. Aside from holding firm on this issue, sellers have a few other good choices. One is to always sell to a buyer who is "bigger, better, and faster." The buyer in such instances should be prepared to have all significant owners guarantee the debt. A second choice is to have the buyer utilize bank financing. While this step may not cover the entire purchase price, it greatly reduces a seller's risk and can resolve the need to have a buyer's spouse sign the purchase agreement.

One other area to be cognizant of in this area is an advisor who is selling and is in the midst of a divorce. It happens. Every situation is different, and the applicable state's laws must be taken into account in determining how best to deal with the issue, but having a spouse sign in such a situation would not be unusual.

Electronic Signatures   Electronic contracts and electronic signatures are every bit as legal and enforceable as traditional paper contracts signed with a pen. The Electronic Signatures in Global and International Commerce Act (ESGICA) removed the uncertainty that previously plagued e-contracts (i.e., where no paper or hard copies are even used). In addition, handwritten, stamped, faxed, electronic pen, and even photocopied signatures are all generally adequate to validate a contract absent limitations specified in the contract itself. Electronic and e-mailed signatures are now valid and widely used, but be cautious and verify the exact requirements for electronic signatures in your state.

In fact, there are many ways to "sign" a purchase and sale agreement. What matters isn't how the document is signed, but rather the intent of that party. Courts look to see whether an individual made the "signature," intended to make the signature, and whether that individual intended that signature or mark to signify their agreement to the contract. If the court can find these three things, then the "signature" is usually considered valid and the contract is binding. But the better advice is, don't leave these issues to chance.

It is also possible that a seller could have someone else sign a contract in their place. This can and does occur through a power of attorney and is practical in cases of a disability. Confer with the other party and address such an issue well in advance so there are no last-minute surprises or questions.

Some contracts require the presence of a witness or witnesses to verify that the document is authentic. For example, most states have laws requiring that at least two witnesses authenticate the signing of your last will and testament. Purchase and sale agreements such as those explained in this book and used in the M&A process in this industry usually do not require a witness and do not need to be notarized unless required by state law.

Finally, it bears repeating in this section that buyers (and sellers) need to be very, very careful about not only *who* is selling, but *what* is being sold. The independent financial services industry is mostly composed of "book builders" rather than business builders, a result of the compensation systems commonly in use by independent advisors. Buyers must be very careful that what is being acquired is transferable and is controlled by the seller. If there is any question, buyers should consider having any suspected "book builders" (i.e., advisors who are serving or who have any significant contact with the client base being acquired) sign off on either the purchase and sale agreement or a noncompete, nonsolicitation, no-service agreement (being aware that enforceability without adequate consideration is going to be an issue). This is not an easy task to accomplish as the *quasi-owners* will usually expect and demand some kind of remuneration—which is the seller's responsibility. Buyers should be alert to such issues and address them during the due diligence process.

The range and severity of the legal issues in any given M&A transaction depends on the participants and the circumstances. Every situation is unique. The goal of this chapter was to help advisors, whether buying or selling, better understand what to look for and when to ask questions—in other words, to become an active and knowledgeable participant in the legal process. In the previous chapter, we focused on *Assembling and Managing Your Team*, but when it comes right down to it, the advisors who are parties to such a transaction are the decision makers and the ones who sign *their names* on the bottom line. Understanding at least the basics of everything above that line is part of the job.

CHAPTER 10

The Transition Plan

The goal of the M&A process is to deliver 100% of the client relationships to the buyer, along with the underlying assets and cash flows and responsibilities. The goal isn't 93% or 85% or some other number. It isn't about trying hard or making sure that everyone is doing their best. Those *percentage points* represent real clients who are trusting in their independent financial advisor to make *the* best decision with regard to this exit plan, acting in their best interests, and then to see it through to a satisfactory conclusion.

While a successful transition does not start with the transition plan, this element is woven into the fabric of the entire transaction, beginning with the search for a buyer. The transition planning process should be properly supported through the quality, experience, and dedication of the new advisor (the buyer), a motivating payment or financing structure, and clear, detailed documentation. If the parties get these initial steps right, transitioning the clients in this final stage is much easier and much more successful.

Achieving complete client satisfaction requires a coordinated transition plan that is prepared and drafted prior to closing and approved by both the buyer and the seller. In most cases, the transition plan is memorialized in a consulting agreement. The importance of this singular agreement cannot be overstated as it impacts everything from the final transition rate, to realized value, to the tax structure of the deal. Remember this: you cannot achieve a high level of success with a couple of paragraphs of boilerplate text, and a wheelbarrow full of hope.

Though every plan must be customized for the buyer, seller, and the client base at issue, this chapter will highlight the important elements to consider in the transition planning process. One of the most challenging aspects of the process is navigating the regulatory issues.

REGULATORY ISSUES

Once a transaction between a selling advisor and a buying advisor has been closed, or completed, it is time to tell the clients and request their consent and cooperation. The steps to be taken, and the order in which they are taken, depend on a labyrinth of regulators, rules, contracts, and forms. The regulatory issues of the notification process can be summarized into three basic constructs:

1. Transactions involving fee-only RIAs
2. Transactions in which the buyer and seller are with the same independent broker-dealer
3. Transactions in which the buyer and seller are *not* with the same independent broker-dealer

We'll address the regulatory issues and related rules, contracts, and forms that impact a transition plan in order from easiest to most difficult. Let's start with transactions that involve the stand-alone, fee-only RIA.

Transactions Involving Fee-Only RIAs

It is quite common for a state or SEC-level, stand-alone RIA to sell to another state or SEC-level, stand-alone RIA. We use the term "stand-alone" to refer to an advisor who owns his or her own RIA and who has filed a Form ADV of their own—not the situation in which an advisor works under their broker-dealers' or another advisory firm's RIA. We use the term IAR (Investment Advisor Representative) to refer to an individual who is authorized to provide investment advice for a fee, but who does not necessarily own an RIA.

Assume, for example, that a seller is a stand-alone RIA with $75 million in AUM. Assume also that the buyer is an RIA with $250 million in AUM. Under such a scenario, the seller has two primary choices, post-closing, in terms of regulatory structures. One choice is for the seller to be "absorbed" into the buyer's RIA. In this instance, the seller becomes an IAR under the buyer's RIA for the duration of the transition period as specified in the post-closing consulting agreement. The transition period typically lasts for up to 12 months. The seller would terminate his or her ADV filing shortly after closing to facilitate this particular path.

A second and more common choice is for the seller to maintain his or her RIA and Form ADV in good standing for the 12-month post-closing transition period, but to serve as an IAR under both the seller's RIA and the buyer's RIA. This option is available only where dual registration is permitted, a determination relatively easy to make. If dual registration isn't permitted or practical, the seller maintains his or her ADV until the clients have all signed a new investment advisory agreement with the buyer or have approved the assignment of the current investment advisory agreement to the buyer without change. One strategy isn't necessarily better than the other, but in practice, sellers tend to prefer to maintain their RIA until the transition process has been completed, then electing to terminate their ADV filing/registration. If the seller desires to continue to work with or for the buyer, the seller can move to IAR status under the buyer's RIA at that time.

One of the key aspects of the post-closing transition plan for an RIA-based transaction is notifying the clients, with a focus on "when" and "how" that notification should occur. It is essential that buyer, seller, and all related parties (including the custodian and any third-party money managers and the like) are on the same page as to the method of notification needed and the timing. These are issues that need to be addressed and coordinated during the deal-structuring phase, if not earlier. To those RIAs who are just beginning to consider an exit plan, it would be wise to check your Form ADV and your investment advisory agreement now, perhaps years in advance, to facilitate a seamless transition when the time comes, as discussed further on.

The Investment Advisers Act of 1940 (the "Advisers Act") prohibits the assignment of a client account without the client's permission. An "assignment" is broadly construed to include any transfer of an investment advisory agreement by the advisor, and certainly a complete sale or acquisition of assets or stock, such as with an exit plan, qualifies as an assignment. Neither the Advisers Act nor the rules under the Act are specific as to the manner in which an advisor must obtain client consent to an assignment of an advisory agreement. To that end, in a practical sense, the process is often grounded in the text that advisors actually include in their investment advisory agreements. Time and time again, we see investment advisory agreements with this provision:

> *This agreement may not be assigned by ABC advisor without the* <u>*prior, written consent*</u> *of the client. (Emphasis added.)*

In our opinion, this is a case of over-lawyering. Here is what the law says:

> *The Investment Advisers Act of 1940 § 205(a)(2)-(3). No investment adviser registered or required to be registered with the Commission shall enter into, extend, or renew any investment advisory contract, or in any way perform any investment advisory contract entered into, extended, or renewed on or after the effective date of this title, if such contract . . . (2) fails to provide, in substance, that no assignment of such contract shall be made by the investment adviser*

*without the consent of the other party by the contract; or (3) fails
to provide, in substance, that the investment adviser, if a partnership, will notify the other party to the contract of any change in the
membership of such partnership within a reasonable time after such
change. (Emphasis added.)*

Federal law does not currently require that consent be in writing or
obtained prior to a sale or merger. As an independent owner, an advisor is
certainly free to "raise the bar" in his or her advisory agreement, but why? If
an advisor's investment advisory agreement requires "prior, written consent,"
then, as a seller, you cannot close on the transaction until you obtain each
client's permission *before* you've sold or been paid anything. In other words,
you must disclose the name of the seller, the basics of the transaction, and get
the client to say "Yes" to all this before they've even met the prospective buyer.
Why would your clients be willing to do this? In fact, expect that your clients
will want to meet your buyer—before closing—before you've been paid anything or the deal has been finalized. This is not a good position for a seller
to be in. And it can get more complicated—consider the possibility that, for
some reason, after all the necessary disclosures and approvals, the transaction
doesn't close. The buyer walks away. Sometimes that happens. Now what?

Our reading of the law is that it does not require a client to approve a
prospective or possible assignment, only an actual assignment, and that cannot happen until the transaction closes and the buyer is firmly committed.
After reviewing your investment advisory agreement text with your compliance officer or consultant, and attorney, consider using this statement in
your investment advisory agreement instead:

*Pursuant to the terms of the Investment Advisers Act of 1940, no as-
signment of this agreement shall be made without the client's consent.*

Or even more simply:

This agreement cannot be assigned without client's consent.

Some compliance specialists and attorneys like to add in more precise
text to obtain "negative consent," even specifying the number of days the
client has to object to the assignment such as this:

*ABC advisor may assign this agreement by either the written con-
sent of the client or by forwarding a "negative consent" letter to
the client, whereby if the client does not notify ABC advisor of an
objection within 45 days of receipt of the letter, the assignment shall
become effective.*

Our advice is to keep it simple. Every element added to your investment advisory agreement, as a seller or potential seller one day, is a higher level that you must adhere to. You be the judge, but make the decision for yourself with full knowledge of the rules and the possible outcomes. If you're thinking about selling in the next five years, adjust your investment advisory agreement well in advance to accommodate your plan or the possibility of such a plan. Going forward, the advice in this chapter assumes that your investment advisory agreement adheres strictly to the Advisers Act, and *does not require* "prior, written consent."

There may also be a scenario in which the buyer asks an acquired client to sign his or her own investment advisory agreement. The new contract solves the issues handily in most cases. However, some buyer/seller teams prefer to handle this task later, after the buyer and the clients have gotten to know each other a little better. Moreover, trying to sign perhaps 100 new agreements with clients who don't know the buyer, within a condensed period of time after closing, is often not a very practical solution.

As a buyer of an RIA practice or business, be sure to review the seller's investment advisory agreement(s) and check what is required under their assignment clause. Also check copies of the seller's investment advisory agreements from years past as both the agreement and the assignment clause may have evolved or changed, and not every client may have signed an updated advisory agreement. As a buyer, the structure and notification requirements of your transition plan often center on this point.

Recently, the SEC has begun to recognize that the use of electronic means to disseminate information can be a benefit to investors and service providers. In an effort to provide guidance on these matters, the SEC has published several interpretive releases addressing the use of electronic media for delivering information to investors. One of the types of information that can be delivered or handled electronically includes a client's consent to assignment of an investment advisory contract under Section 205(a)(2) of the Advisers Act.

One of the key issues with electronic delivery, however, is evidence of delivery—you must prove delivery of the notice. Understand that "access" does not necessarily equal "delivery" from the SEC's point of view. In other words, posting something on your website and inviting your clients to read it will not likely satisfy notice requirements without something more. Check with your compliance officer or consultant if you're considering one of these avenues.

(Sample letters to a client to notify them of a transaction between two fee-only RIAs can be found further on.)

Transactions in which Buyer and Seller Are with the Same IBD /Custodian

Although many sellers prefer to find a buyer who is with the same independent broker-dealer (IBD)/custodian, it can still be a smart strategy to cast a wider net. Conversely, enjoying the benefits and value of an open market search also doesn't mean that it isn't smart to find a buyer within the same broker-dealer/custodian, if at all possible. The point is, whomever you sell to should be *the best* of all the possible reps or advisors out there, not *the easiest* transaction from the seller's point of view.

Generally, an intra-broker-dealer/custodial transfer is a fairly seamless process. The use of an ACATS (Automated Customer Account Transfer Service) form is generally not needed for this type of transition. However, depending on the IBD/custodial platform, there may be changes to client account numbers, rep IDs, paperwork, and in the worst-case scenario, a complete *re-papering* of the client accounts and agreements. To ensure that all the details are identified, both buyer and seller should consult with their shared broker-dealer/custodian to ensure all issues are identified and resolved prior to the transaction being finalized. Most IBDs and custodians will provide in-house forms and some level of support to guide advisors and registered representatives through this process, and most do so at little to no cost.

The more challenging problem is that most sellers also have many fee-based clients as well as brokerage clients. Advisory account clients are treated differently from brokerage account clients, again triggering the notice requirements of an assignment of the account. Advisors who work under their IBD's RIA are typically required to obtain approval in writing. Most IBDs and their RIA affiliates have a short form ready to go for this purpose. In the event of a hybrid model or a situation in which an advisor has a stand-alone RIA of their own (and a separate IBD affiliation), it is up to the advisor to follow the requirements in the Advisers Act and their investment advisory agreement. In this case, which is quite common, the entire preceding section on client notification applies.

In a transaction that involves brokerage and possibly fee-based accounts and perhaps insurance-related income, proper licensure is an important consideration. The parties to a transaction should make sure that the buyer is properly licensed, registered, or appointed, as necessary, *by the closing date* in order to service and be paid on all newly acquired accounts. The date of closing, or the effective date, should be carefully coordinated with this goal in mind. For registered representatives and IARs at independent broker-dealers, the compliance and licensing departments will usually provide support for this process and help to ensure proper timing, but again, advisors should coordinate with their broker-dealer and/or custodian(s) well in advance to ensure that the U-4 and U-5 processing happens in conjunction with the carefully orchestrated transaction timeline and transition plan.

(Sample letters to a client to notify them of a transaction on an intra-broker-dealer basis can be found further on.)

Transactions in which Buyer and Seller Are *Not* with the Same IBD/Custodian

It is not uncommon for a buyer and a seller to be with different broker-dealers and/or custodians. A selling advisor who utilizes a larger IBD, in terms of number of registered reps, and who lives in and works in or near a major metropolitan area where many of these reps also work, can often successfully sell using a *closed market approach*. Finding another advisor within the same network who is also an excellent match in all other regards is a distinct possibility. In contrast, a seller within a smaller IBD, or who lives and works in a smaller city or a more rural setting, may need to find his or her best match with an advisor who is affiliated with a different IBD. In this instance, one party will always need to switch affiliation immediately after closing, and the party making the change is usually the seller.

In most cases, when the seller changes to the buyer's IBD/custodian (or the buyer simply adds the seller's custodian), the assumption is that the buyer is also larger, perhaps much larger, than the seller. If the facts were reversed, the next most logical pattern is for the buyer to change to the seller's IBD. If there is a third variance, it is this: the party with the smallest, least-known IBD changes to the party with the larger, better-known IBD (measured from the clients' point of view, both current clients and prospective new clients and referrals). The change of broker-dealer should be accomplished immediately after closing. Be certain that the new, incoming advisor is fully vetted and approved by the receiving IBD prior to closing, which necessarily implies that the parties should perform adequate, even additional due diligence, with this change in mind.

That said, during the due diligence period, the buyer and seller should be extremely careful to maintain confidentiality and observe all privacy policies that impact the process. A signed and mutual nondisclosure agreement is a must, but that's probably not enough. Each advisor should obtain and read through their IBD's/custodian's privacy policy statements and work with a qualified intermediary and/or attorney on these issues. Share only general client information during the due diligence stage, mostly in the aggregate. Some of the information the buyer wants to know simply has to wait until after closing, or at the earliest, on the eve of closing. Using formal systems, processes, and contract procedures will help to streamline and simplify these steps.

The process of having a seller, for instance, transfer to the buyer's IBD means the seller must apply for affiliation with the buyer's IBD prior to closing. The review process is unique to each IBD, but expect that it will include a FINRA check, review of registration and regulatory history, a credit and background check, a compliance review, and, finally, on approval, a notification to

FINRA of the desired transfer. Assume that this process will take 30 to 60 days. Most buyers and sellers who face this set of circumstances adjust their due diligence period and their closing date accordingly, allowing the transferring party a 30-day head start on the closing process, with final approval timed as precisely as possible around the closing date. The timing of the U-4 and U-5 events must be properly executed to ensure the selling (or transferring) representative maintains legal access to potentially private, client-level information, until such time as the clients are fully transitioned to the new IBD.

The following five paragraphs contain detailed information about the ACATS transfer process. For readers who are familiar with this process, please feel free to move ahead to the more salient parts of this explanation.

> *The transfer of client accounts, assets, and data will occur inter-IBD/custodian via one of three methods, immediately after closing: (1) block transfers; (2) ACATS, or; (3) non-ACATS. For the vast majority of financial service providers, block transfers are no longer a possibility due to their cost and complexity. Generally speaking, these are done only between very large financial institutions like broker-dealers. If your transaction is of such scale, and/or you feel that there is merit to looking into this type of transfer process, you should consult with your IBD/custodian directly to see if they would be willing to support such an undertaking.*
>
> *The second and most common transfer approach is the ACATS process. (U.S. brokerage firms utilize a standardized system to transfer customer accounts from one broker-dealer/custodian to another. This system, known as the Automated Customer Account Transfer Service, or ACATS, allows assets to move seamlessly between brokerage firms in a unified time frame.) ACATS transfers are facilitated by a third party, the National Securities Clearing Corporation (NSCC), to assist participating members with timely asset transfers. This standardized system includes transfers of stocks, U.S. corporate bonds, listed options, unit investment trusts, mutual funds, and cash. It does not necessarily allow for the transfer of all assets in all cases as there are still many such assets that are either not DTCC (Depository Trust & Clearing Corporation) or NSCC-eligible.*
>
> *Investors and their advisors must always begin the ACATS transfer process with the receiving firm. An ACATS transfer form or Transfer Initiation Form (TIF) must be submitted and should be verified to ensure all assets and account data match exactly between receiving and delivering firms; client statements and CRM data is often extremely useful in this verification process. The receiving firm takes this request and communicates with the delivering firm*

via ACATS to verify that account and position data is correct and transferable. Any discrepancy at this stage can delay, or stop the account/asset transfer process entirely.

Anticipate that the client transfer process is time consuming and can only proceed as fast as the signed forms can be gathered from the cooperating clients, and will require constant and dedicated follow-up to ensure all accounts and assets transfer in a timely manner. Contact the receiving firm to review the firm's trading policies, available account types, allowable assets, and holding requirements and to verify that the clients' assets are transferable and eligible for custody and trading at the receiving firm before initiating the transfer request. Not all ACATS transferable assets are acceptable for trading or even custody at every brokerage/custodial firm. All outgoing ACATS transfers, full or partial, must be approved by the "delivering firm."

The final transfer option is a non-ACATS transfer. This references any position or account type that cannot be handled through the automated ACATS process with NSCC. As with the ACATS process, a TIF will still be required and should detail any position that will need to be manually reregistered and transferred between delivering and receiving custodians. The usual suspects for these types of transfers are limited partnerships, nontraded REITs, certain mutual funds, hard assets, bank or other notes, and other NSCC-ineligible assets. The process for a non-ACATS transfer is really not considerably different from its automated ACATS brethren, it just takes more time and requires additional follow-up and due diligence to ensure that both custodial entities are talking to one another and don't drop the ball.

Some IBDs assess a transfer fee per client account for this support. FP Transitions includes this issue in its purchase and sale agreement and allows the parties to determine who will be responsible for the costs. In almost every case, the expense item is paid for by the buyer in the transaction and is assumed to be part of the acquisition costs.

It is rare and unusual for an IBD to contest the transition of clients during a sale, even if the IBD is on *the losing end* of the transaction. In almost 20 years, we have not yet seen an independent broker-dealer "cross the line" on this issue. That's saying something. Any delays or difficulties with the transfer process tend not to occur at the IBD/custodian level, but rather with the buyer's and seller's diligence in ensuring that the paperwork, assets, accounts, and data are correct, verified, and accounted for. Plan accordingly and allow for extra time when a transfer of clients from one IBD to another is involved.

(Sample letters to a client to notify them of a transaction on an inter-broker-dealer basis can be found in the following pages.)

TRANSFERRING FEE-BASED ACCOUNTS

If the buyer and seller each have stand-alone RIAs who rely on different custodians, the common solution is for the buyer to *add* the seller's custodian. It is a distinct advantage to be able to have more than one custodian and another reason why transitioning a fee-only RIA tends to be easier than transitioning a FINRA-based model.

Most registered investment advisors (RIAs), and their underlying investment advisor representatives (IARs), charge a quarterly fee (either in advance or in arrears). Make the determination of this payment and collection aspect a part of the due diligence process, as a buyer and as a seller, because adjusting the seller's system to fit the buyer's system isn't always easy, even if the buyer already uses the same custodian or is willing to add the seller's custodian to their existing systems and processes. The good news is, it is a one-time adjustment. That said, it can create some turbulence in the transition process in the months immediately following the closing.

Here is an example. Assume that the seller charges fees quarterly in arrears. The buyer, who is otherwise a perfect match, charges quarterly fees in advance. Most buyers are not willing to "mix billing systems" on a permanent basis and will need to convert the acquired clients to their current system (even though buyers often honor the seller's *fee schedule* for at least a couple of years post-closing). Of course, this will necessitate the clients' signing a new investment advisory agreement, or at least an amendment to their existing and assigned agreement. From the clients' perspective, depending on the fact pattern, it can seem as if they are getting billed twice—once at the end of the seller's completed quarter, and then immediately again at what amounts to the start of the next quarter under the buyer's billing system.

Buyer and seller will need to work together to coordinate their messages and integration of the new billing protocol, and trust that most clients will adapt. One possible solution is that the buyer agrees to forgo the initial calendar quarter's billing so as to accommodate and *welcome* the client into the new advisory firm and *make an investment* in the long-term relationship. That all sounds good, and it tends to work well, but it also can affect the buyer's anticipated cash flow and the seller's value proposition in that it can affect contingencies tied to the final purchase price based on client delivery and retention (goals that are almost always tied to and measured by gross revenue receipts). These are solvable problems, assuming a well-thought-out transition plan and a buyer and seller who work well together. This is *not* something that needs to be addressed at the letter of intent or term sheet stage, but it does need to be included in the purchase and sale contract.

The use of discretion versus nondiscretion is also relevant, but usually easier to resolve. Some RIAs or IARs have full discretion to implement changes to a client's portfolio without advance, written permission, and some operate only with nondiscretion. Most sellers prefer to find buyers who do things the way they do things, and will agree to maintain their methods and fees charged for at least the first couple of years. Once the post-closing transition period (usually 6 to 12 months) is cleared and any contingencies have been eliminated, it is up to the buyer to proceed as they deem appropriate.

SETTING UP FOR THE POST-CLOSING TRANSITION

Most successful transition plans center around a well-coordinated, carefully choreographed post-closing transition period that lasts 6 to 12 months. Though many transitions proceed more quickly, it is important that the clients and staff know that the seller is ready, willing, and able to work with the buyer for up to 12 months. This facet of the process is memorialized in the consulting agreement that is, or should be, a standard part of the documentation package. Under this agreement, the seller is "the consultant" and works alongside the buyer as a 1099 contractor.

This post-closing transition period is an important part of the messaging to the clients being transferred to a new advisor (whether a practice, business, or firm), as well as the functionality of the plan. Rather than a sudden departure, the seller can honestly (and contractually) promise to continue to be a part of the clients' relationship for at least "one more year" after closing, working closely with a hand-picked advisor who now has time to step in and get to know the clients better, gradually.

As discussed in Chapter 8, the consulting agreement is a key component of the entire documentation package, and is the cornerstone of the transition plan. In many ways, it defines the "tone" of the plan. The consulting agreement needs to anticipate how the seller will assist the buyer, specifying his or her duties, and laying the groundwork for the upcoming "economic marriage." This is particularly important for practices in which the seller has been a dynamic force in the clients' economic lives and now needs to gracefully execute his or her own exit plan.

The following list includes the key components of a solid and effective consulting agreement:

- Formal appointment by buyer of seller for delivery of services and support post-closing
- Term of appointment—generally no more than 12 months
- Description of duties: including weekly/hourly commitment up through completion of client transfer
- Licensing, registration requirements necessary to fulfill the consulting duties
- Agreement regarding extended absences by seller (vacation, health issues, etc.)

In addition, the consulting agreement should detail the actual steps required to transition the clients and include these elements:

- Coordination of all post-closing duties and client contacts by the selling advisor
- Preparation of transition letter(s)
- Calls and preparation of supporting scripts
- Individual meetings as well as group meeting(s) to introduce buyer to the clients
- Completion of consent forms
- Completion of client transactions that were "in progress" at the time of closing
- Phone availability of seller
- Providing background notes/histories on clients
- Assistance in increasing AUM (and any related compensation)

The seller, now a consultant to the buying advisor, must still maintain necessary and appropriate licensing and registration; this is a key component of the transition plan and should also be spelled out in the consulting agreement—in other words, put it in writing. Generally, the agreement will also provide a damages clause should the seller allow any of the necessary licenses to lapse and be unable to fully implement the transition plan.

Consider beginning the transition process with the smaller or easier clients until both buyer and seller develop the necessary transition skills and a clear, well-rehearsed, well-delivered, and coordinated message. In general, the seller should initiate the first contact during the transition period, informing each client as to what is happening and relying on a written script, promising to deliver more information by mail in the next 7 to 10 days. Buyer and seller should follow up the delivery of each client-specific notification letter with a personal meeting attended by both parties and any key staff members who are part of the transition team, especially those who will remain on board with the buyer in the years to come. Here are some additional transition strategies to consider when designing your transition plan and executing a supporting consulting agreement.

- Divide the client base into three to five groups based on size, anticipated transition difficulty, geography, or importance of retention. List the largest or more difficult clients to transition at the top of the list and smaller or easiest clients to transition at the bottom of the list.
- Develop a phone script in order to deliver a concise, clear, and consistent message, based in part on the transition letter to follow. Five minutes

with each client is sufficient and necessary in order to reach all clients within a reasonable period of time.

- Buyer and seller should jointly prepare a short written synopsis, or "elevator speech," of what they want to communicate to each client, or group of clients when a client calls or otherwise asks a question about the transition process. This text should be shared with everyone in the buyer's and seller's offices.
- Buyer and seller should jointly prepare and provide basic, written transition information to each participating staff member so that communications and messages are tightly controlled and consistently delivered at all levels, from receptionist to advisor to owner.

Finally, and especially when there is a transfer between two different IBDs, assign someone in the office to confirm (and confirm again) that *all* assets were correctly and fully transferred. It is not unusual to see five out of six accounts transferred correctly. Occasionally, the orphaned account may show as transferred but not have been fully completed. Essentially, the account ends up "orphaned" because of a regulatory requirement or new signature requirement (e.g., the receiving firm requires a copy of a trust certification, or minor children have become adults, which requires new signatures, etc.).

E&O INSURANCE (TAIL COVERAGE)

Although most advisors carry errors and omissions insurance ("E&O" insurance or coverage), very few fully understand its mechanisms. This is especially true for those who have paid premiums for many years, but have never made a claim for coverage. The application of E&O coverage to a sale or merger is yet another level to consider and plan for.

For a claim to be covered, the alleged error or omission must be covered by the policy *and* must have taken place on or after the date of coverage, but before the policy's expiration date; and the claim *must be made while the policy is still in force*. The claim must also be reported to the insurance carrier within the time frame stipulated by the policy. All this is highly relevant to a seller who is ending his or her career and *shutting things down*, but perhaps not immediately after the sale as he or she continues to assist the buyer in transitioning the client base.

What happens if, as a seller, you choose not to renew your E&O policy the day after closing? If, months later, a client files an arbitration claim for a loss that has just come to their attention, there is arguably no coverage for this incident from the seller's perspective because the E&O policy is no longer in force, even though the policy may have been active when the error was made. If an advisor allows his or her claims-made policy to lapse, coverage for prior acts may be lost as well. This is where the issue of "tail coverage" comes into play.

Advisors can purchase coverage for an extended reporting period beyond their policy's expiration date, allowing continuous coverage for any claims that may be brought after a practice or business has ceased. This extension, known as tail coverage, typically lasts from one to five years. Tail coverage only includes claims related to errors and omissions that take place after the retroactive coverage date of inception and while the practice or business was still operational; it doesn't cover claims related to work you may do after your practice or business has formally closed. This is why this issue needs to be carefully coordinated with the buyer and as pertains to the duties involved in the post-closing transition period, and certainly any activities beyond this point. Costs for tail insurance coverage vary, as can the length of time coverage is extended, so ask your insurance provider for details.

In most cases, the seller will agree to remain licensed and covered by E&O insurance during the 12-month, post-closing transition period. The cost of the coverage is negotiable between the buyer and seller, but more often than not, it is considered the seller's responsibility. In a Sell and Stay type of transaction, or if the seller agrees to remain a part of the buyer's team for several years after the sale, the responsibility for the cost of E&O coverage would likely shift to the buyer.

SAMPLE CLIENT LETTERS

The following is a series of letters that past sellers and buyers have successfully used to inform clients of a change of control and to implement the transition planning process. The letters are not presented in any specific order or level of recommendation, but simply represent a compilation of letters that have worked well in the field.

A transition or announcement letter is typically prepared by the seller (often with help from a qualified intermediary), since they know the clients best, but with input and final approval by the buyer. Because such a letter will be sent immediately after closing, it can and should be prepared in advance. Depending on the circumstances of the transition and the size and diversity of the client base, more than one version or style of letter may be appropriate for different clients. This is especially true for advisors who have a fee-based practice and stand-alone RIA, with an IBD affiliation.

Each sample letter in this section should be personalized by the seller; it cannot look like or read like a form letter. Professionally merge-print each letter so that each client is addressed individually and cordially—a handwritten note on each letter helps in this regard. It is good idea to always call the client before sending a transition or announcement letter. Calling clients before sending a letter takes extra time, but advisors will get much better results in return for the extra time and effort. These calls should be lightly scripted to ensure that the proper message is delivered clearly and succinctly and consistently, and so that the selling advisor can speak to all clients in a relatively short period of time. Avoid falling into the trap of reciting the entire story at the time of the phone call. The purpose of the call is simply to notify the client that a change has occurred and that more complete information is forthcoming in a letter.

Format your letter to address these key issues, as may be appropriate, stressing the commonalities between past and future advisors, and all the things that are not going to change:

Address relationship between the seller and client, citing

- Appreciation
- Trust
- Length of relationship
- Commitment
- Core values

Explain the relationship between the buyer and seller

- Handpicked, "best match," competitive search process
- Common background
- Common values
- Common philosophies
- Continuing employment by the buyer of one or more of the seller's key staff members

Introduction of buyer/buyer's business or firm, stressing key attributes as appropriate

- Similarities
- Reputation
- Education
- Designations
- Publications
- Rewards
- Community service
- Faith
- Family
- Core values
- Regulatory structure (IBD, RIA, etc.)

Instructions for next steps, follow-up by seller or buyer,
including

- Phone call
- Letter (notice provisions, negative consent)
- Client appreciation event
- Paperwork to be completed
- Who to call with questions
- Next meeting date

Client letters should be reviewed by each advisor's compliance department or compliance officer before use. Each and every reference that follows the use of "[Client's Name]" assumes that the user will insert a client's actual name in these spaces, just in case that wasn't obvious.

LETTER NO. 1: ANNOUNCING SALE/MERGER TO A THIRD-PARTY BUYER (WITH BROKER-DEALER/CUSTODIAN CHANGE)

Dear [Client's Name],

I hope this letter finds you well. As I recently shared with you, as a part of my commitment to provide you with outstanding independent financial services and advice, I have decided to change my broker-dealer affiliation from [Broker-Dealer/Custodian One] to [Broker-Dealer/Custodian Two]. This move is made in concert with my merger into a slightly larger advisory firm, [New Advisory Firm Name], a group that I have hand-picked and one that holds the same values I do.

This merger with [New Advisory Firm Name] and our new affiliation with [Broker-dealer/Custodian Two] will enable us to provide multigenerational services and incorporate state-of-the-art technology and reporting systems. These are changes that have been long overdue. We will now be able to provide you (and your children and grandchildren when they're ready!) with the most timely advice and research, and we will be able to expand our services to you—steps that we think are critically important in this day and age.

As a part of this merger process, I am delighted to announce that I have a new associate, [Buyer's Individual Name], CFP™, MBA. For the past three years I have been searching for a Certified Financial Planner™ like [Buyer's First Name] with the experience and expertise (and personality) to provide you with the highest level of service and to enable me to focus more of my time on strategic planning and investment research. [Buyer's First Name] has been providing financial advice and services since _____ and has been a part of [New Advisory Firm Name] for the past ___ years. Many of you have asked me about my retirement plans and who will take care of your financial advisory needs in the future; this is my solution, though I do intend to stick around for a while longer. In the meantime, I very much look forward to introducing [Buyer's First Name] and the rest of the crew to you when we next meet.

All of my key staff members [insert names] will continue to work alongside of me and will help make these changes easier.

In order to complete the transition to our new broker-dealer and our new advisory firm, I have enclosed forms for you to review and sign. Please overnight all of the signed documents in the enclosed envelope and, as always, feel free to contact me or any member of my staff with any questions. We look forward to providing great service to you and your family for generations to come.

Sincerely, [Seller's Name]

LETTER NO. 2: ANNOUNCING INTERNAL EXIT PLAN WITH KEY EMPLOYEE

Dear [Client's Name],

Let me begin by saying how wonderful it has been to be able to work with you to help you reach your financial goals. Over the past 12 years, I have met many wonderful people and feel fortunate to have been a part of your lives.

In the past few years, many of you have asked me about my own goals, including that of retirement. Let me now provide a more definitive answer by saying that I have started a gradual and professional transition period by training and mentoring my eventual replacement, [Employee Buyer's Name]. We are now entering a new phase of this transition with the formal introduction of our clients to [Employee Buyer's Name] and his/her greater responsibility for advice and decision making on your behalf. You will see his/her name appear on your next statements. Our wonderful office staff headed by _____, Office Manager, will continue without interruption. I will be in the background for a while longer, so feel free to call with any questions.

(Continued)

(Continued)

[Employee] has an outstanding list of qualifications and credentials to serve you, including (list designations, degrees), and has over ____ years of financial experience. He/She is well prepared to give you the kind of service you are accustomed to receiving and maybe even some new ideas as we all struggle to cope with uncertainties on the horizon. [Employee] is strongly committed to the financial planning process and will do the necessary work needed to help you reach and maintain your financial goals.

Both of us have worked hard to make sure you will be in good hands after I leave. [Employee] will use the same team approach that I have over the years and I am certain that you will enjoy and profit from his/her expertise. I would consider it your continuing faith in the work I have done for you over the years to accept [Employee] and his/her team in my stead. After the transition is completed over the next 12 months or so, it will be time for me to join many of you in retirement. I am looking forward to long-postponed travels and pursuing some new hobbies, and expect to cross paths with many of you while doing so.

We will announce a client appreciation event in the fall and look forward to seeing you there. As they say, old financial planners don't die, they just slowly fade away. It is now my time to do so.

If you have any questions, please give either [Employee] or me a call. My best wishes, as always.

Sincerely, [Seller's Name] and [Employee]

LETTER NO. 3: RIA SALE TO THIRD-PARTY AND NEGATIVE CONSENT LETTER

Dear [Client's Name],

As my practice as grown over the years, I have set important goals for myself, just as I have encouraged you to do. One of those goals, a very important one to be sure, was to have a succession plan in place by the time I turned 65. That momentous event occurred this past August and so now is the time to share my plans with you.

In a financial planning and advisory practice such as ours, the death or disability of the principal planner can have a significant impact, not only to the family of that person, but also to all of the clients who rely professionally on that person. So, even though I am in good health and plan on continuing as an active financial planner for some time to come, I want to make sure that, regardless of what lies ahead, your financial needs and goals will not be affected or interrupted.

As I mentioned during our recent phone call and discussion, [New Advisor's Name] and I signed an agreement for him/her to become the owner of [Seller's Practice Name]. I will remain active in the business and continue to work with you and my other clients for at least one more year, but the primary contact will be with [New Advisor's Name]. I will be working hard behind the scenes to make sure that your needs are fully addressed and that [New Advisor's Name] understands the goals that we have been working toward and which you have entrusted to me.

I would have more difficulty making this announcement and taking this step if I did not have supreme confidence in [New Advisor's Name], who shares my passion for financial planning and a penchant for customer service. We both firmly believe that making your quality of life as rewarding as possible is of equal importance to recommending appropriate investments and guiding our financial journey. I believe that in every sense of the words, this step that I take on your behalf will add value to your financial plans and goals.

Unless I hear differently from you in the next 30 days, your account and trust in me will be transferred to [New Advisor's Name], who is ready and willing to accept such responsibility. We wanted to let you know about our plans now so that you receive this news directly from us. We believe this is an important and necessary step to help you plan for your future even as I plan for mine. If you have any questions or concerns, please call me directly.

Sincerely, [Seller's Name]

LETTER NO. 4: RIA MERGER ANNOUNCEMENT LETTER

Dear [Client's Name],

On behalf of everyone at [Company Name], I am pleased to share with you an exciting development resulting from many, many hours of careful planning and deliberation. As you know, we take great pride in providing you with excellent service—we are committed to professionalism and

(Continued)

(Continued)

personal attention above all else. We are ever vigilant in our search for better market intelligence, planning ideas, and sound advice in our ever-changing and complex world. We believe that, to remain committed to the promises we made to you, we also need to strengthen our own business model to help you achieve your goals now and long into the future.

For all these reasons, we have identified and selected [New Advisory Firm Name] as our new strategic partner. Organizationally speaking, we will begin taking steps to merge our two operations over the course of the next several months. [New Advisory Firm Name], like [Company Name], is an SEC-registered, fee-only investment advisor whose founding principles closely parallel our own beliefs. The evidence of natural synergies and commonalities also allows for the obvious sharing of intelligence and cost efficiencies.

[New Advisory Firm Name] has approximately 25 employees with offices in [list cities]. Their offices are managed by a group of seasoned investment professionals who are accredited with professional designations such as Chartered Financial Analyst (CFA), Certified Financial Planner (CFP), and Certified Public Accountant (CPA), much like our office. They are disciplined financial professionals who we believe will support and enhance our own comprehensive wealth management platform.

There will be no changes made to the process and manner in which we deliver our services. All of our support staff will continue to perform as they always have and will remain vital to the growth of our business. We look forward to continuing our work for you without interruption.

More information will follow as part of our work is to keep you properly informed on financial matters, but always feel free to call me directly if you have any questions or concerns. I am so proud to share this information with you. Thank you for your time.

Sincerely, [Seller's Name] and a signatory of [New Advisory Firm]

LETTER NO. 5: ANNOUNCING SALE OR MERGER TO A THIRD-PARTY BUYER (NO BROKER-DEALER/CUSTODIAN CHANGE)

Dear [Client's Name],

As a follow-up to our earlier discussion, and after considerable research over the past year, I have made a decision that is important to the way that I will provide services to you, our valued client, in the future. I have put a lot of thought into the amount of time and the level of dedication required to ensure that your long-term financial goals are met, and I think you will find that these are necessary steps to that end.

As a sole practitioner, I have long been concerned about the continuity of financial management services for you and your family if something should happen to me, or when I ultimately retire. Prudence dictates the wisdom of having additional experienced and competent advisors in place to serve your needs and those of your children and grandchildren. Therefore, I will be merging my practice into [Buyer's Firm Name]. As I grow older and move closer to retirement, I wanted to find a larger advisory business to step in, but also a group of individuals who impressed me as intelligent, principled, and caring advisors—a small group highly qualified to work with my clients in the manner to which you are accustomed. After numerous discussions with [Buyer's Name], I believe he/she and his/her colleagues share an approach very similar to mine in financial planning and investment management. This is the group that I would like you to work with after my retirement.

Happily, my capable Administrative Assistant, [First Name], will be joining [Buyer's Name] and me at [Buyer's Firm Name]. Together, we are committed to making this transition as easy as possible and we intend that this adjustment and improvement to our practice model will ensure the continuation of services to you and your family, without interruption, for generations to come.

I will remain at the address on the letterhead through [Date], and available to assist you in making this transition. After that date, I can be reached at the [Buyer's Firm Name and Phone Number]. My affiliation with [broker-dealer name] will remain unchanged, as will your fee schedule and the billing process you've grown accustomed to at least into the near future.

Please feel free to call me or [Administrative Assistant's Name] to answer any questions. I look forward to our continued relationship and to helping you achieve your financial goals. We will be reaching out to you very shortly to schedule a formal meeting so that I may introduce you to the new team and we will complete any additional paperwork during that visit.

Sincerely, [Seller's Name]

NEGATIVE CONSENT FORM

Dear [Client's Name],

As mentioned in my previous letter, and as we discussed by phone, I have joined [Buyer's Business Name] to better serve your long-term needs as I get closer to retirement. In fact, my entire team is physically moving to [Buyer's Business Name]'s location here in [City/State]. [Buyer's Name] is an investment advisor registered with the Securities and Exchange Commission and has been expertly serving clients like you since ____. I have hand-picked this group of professionals because I think they are the best and will do a great job in supporting your goals and honoring the steps we've taken together over many years.

I will be assigning your client account agreement(s) to [Buyer's Business Name] effective _____, ___. Your accounts will continue to be custodied at [Name of Custodian] and your account numbers will not change. If I do not hear from you within 30 days of the date of this letter, I will assume that you agree with my decisions on your behalf and your account will be formally assigned to [Buyer's Business Name]. We will continue to service your accounts thereafter with few changes and no interruption of the services you have enjoyed in years past.

We have also enclosed Part 2 of [Buyer's Business Name] Form ADV, which discloses important information about its business. This is a regulatory requirement and is aimed at helping you more fully understand how the new advisory team works and delivers its services.

We so appreciate working with you over the years. If you have any questions about this process, please contact me directly at [Phone Number]. Thank you.

Sincerely, [Seller's Name]

CLIENT ACKNOWLEDGMENT AND CONSENT

(This form is intended to be handed to a transitioning client at the conclusion of a face-to-face meeting and following an appropriate explanation. It can be placed on either the seller's or buyer's letterhead.)

The undersigned consents to the assignment of the attached Investment Advisory Agreement and/or Financial Planning Agreement dated the ___ day of _____, with [Seller's Practice Name] to [Buyer's Business Name]. The undersigned acknowledges receipt of Part 2 of Form ADV for [Buyer's Business Name].

Name(s) of Client(s) (list all if more than one)

_____

Signature   Date

_____

Signature   Date

Conclusion

Vince Lombardi once spent over eight hours describing the intricacies and variabilities of a single, seemingly simple, running play that, when executed, lasted for all of 3 to 5 seconds. He coached not only his players, but in the off-season the other coaches too. He was a master of the details of his profession. That is what we do at FP Transitions, literally. When our clients and their coaches come to our offices for a visit, we sometimes spend an entire day "whiteboarding" a single concept—one advisor's set of plans.

The planning process, be it an exit plan, a succession plan, or a continuity plan, is unique to each advisor and to the book, practice, business, or firm he or she has built or is trying to build. As the day of planning comes to a close, we inevitably hear two common refrains: (1) "I had no idea how much I didn't know," and (2) "I wish I had embarked on this journey 10 years earlier." Take the lessons not only from books like these, but also from the experiences of other advisors.

Our goal with this book is not to convince you to buy or sell a financial services or advisory practice. That is up to you. As an independent advisor, you have earned the right to decide for yourself what course your career will follow. The takeaway from this book is that advisors need to take control of the process and the elements of their own individual plans. An endgame strategy should never be something that happens to you, but rather something that is woven into the fabric of the work you do from the first day on the job. Handing off the baton is inevitable; it is not something to avoid, or even something that is avoidable. It is going to happen, so take control of the event. Gathering information is step one, but step two is *doing something*, committing to a specific course of action, and doing what is best for the clients you serve. Embrace the challenge and enjoy the well-earned results.

With that, we wish you good luck and good planning.

Sample Documents

This appendix includes sample documents for use in the mergers and acquisitions (M&A) space. These sample documents are provided to help readers better understand the documentation process. Do not use or rely on these documents without consulting an attorney. Visit the companion website for this book to download files to adapt to your use with legal assistance. Samples of the following are available here and online:

- Mutual Nondisclosure Agreement
- Buyer's Due Diligence Checklist
- Seller's Due Diligence Checklist
- Letter of Intent for purchase of assets
- Buyer Acquisition Profile

MUTUAL NONDISCLOSURE AGREEMENT

Date: _____ (the "Effective Date")
Parties: _____ ("Seller")
    and
    _____ ("Buyer")

RECITALS:

Prospective Seller is a(n) _____ organized under the laws of the State of _____ having its principal place of business in the State of _____ and having its offices located at _____.

    Prospective Buyer is a(n) _____ organized under the laws of the State of _____, having its principal place of business in the State of _____ and having its offices located at _____.

(Continued)

249

(Continued)

WHEREAS Seller and Buyer (collectively the "Parties" or individually a "Party") wish to discuss and review potential business arrangements between the Parties ("Purpose"); and,

WHEREAS the Parties wish to clarify the manner in which any Confidential Information disclosed in the course of such discussions is to be treated and protected by the Parties.

NOW, THEREFORE, in consideration of the mutual promises contained herein and other good and valuable consideration, the receipt and sufficiency of which are hereby acknowledged, the Parties hereto agree as follows:

SECTION 1. DEFINITIONS

Definitions. In this Agreement, the following terms will have the following meanings:

"Affiliate" means, with respect to any individual or entity, any other individual or entity directly or indirectly controlling or controlled by, or under direct or indirect common control with, such individual or entity or one or more of the other Affiliates of that individual or entity (or a combination thereof). For purposes of this definition, an individual or entity shall control another entity if the first individual or entity: (i) owns, beneficially or of record, more than fifty percent (50%) of the voting securities of the other entity, or (ii) has the ability to elect a majority of the directors of the other entity.

"Confidential Information" means all documents, data, and information of a Disclosing Party or any of its Affiliates that has been, or may hereinafter be, disclosed to the Receiving Party in the course of the Parties' discussions or other investigations by the Receiving Party, directly or indirectly, whether in written, oral, graphic or any other form, and which is identified as, or would reasonably be understood to be, confidential and/or proprietary to the Disclosing Party. Without limiting the generality of the foregoing, Confidential Information shall include without limitation: (i) any trade secret, technical, financial, or business information, customer information, business processes, personal information commercial activities, intellectual property, idea, concept or know-how that is considered and treated as being confidential or proprietary by Disclosing Party; (ii) the fact that discussions and an exchange of information between the Parties have been or are taking place; and, (iii) the existence or terms and conditions of this Agreement. Confidential Information disclosed in tangible or electronic form may be marked or otherwise identified by Disclosing Party with a legend as being confidential, but in no event shall the absence of such a mark or legend relieve a Receiving Party of the obligation to treat as confidential information that would be considered confidential by a person exercising reasonable business judgment.

"Competitor" means, with respect to a Party or its Affiliates, any person who offers products or services that compete with products or services provided by such Party or its Affiliates.

"Disclosing Party" means either Party, or any of their respective Affiliates, that furnishes or discloses Confidential Information pursuant to, or in any connection with, this Agreement.

"Receiving Party" means either Party, or any of their respective Affiliates, that receives Confidential Information pursuant to, or in any connection with, this Agreement.

SECTION 2. USE AND DISCLOSURE OF CONFIDENTIAL INFORMATION

2.1 Obligations. Each Party agrees that it shall use the Confidential Information of a Disclosing Party only in connection with, and to the extent required for, the Purpose. Each Receiving Party agrees that it shall protect the Disclosing Party's Confidential Information from all harm, loss, theft, interference, corruption, destruction, and unauthorized reproduction or access. Subject to Sections 2.2 and 2.4 hereof, each Receiving Party shall ensure that such Confidential Information is not disclosed, published, copied, released, transferred, or otherwise made available in any form to or for the use or benefit of any other person except as expressly permitted by this Agreement or as may otherwise be agreed to in writing by the Disclosing Party.

2.2 Permitted Disclosure. A Receiving Party:

2.2.1 Shall be permitted to disclose relevant aspects of a Disclosing Party's Confidential Information to its officers, directors, employees, or professional advisors who need to know such Confidential Information for the Purpose. Disclosure of this Agreement and of information related to the Purpose, other than a Disclosing Party's Confidential Information, may be made to a Receiving Party's potential business partners and their respective investors, designated intermediaries, or investment bankers, provided that such potential business partners are not the Disclosing Party's Competitors, nor Affiliates of

(Continued)

(Continued)

such Disclosing Party's Competitors, including to such persons' officers, directors, employees, or professional advisors, in connection with the due diligence review of Receiving Party by such business partners, investors, or investment advisors; and,

2.2.2 May disclose Confidential Information that:

2.2.2.1 The Receiving Party can show, by documented and competent evidence, was in the possession of the Receiving Party prior to its disclosure to the Receiving Party by or on behalf of the Disclosing Party, provided that such disclosure was not in contravention of this Agreement and was not made by any other person in contravention of an obligation of confidentiality to the Disclosing Party or any other party that is known or reasonably ought to be known by the Receiving Party;

2.2.2.2 Is or becomes generally available to the public other than as a result of a disclosure directly or indirectly by Receiving Party in breach of this Agreement;

2.2.2.3 Is or becomes available to the Receiving Party on a non-confidential basis from a source other than Disclosing Party, provided that such source is not in breach of its obligations under this Agreement and was not made by any other Person in contravention of an obligation of confidentiality to the Disclosing Party or any other party that is known or reasonably ought to be known by the Receiving Party;

2.2.2.4 Receiving Party can show, by documentary and competent evidence, to have been developed independently by Receiving Party without using such Confidential Information; or,

2.2.2.5 The Disclosing Party has authorized, in writing, the disclosure of.

2.3 Third Party Disclosure. Prior to providing any Confidential Information of a Disclosing Party to another person as is permitted by Section 2.2, the Receiving Party shall:

2.3.1 Inform such persons of the confidential nature of the Confidential Information; and,

2.3.2 Ensure that such persons and parties agree with the Receiving Party to be bound by a written confidentiality agreement containing terms materially and substantially similar to the confidentiality obligations contained in this Agreement, or that such persons are otherwise bound by professional duties of confidentiality to the person from whom such Confidential Information is received, and the Receiving Party shall be responsible and liable for all persons to whom it discloses such Confidential Information with respect to their use of such information.

2.4 Disclosure Compelled By Law. In the event that a Receiving Party becomes legally compelled by law, regulation or order of court or administrative body of competent jurisdiction to disclose any Disclosing Party's Confidential Information, the Receiving Party shall be entitled to disclose such Confidential Information to the extent that it complies with, and within the constraints of, this Section 2.4. The Receiving Party shall provide Disclosing Party with prompt prior written notice of its obligation to disclose so that the Disclosing Party may seek a protective order or other appropriate remedy and/or waive compliance with the terms of this Agreement, which waiver shall not be unreasonably withheld. In the event that such protective order or other remedy is not obtained, or that the Disclosing Party waives compliance with the provisions hereof, the Receiving Party agrees to furnish only that portion of Disclosing Party's Confidential Information which it is legally required to disclose and to exercise best efforts to obtain assurances that the Confidential Information will be treated in confidence. In addition, the Receiving Party will take reasonable steps to remove from the Confidential Information that is required to be disclosed, any information that is commercially sensitive to the Disclosing Party.

SECTION 3. NO IMPLIED OBLIGATIONS

The Parties agree that unless a written agreement between the Parties with respect to the Purpose is executed, if any, and except for the matters specifically agreed to herein, neither Party will be under any legal obligation of any kind whatsoever with respect to the Purpose or otherwise by virtue of this Agreement or any written or oral expression with respect to the Purpose by any of their respective directors, officers, employees, or agents.

SECTION 4. OWNERSHIP

Except as is expressly set forth in this Agreement, nothing in this Agreement shall grant, or shall be construed as granting, a Receiving Party any right, title, ownership, license, or other right or interest in

(Continued)

(Continued)

or to any of a Disclosing Party's Confidential Information, or in or to any of a Disclosing Party's intellectual property or other proprietary rights. Any Confidential Information provided by a Disclosing Party shall remain the sole and exclusive property of the Disclosing Party.

SECTION 5. INDEPENDENT DEVELOPMENT

Each Party acknowledges that the other Party may currently, or in the future, be developing information internally or receiving information from third parties that may be similar to a Disclosing Party's Confidential Information. Accordingly, nothing in this Agreement shall be, or shall be construed as, an agreement, restriction, limitation, representation, or inference that a Receiving Party will not independently and originally develop, communicate, or use (without copying or misappropriating any Confidential Information) technology, information, concepts, systems, techniques, or products that, without any breach of this Agreement whatsoever, compete with or are the same or similar to the technology, information, concepts, systems, techniques, or products contemplated by or embodied in Disclosing Party's Confidential Information.

SECTION 6. NO WARRANTY OF ACCURACY

Neither Party makes any representation or warranty whatsoever with respect to any Confidential Information disclosed by it hereunder, including as to the quality, currency, accuracy, or completeness of such Confidential Information. Each Party agrees that the Confidential Information it provides is provided strictly on an "as is" basis and that a Disclosing Party will not have any liability to a Receiving Party resulting from, arising out of or in any connection with any use of, or reliance on, a Disclosing Party's Confidential Information by the Receiving Party.

SECTION 7. TERM AND RETURN OF CONFIDENTIAL INFORMATION

7.1 The term of this Agreement shall commence on the Effective Date set forth at the beginning of this Agreement, and unless superseded by another form of writing, shall continue in full force and effect for a minimum of five (5) years, and thereafter for such period of time as a court of competent jurisdiction may determine is fair and reasonable in the circumstances of each case.

7.2 Upon the request of a Disclosing Party, a Receiving Party will promptly return to the Disclosing Party, or destroy:

7.2.1 All of the Disclosing Party's Confidential Information, including all copies thereof, that is in receiving Party's possession, under its control or in the possession of other persons to whom it has been provided as permitted hereunder; and,

7.2.2 All analyses, studies, notes, or other materials, or such part thereof, that were created by Receiving Party and that are based on or contain Disclosing Party's Confidential Information.

7.3 Upon the request of a Disclosing Party, a senior officer of the Receiving Party shall certify in writing, on behalf of the Receiving Party, that all Disclosing Party's Confidential Information required to be returned or destroyed pursuant to this Agreement has been returned or destroyed, as applicable.

SECTION 8. REMEDIES

8.1 Equitable Relief; Waiver of Immunities. Each Party acknowledges and agrees that a breach of this Agreement by a Receiving Party will result in immediate and irreparable harm to the Disclosing Party and that damages may not be an adequate remedy for such a breach. Neither Party, and nothing in this Agreement, shall interfere with, delay, obstruct, defend against, or prevent either Party from taking, or require any Party to take, any steps prior to taking action to seek an interim and interlocutory equitable remedy on notice, or ex parte, to enforce any provision herein to protect their respective rights. Each Party covenants and agrees not to contest, object to, defend against or otherwise oppose an application for equitable relief by the other Party in such circumstances and each Party waives any and all immunities from any equitable relief to which it may be entitled. Any such relief or remedy shall not be exclusive, but shall be in addition to all other available legal or equitable remedies. Each Party agrees that the provisions of this Section are fair and reasonable in the commercial circumstances of this Agreement, and that neither Party would have entered into this Agreement but for each Party's agreement with the provisions of this Section. The breaching Party agrees to reimburse the nonbreaching Party for all costs and expenses (including reasonable legal fees and disbursements) incurred by such nonbreaching Party in

(Continued)

(*Continued*)

connection with a successful application to enforce its rights as provided for in this Section.

8.2 Indemnity. A Receiving Party agrees that it shall indemnify and hold harmless a Disclosing Party from any and all losses, harm, injury, liabilities, damages, costs and expenses, including all reasonable legal fees, costs and expenses, arising out of, relating to, or in any connection with a breach by such Receiving Party of its obligations pursuant to this Agreement.

SECTION 9. MISCELLANEOUS PROVISIONS

9.1 Assignment. This Agreement and any obligation or interest herein may not be assigned or transferred by a Party without the prior and express written consent of the other Party.

9.2 Governing Law. This Agreement shall be governed by, construed, and interpreted in accordance with the laws of the State of

_____.

9.3 Arbitration Agreement. Any controversy or claim arising out of this Agreement or the interpretation of any of the provisions in this Agreement shall be resolved by binding arbitration by one arbitrator. Each party shall be responsible for its own attorney fees and costs.

9.4 Notices. All notices required or permitted to be provided pursuant to this Agreement shall be given in writing and sent by: (i) registered mail; (ii) fax transmission; or, (iii) be personally delivered in exchange for an acknowledgment of receipt to the following addresses:

SELLER:　　　　　　　　　**BUYER:**

_____　　　_____
_____　　　_____
_____　　　_____

or to any other person or address of which either Party may notify the other in writing from time to time. All notices shall be presumed to have been received: (i) at the time delivered if by personal delivery; (ii) five (5) Business Days after the date of their mailing if by mail; or (iii) on the next Business Day following the day of transmission if by fax transmission.

9.5 Severability. If any provision contained in this Agreement is found by a court of competent jurisdiction to be invalid, illegal, or unenforceable, such determination shall not impair or affect the validity, legality, or enforceability of the remaining portions of this Agreement and each provision or portion thereof is hereby declared to be separately severable and distinct and shall be valid and enforceable to the extent permitted by law.

9.6 Waiver. All waivers must be in writing and signed by the Party waiving its rights. No failure or delay in exercising any right, power, or privilege hereunder shall operate as a waiver thereof, nor shall any single or partial exercise thereof preclude any other or further exercise thereof or the exercise of any right, power, or privilege hereunder.

9.7 Amendment. This Agreement may only be amended by written agreement duly executed by authorized representatives of each of the Parties.

9.8 Language. This Agreement has been drawn up in English at the express wish of the Parties.

9.9 Entire Agreement. The Parties agree that this Agreement constitutes the complete and exclusive statement of the terms and conditions between them with respect to the subject matter hereof and supersedes all prior and contemporaneous agreements, understandings, negotiations, and discussions, whether oral or written, of the Parties.

9.10 Counterparts. Fax and Email Transmission. This Agreement may be executed in counterparts, each of which taken together shall constitute one single agreement between the Parties. The Parties agree that this Agreement may be executed by fax or email transmission and that the reproduction of signatures by fax or by email shall be treated as binding as if originals and each Party agrees and undertakes to provide the other Party with a copy of the Agreement bearing original signatures forthwith upon demand by the other Party.

IN WITNESS WHEREOF, the Parties have executed this Agreement as of the date first set forth above.

SELLER: BUYER:

_____   _____

BUYER'S DUE DILIGENCE CHECKLIST

NOTE: This checklist is not a complete list, but is intended to cover some of the more common areas in which buyers have conducted due diligence about the seller and/or the seller's business. Every transaction is unique and the due diligence process must be adapted to the situation. All items in this checklist may not apply to your particular situation. Please consult your attorney and CPA for additional information and due diligence steps.

ORGANIZATIONAL / ENTITY STRUCTURE OF SELLER

Point of Contact: _____

- ❑ Entity or business structure
- ❑ Ownership structure
- ❑ Review the following documents of seller:
  - ■ Articles of Incorporation, Articles of Organization, or similar documents, including any amendments thereto;
  - ■ Bylaws, Operating Agreements, and/or Partnership Agreements;
  - ■ Shareholder, Director, and Committee Minutes, Consents, and/or Resolutions;
  - ■ Stock Ledgers, Membership Ledgers, or other similar documents, including amendments thereto; and,
  - ■ All other documents in the company's minute book
- ❑ Bylaws, operating agreements, partnership agreements, joint venture agreements of any entity in which the seller or its subsidiary is an owner
- ❑ Certificate of Good Standing from state of incorporation
- ❑ Active status reports in the state of incorporation for the past three years
- ❑ List of all of the seller's assumed names and copies of registrations thereof
- ❑ List of all states in which the company is authorized to do business and annual reports for the past three years
- ❑ List of all states, provinces, and countries where the seller owns or leases real property, maintains employees, and/or conducts business
- ❑ Copies of agreements with owners relating to options, voting trusts, warrants, puts, calls, subscriptions, and convertible securities

FINANCIAL AND TAX INFORMATION OF SELLER

Point of Contact: _____

- ❑ General ledger, balance sheets, income statements, and cash flow statements for the past three years, including interim statements for the year to date
- ❑ Auditor's letters or reports for the past three years

❑ Federal, state, and local tax returns and reports for at least the last three years
❑ Projections, capital budgets, and strategic plans
❑ Breakdown of revenue including the quality, type, and quantity of revenue sources
❑ Analyst reports, including any analyses of fixed and variable expenses or of gross margins
❑ Tax settlement documents for the past three years
❑ Schedules of the following:
  ▪ Indebtedness and contingent liabilities;
  ▪ Inventory;
  ▪ Accounts receivable;
  ▪ Accounts payable.
❑ Documents and correspondence related to any pending or threatened audit or tax claim against seller or seller's assets
❑ Depreciation and amortization methods for the past five years
❑ Changes in accounting methods during the past five years
❑ Description of seller's internal control procedures
❑ UCC filings, tax liens, or other liens against the seller's business assets
❑ Recent formal valuation or appraisal, if any
❑ Determine if seller's reported gross income includes bonuses, awards, or other forms of nonrecurring revenues
❑ Amount of the broker-dealer override. If the seller is an investment advisor, determine the annual fees typically charged, the amount of any broker-dealer override on the investment advisory accounts, if any, and whether fees are charged in arrears or in advance.
❑ Confirm that the FP Transitions' *Seller Listing Form* represents reasonably accurate data. Determine any material changes since the date of listing and the reasons for the changes.

PURCHASE / NEGOTIATION ISSUES
Point of Contact: _____
❑ Determine the general terms of the transaction, including but not limited to:
  ▪ Whether it is an asset sale or a stock sale;
  ▪ Purchase price;
  ▪ Down payment amount, if any;
  ▪ Terms of earn-out arrangement;
  ▪ Whether the buyer will obtain financing;
  ▪ Seller financing, security/collateral;
  ▪ Compensation to the seller for additional referrals to the buyer after closing;

(Continued)

(Continued)

- Noncompetition/nonsolicitation agreements for seller and its employees;
- Life insurance and/or disability insurance;
- Dispute resolution;
- Continuation of the seller's license(s) after closing;
- Terms of the transition period (i.e., length of seller's involvement after closing, extent of seller's involvement, duties of seller after closing); and,
- Closing date.

LICENSING / REGULATORY / COMPLIANCE INFORMATION

Point of Contact: _____

- ❏ Current FINRA Form U-4 and, if applicable, SEC Form ADV for the seller and each of its employees, along with proof of filing. Confirm the filing status of these forms and any disciplinary history using FINRA's online verification process.
- ❏ Determine the date of the peer review, or the last regulatory audit conducted by state, federal, or self-regulatory agencies. Review deficiency letters and any related correspondence. Request information pertaining to resolving any deficiencies from the appropriate regulatory agency and/or from the seller.
- ❏ Obtain copies of each report or other documents filed with governmental agencies that have regulatory power over the seller.

CLIENT PROFILE / TRANSFERABILITY ISSUES

Point of Contact: _____

- ❏ Written list of the client base with the following information:
  - Age ranges and demographics;
  - Number of years each client has been with the seller's practice;
  - How each client selected the seller as their advisor;
  - Relevant cultural information (e.g., holidays, customs to be observed during meetings, etc.); and,
  - Multigenerational and family-related wealth and wealth transfer issues
- ❏ If the transition involves moving clients from one broker-dealer to another, check with your and the buyer's broker-dealers regarding their policies and portability of client information (Reg S-P).

LEGAL / LITIGATION

Point of Contact: _____

- ❏ Description of all pending or threatened litigation, administrative proceedings, discrimination claims, grievances, wrongful termination claims, arbitration cases, workers' compensation cases, governmental investigations, or inquiries against or involving the seller or any of its related companies
- ❏ Insurance agreements, including general liability, personal and real property, errors and omissions insurance, directors and officers, worker's compensation, and other insurance
- ❏ Seller's insurance claims for the past three years
- ❏ Correspondence from clients relating to complaints or disputes about the seller's practice
- ❏ Documents relating to any settlements or injunctions to which the seller is a party
- ❏ List of unsatisfied judgments

BUSINESS MATTERS

Point of Contact: _____

- ❏ Business plans, descriptions of the company, and/or brochures
- ❏ Seller's office manual, compliance manual, and privacy policy
- ❏ Seller's law firms, accounting firms, consulting firms, and similar professionals engaged during the past five years
- ❏ Material agreements related to the seller, including loans, financing agreements, and lines of credit; security agreements; guaranties; noncompetition, nondisclosure, and nonsolicitation agreements; professional and consulting agreements
- ❏ Leases for all real and personal property related to the business
- ❏ Real estate leases, deeds, mortgages, title policies, surveys, zoning approvals, variances, and use permits
- ❏ Business licenses and permits

MARKETING

Point of Contact: _____

- ❏ Market niches the seller has developed
- ❏ Agreements relating to marketing, including all advertisements and professional dues
- ❏ Articles and press releases relating to the seller during the past three years
- ❏ Search online to determine if there is any negative publicity or customer complaints about the seller's business(es)

(Continued)

(*Continued*)

EMPLOYMENT AND LABOR MATTERS

Point of Contact: _____

- List of employees with titles, job classifications, licenses held, compensation, bonuses, benefits, and location of employment
- Agreements with the seller's employees, officers, directors, shareholders, and their affiliates, including but not limited to employment agreements, bonus arrangements, employee stock-ownership plans, covenants not to compete, confidentiality agreements, and other restrictive covenants
- Employee handbook or other personnel policy manuals
- Discuss with the seller which employees are vital to a successful transition
- Agreements with key employees
- Summary plan descriptions of all qualified and nonqualified retirement plans
- List and description of benefits of all employee health and welfare insurance policies or self-funded arrangements
- Workers' compensation claim history
- Unemployment insurance claims history

PERSONAL PROPERTY (IF APPLICABLE)

Point of Contact: _____

- List of all personal property being transferred in the sale and the locations thereof
- Inspect all personal property being transferred in the sale
- Warranties, instructions, and purchase receipts for the assets
- Service agreements and equipment leases
- Determine ongoing costs for service and maintenance of the assets
- Schedule of sales and purchases of major capital equipment during the last three years

This Due Diligence Checklist is designed to provide general guidance to a wide variety of buyers of stock or business assets related to a financial services practice and may not be suitable for all users or situations. This document is provided and is to be used with the understanding that the publisher is not engaged in rendering legal, accounting, tax, or other professional advice or service. If legal, accounting, tax, or other professional advice or assistance is needed, it is the user's responsibility to seek the services of a competent professional.

FP Transitions suggests that buyers and sellers enter into a contingent payment structure in which at least a portion of the purchase price is paid contingent upon the delivery and retention of client accounts, assets, and cash flows. The use of such a payment structure tends to mitigate poor or incomplete due diligence or a sudden post-closing change in economic conditions affecting the practice. Conversely, the larger the cash down payment or the fewer deal payment contingencies, the more thorough and accurate the due diligence process needs to be.

SELLER'S DUE DILIGENCE CHECKLIST

NOTE: This checklist is not a complete list, but is intended to cover some of the more common areas in which sellers have conducted due diligence about the buyer and/or the buyer's business. Every transaction is unique and the due diligence process must be adapted to the situation. All items in this checklist may not apply to your particular situation. Please consult your attorney and CPA for additional information and due diligence steps.

The thoroughness of a seller's due diligence on a buyer will vary depending on the transaction structure. For example, if the buyer is paying the seller in full at the time of closing (cash and not with stock), and with no contingencies or bank loans involved, a seller's due diligence on a buyer will be greatly reduced. If, on the other hand, a seller is financing the majority of the sale price, and or the seller is being paid in whole or in part with the buyer's stock, a seller's due diligence on a buyer will be greatly increased.

ORGANIZATIONAL / ENTITY STRUCTURE OF BUYER

Point of Contact: _____

☐ Entity or business structure
☐ Ownership structure
☐ Review the following documents of the buyer:
  ■ Articles of Incorporation, Articles of Organization, or similar documents, including any amendments thereto;
  ■ Bylaws, Operating Agreements, and/or Partnership Agreements;
  ■ Shareholder, Director, and Committee Minutes, Consents, and/or Resolutions;
  ■ Stock Ledgers, Membership Ledgers, or other similar documents, including amendments thereto;
  ■ Organizational chart; and,
  ■ All other documents in the company's minute book
☐ Bylaws, operating agreements, partnership agreements, joint venture agreements of any entity in which the buyer or its subsidiary is an owner
☐ Certificate of Good Standing from state of incorporation
☐ Active status reports in the state of incorporation for the past three years
☐ List of all of the buyer's assumed names and copies of registrations thereof

❑ List of all states in which the company is authorized to do business and annual reports for the past three years

❑ List of all states, provinces, and countries where the buyer owns or leases real property, maintains employees, and/or conducts business

FINANCIAL AND TAX INFORMATION OF BUYER

Point of Contact: _____

❑ Buyer's credit score/credit report

❑ Recent formal valuation or appraisal results

❑ General ledger, balance sheets, income statements, and cash flow statements for the past three years, including interim statements for the year to date

❑ Auditor's letters or reports for the past three years

❑ Federal, state, and local tax returns and reports for at least the last three years

❑ Projections, capital budgets, and strategic plans

❑ Breakdown of revenue including the quality, type, and quantity of revenue sources

❑ Analyst reports, including any analyses of fixed and variable expenses or of gross margins

❑ Tax settlement documents for the past three years

❑ Schedules of the following:
  ■ Indebtedness and contingent liabilities;
  ■ Inventory;
  ■ Accounts receivable;
  ■ Accounts payable.

❑ Documents and correspondence related to any pending or threatened audit or tax claim against buyer or buyer's assets

❑ UCC filings, tax liens, or other liens against buyer's business assets

PURCHASE / NEGOTIATION ISSUES

Point of Contact: _____

❑ Determine the general terms of the transaction, including but not limited to:
  ■ Whether it is an asset sale or a stock sale;
  ■ Purchase price;
  ■ Down payment amount, if any;
  ■ Terms of earn-out arrangement;
  ■ Whether the buyer will obtain financing;

(Continued)

(Continued)

- Seller financing, security/collateral;
- Compensation to the seller for additional referrals to the buyer after closing;
- Noncompetition/nonsolicitation agreements for seller and its employees;
- Life insurance and/or disability insurance;
- Dispute resolution;
- Continuation of the seller's license(s) after closing;
- Terms of the transition period (i.e., length of seller's involvement after closing, extent of seller's involvement, duties of seller after closing);
- Closing date.

LICENSING / REGULATORY / COMPLIANCE INFORMATION
Point of Contact: _____

- ❏ FINRA Form U-4 and, if applicable, SEC Form ADV for the buyer along with proof of filing. Confirm the filing status of these forms and any disciplinary history using FINRA's online verification process.
- ❏ Date of the peer review, or the last regulatory audit conducted by state, federal, or self-regulatory agencies. Review deficiency letters and any related correspondence. Request information pertaining to resolving any deficiencies from the appropriate regulatory agency and/or from the buyer.
- ❏ Each report or other documents filed with governmental agencies that have regulatory power over the buyer.

CLIENT TRANSFERABILITY ISSUES
Point of Contact: _____

- ❏ If the transition involves moving clients from one broker-dealer to another, check with the buyer's broker-dealer and your broker-dealer regarding its policies and portability of client information (Reg S-P).

LEGAL / LITIGATION
Point of Contact: _____

- ❏ Buyer's continuity plan and succession plan
- ❏ Description of all pending or threatened litigation, administrative proceedings, discrimination claims, grievances, wrongful termination claims, arbitration cases, workers' compensation cases, governmental

investigations, or inquiries against or involving the buyer or any of its related companies

❑ Insurance agreements, including general liability, personal and real property, errors and omissions insurance, directors and officers, worker's compensation, and other insurance

❑ Insurance claims for the past three years

❑ Correspondence from clients relating to complaints or disputes about the buyer's practice

❑ Insurance policies that may provide coverage for pending and threatened litigation

❑ Documents relating to any settlements or injunctions to which the buyer is a party

❑ List of unsatisfied judgments

BUSINESS MATTERS

Point of Contact: _____

❑ Buyer's previous acquisition history, including seller references

❑ Business plans, descriptions of the company, and/or brochures

❑ Office manual, compliance manual, and privacy policy

❑ Leases for all real and personal property related to the business

❑ Real estate leases, deeds, mortgages, title policies, surveys, zoning approvals, variances, and use permits

❑ Business licenses and permits

MARKETING

Point of Contact: _____

❑ Articles and press releases relating to the buyer during the past three years

❑ Search online to determine if there is any negative publicity or customer complaints about the buyer's business(es)

EMPLOYMENT AND LABOR MATTERS

Point of Contact: _____

❑ Discuss with the buyer which employees are vital to a successful transition.

This Due Diligence Checklist is designed to provide general guidance to a wide variety of buyers of stock or business assets related to a financial services practice and may not be suitable for all users or situations. This document is provided and is to be used with the

(Continued)

understanding that the publisher is not engaged in rendering legal, accounting, tax, or other professional advice or service. If legal, accounting, tax, or other professional advice or assistance is needed, it is the user's responsibility to seek the services of a competent professional.

FP Transitions suggests that buyers and sellers enter into a contingent payment structure in which at least a portion of the purchase price is paid contingent upon the delivery and retention of client accounts, assets, and cash flows. The use of such a payment structure tends to mitigate poor or incomplete due diligence or a sudden post-closing change in economic conditions affecting the practice. Conversely, the larger the cash down payment or the fewer deal payment contingencies, the more thorough and accurate the due diligence process needs to be.

NONBINDING LETTER OF INTENT FOR PURCHASE OF ASSETS

TIME FRAME
Today's Date: _____ Listing Number: _____
Due Diligence Period: days (begins when buyer receives signed LOI)
Proposed Closing Date: _____

PARTIES

Buyer: Seller:
Individual Name: _____   Individual Name: _____
Company Name: _____   Company Name: _____
Address: _____   Address: _____
Phone: _____   Phone: _____
Email: _____   Email: _____

TERMS OFFERED
Purchase Price: $ _____.00
Payment Structure:
   ☐ Seller Financing:

   Down Payment $ _____.00 (to be paid at Closing)

   (including earnest-money deposit [1% of purchase price] paid
      within 10 days of Seller's acceptance)

Buyer should be prepared to provide written verification of all fund
sources

   Promissory Note: $ _____ Term: _____
      Interest Rate: _____% First Payment: _____
      Payment Frequency: ☐ Monthly ☐ Quarterly ☐ Annually
         ☐ Other: _____
      Look Back Provision? ☐ Yes ☐ No
      Look Back Period: Adjustment at ☐ 3 months ☐ 6 months
         ☐ 9 months ☐ 12 months ☐ Other: _____
   ☐ Earn Out: $ _____ Years: _____ Percent Paid: _____%
      Fixed time period: ☐ Monthly ☐ Quarterly ☐ Annually
         ☐ Other: _____
      Fixed amount: $ _____
   ☐ Cash Buyout: $ _____ (to be paid at Closing)

(Continued)

(Continued)

BUYER'S SOURCE OF FUNDS
☐ Personal Funds   ☐ Broker-dealer/Custodian
☐ Bank Loan   ☐ Home Equity
☐ Retirement Accounts   ☐ Other: _____

PREQUALIFICATION
Buyer represents that (s)he ☐ has ☐ has not been prequalified for a loan through _____ for all or part of the Purchase Price plus any related costs and fees associated with this transaction.

BROKER-DEALER/CUSTODIAN
☐ Buyer intends to maintain the acquired accounts at _____
OR
☐ Buyer intends to transfer all of the acquired client accounts listed in Exhibit 1 to _____

CONTRACTS
☐ Buyer will assume Seller's Current Office Lease(s)
☐ Buyer will hire Seller's staff ☐ subject to any existing employment agreements
☐ Buyer will assume all other contracts owned by Seller, including but not limited to employment contracts, contracts for services or maintenance, contracts for software, or other similar contracts existing or related to or connected to the operation of Seller

TERMS AND CONDITIONS
Subject to successful Due Diligence, Buyer offers to purchase from Seller the Assets for the Purchase Price set forth herein. This Letter of Intent is subject to Buyer's satisfactory completion of due diligence and any other contingencies as may be separately listed on any attached Addendum.

    This Letter of Intent for Purchase of Assets, including the Terms and Conditions set forth herein (the "LOI"), effective when executed by Buyer and Seller (the "Parties"), will evidence the current mutual intent of the Parties. The Parties recognize that the transaction will require further documentation and approvals, including the preparation and approval of one or more formal agreements setting forth the terms and conditions of the proposed purchase (collectively, the "Purchase Agreement"). Nevertheless, Buyer and Seller execute this

Nonbinding LOI to evidence their intention to proceed in mutual good faith to complete work required to negotiate terms of a Purchase Agreement consistent with this letter.

The matters set forth herein, including **SECTION I. THE TRANSACTION** below are not intended to and do not constitute a binding agreement of the Parties with respect to the Transaction; any such binding agreement will arise only upon the negotiation, execution and delivery of a mutually satisfactory Purchase Agreement and the satisfaction of the conditions set forth therein. The matters set forth in **SECTION II. BINDING PROVISIONS** below shall constitute binding agreements of the Parties. In consideration of the rights and obligations of the Parties hereunder, and for other good and valuable consideration, the receipt and sufficiency of which are hereby acknowledged by the Parties, the Parties hereby agree as follows:

SECTION I. THE TRANSACTION

A. Assets Purchased. Seller plans to sell to Buyer and Buyer plans to purchase from Seller, on the terms and conditions set forth in this LOI, all of Seller's rights, title, and interest in and to the following assets ("Assets"):

1) All clients and client accounts associated with this listing (including their immediate family members, heirs, and assigns), as well as supporting information, client histories, computer records, all as set forth more definitively in the Purchase Agreement to be executed (the "Client Accounts");

2) Seller's business name/trade name;

3) Seller's individual goodwill;

4) Seller's continued assistance in the transition of the Client Accounts to buyer, for a period of months set forth in a separate Consulting Agreement;

5) Seller's agreement not to compete with or solicit the Client Accounts for a period of time as set forth in a separate Noncompetition/Nonsolicitation Agreement;

6) All commissions and/or client fees earned and recognized as of the date immediately following Closing with respect to the Business, as well as all future commissions, trail commissions, and other revenue derived from the Assets and Client Accounts after Closing;

(Continued)

(Continued)

   7) All fees and other revenue derived from the Assets and Client Accounts after Closing, based on when it was earned; and,

   8) All other assets as listed on Addendum A.

B. Excluded Assets. Excluded from this sale is Seller's cash and accounts receivable defined as work completed and billed prior to Closing. Buyer and Seller agree to divide all recurring fees, trails, and 12b-1 fees, whenever earned and billed, on a pro rata basis as of the actual date of Closing.

C. No Liabilities or Obligations Assumed. All obligations and liabilities of Seller of whatever nature ("Excluded Liabilities") shall remain the obligations and liabilities solely of Seller and shall not be assumed by Buyer.

D. Purchase Price. Buyer represents that buyer has sufficient funds available to close this sale in accord with this LOI and is not relying on any contingent source of funds unless otherwise disclosed herein. If Buyer requires an institutional or bank loan and this contingency is disclosed on the attached Addendum by Buyer, this transaction is subject to Buyer qualifying for that loan and obtaining funds. Buyer agrees to make written loan application not later than 10 days from the effective date of this LOI, complete necessary papers, and exert best efforts, including payment of all application, valuation, and processing fees in order to close the loan.

E. Standard Form Contracts; Tax Allocation. The Parties agree to use the standard form agreements, and the standard tax allocation for asset sales of independent financial service practices provided by FP Transitions to fulfill the provisions set forth in this LOI.

F. Post-Closing Support. As a part of the overall payment structure and for compensation included as a part of the Purchase Price, Seller agrees to enter into a Consulting Agreement (form to be provided by FP Transitions) that provides for Seller's assistance and support in delivering the client accounts/relationships to be acquired, and to support Buyer's efforts to retain those client accounts for up to 12 months following Closing, or as set forth above if for a lesser period.

G. Noncompetition / Nonsolicitation Agreement. The Asset Purchase Agreement shall require that, among other things, Seller enter into a noncompetition / nonsolicitation agreement with Buyer for a period equal to at least the length of financing, or as may be allowed by law.

H. Collateral and Security. Buyer will personally guarantee any unpaid balance after the down payment. In addition, as security for the full and prompt payment, Buyer will execute a Security Agreement for the acquired assets and acknowledges that Seller will file a UCC-1 Financing Statement perfecting such security interest.

SECTION II. BINDING PROVISIONS

A. Expenses. Each party shall bear its own costs associated with negotiating and performing under this LOI.

B. Confidentiality. Each party shall refrain from disclosing or copying any information regarding this transaction without first obtaining the other party's written consent. Notwithstanding the foregoing, each party may disclose information to the extent required by law and to its attorneys, accountants, lenders, or consultants providing services related to this transaction.

C. Best Efforts. Buyer and Seller will negotiate in good faith and use commercially reasonable efforts to arrive at a mutually acceptable Agreement for approval, execution, and delivery on the earliest possible date. Buyer and Seller will thereupon use their best efforts to complete all tasks by the Closing Date. Time is of the essence in this Agreement. Seller agrees that between the date of this agreement and the Closing Date that seller will continue to operate the business in its usual and ordinary course and in conformity with all applicable laws, ordinances, regulations, rules, and orders.

D. Closing by Stewart Title. This transaction shall be closed by Stewart Title in Oregon. Costs of escrow shall be split equally between buyer and seller upon Closing; fees will be deducted by escrow. The escrow account will be opened on behalf of Buyer and Seller for submission of an earnest money deposit by the buyer within 10 days of this letter being accepted and signed by both parties.

E. Attorney Fees. In the event it becomes necessary for either party to file a suit to enforce the binding provisions of this LOI, the prevailing party shall be entitled to recover, in addition to all other remedies or damages, reasonable attorney fees and costs incurred.

(Continued)

(Continued)

F. Earnest Money Deposit Payment/Refund. Buyer is entitled to a full refund of all earnest money at Buyer's sole discretion at any time prior to the expiration of the due diligence period set forth above. If Buyer fails to complete this transaction after the due diligence period has ended for any reason not addressed in this LOI or through no fault attributable to Seller, then all earnest money paid (or agreed to be paid) shall be paid to Seller as liquidated damages or as allowed by law.

G. Noninclusive; Nonbinding. This LOI does not contain all matters upon which agreement must be reached in order for the transaction to be completed. This LOI does not create and is not intended to create a binding and enforceable contract between the parties with respect to the provisions of Section I and the subject matter of the transaction, and may not be relied upon by a party as the basis for a contract by estoppel or otherwise. A binding commitment with respect to the transaction can only result from the execution and delivery of the mutually satisfactory Purchase Agreement.

H. Arbitration. Any controversy or claim arising out of this LOI or the interpretation of any of the provisions herein shall be resolved by binding arbitration by one arbitrator.

I. Entire Agreement. This LOI constitutes the entire agreement of the parties relating to the subject matter hereof and supersedes all prior discussions, agreements, or understandings, whether oral or written, relating to such subject matter. There are no other written or oral agreements or understandings between the parties. Any amendment of this LOI must be written and signed by all parties.

SEE ATTACHED ADDENDUM FOR ADDITIONAL DETAILS. AN ADDENDUM, IF ATTACHED, IS INCORPORATED AS A PART OF THIS LETTER OF INTENT.

If this offer is not accepted within 10 days of the date Buyer signs this Letter of Intent, the offer will be void.

_____		_____	
Buyer	Date	Seller	Date

This Letter of Intent is designed to provide general guidance to a wide variety of buyers and sellers of stock or business assets related to a financial services practice and may not be suitable for all users or situations. If the user does not understand a term or condition in this Letter of Intent, user is advised to seek competent legal advice before signing. This document is provided and is to be used with the understanding that the publisher is not engaged in rendering legal, accounting, tax, or other professional advice or service. If legal, accounting, tax, or other professional advice or assistance is needed, it is the user's responsibility to seek the services of a competent professional. All refunds of earnest money must be approved by both buyer and seller. Whenever the buyer is an entity, a Personal Guaranty by the shareholder(s) or member(s) of the entity should be obtained.

BUYER ACQUISITION PROFILE

YOUR CONTACT INFORMATION

First Name: _____   Business Name: _____
Last Name: _____   Street Address: _____
Phone: _____   Street Address 2: _____
Email: _____   City: _____
                           State: _____
                           Zip: _____

Role: Owner
Affiliation/Broker-Dealer/Custodian(s): _____
Are you a licensed advisor? Yes ☐   No ☐

ADVISOR INFORMATION

Type: RIA
Birth Year: _____
Years in Industry: _____
Years in Business: _____

CONTINUITY PLANNING

Do you have a continuity plan in place to protect your practice in the
event of your death or disability? Yes ☐   No ☐

SUCCESSION PLANNING

Do you have a formal, written succession plan for transfer of
ownership? Yes ☐   No ☐
If yes, what is your succession time frame?

TOTAL PRACTICE REVENUE (GDC)

Trailing 12 Months $ _____
2015 $ _____
2014 $ _____
2013 $ _____

REVENUE MIX

Fee Income _____ %
Commission/Securities _____ %
Hourly _____ %
Insurance _____ %
Other _____ %

REVENUE BALANCE

Recurring Revenue _____ %
Fees, Trails, Renewals _____ %
Nonrecurring _____ %

Do you have a website?
Web Address: _____

VALUATION

Have you completed a formal valuation of your practice?
Yes ☐ No ☐
If yes, when was the valuation performed (if not completed by FP
Transitions)?
What was the result of your valuation (if not completed by FP
Transitions)?

COMPANY PROFILE

Assets Under Management: _____
Total Number of Clients/Households: _____
Average Client Tenure: _____
Number of Owners: _____
Number of Licensed Employees: _____
Total Number of Employees: _____
Licenses Held:

☐ 3   ☐ 7   ☐ 24   ☐ 62   ☐ Exempt
☐ 5   ☐ 15   ☐ 42   ☐ 63   ☐ Other
☐ 6   ☐ 22   ☐ 52   ☐ 65

Designations:

☐ CFP   ☐ CFA   ☐ AIF   ☐ ChFC
☐ CFS   ☐ MBA   ☐ CPA

Other Licenses or Designations: _____
Professional Affiliations (NAPFA, DFA, FPA, etc.): _____

About the Author

David Grau Sr., JD, is one of the original founders of FP Transitions and is the company's president. As a former securities regulator (the operative word being "former") and securities attorney, David has spent almost half his life in this industry, helping advisors set up their practices, build them into sustainable businesses, and sell or merge them when that is the best and most appropriate course of action.

Buying, Selling, and Valuing Financial Practices: The FP Transitions M&A Guide, is David's second book. David previously authored the best-selling *Succession Planning for Financial Advisors: Building an Enduring Business*, published by John Wiley & Sons in 2014. David has also written 90 nationally published articles, white papers, and manuals on continuity issues, income perpetuation strategies, mergers and acquisitions, succession planning, tax strategies, and internal ownership tracks. David was named one of the most influential people in the profession in an industry survey of financial advisors by *Financial Planning* magazine.

David is a current member of the Oregon State Bar and a past board member of the Oregon and SW Washington chapter of the Financial Planning Association. David is a graduate of Purdue University, with highest honors, and Northwestern School of Law. Most important, David is a perennial Diamond Medallion Member with Delta Airlines and, yes, it is all about the miles (almost 2 million to date)!

About the Website

B *uying, Selling, and Valuing Financial Practices: The FP Transitions M&A Guide* offers readers a companion website at www.wiley.com\go\grau (password: fptransitions17). There you will be able to download some of FP Transitions' most important resources, including:

- From Listing to Closing: An Illustration of the Process
- The Open Market Process
- Case Study #1: Acquisition Wrap-Up: A Seller's Quest to Find the Perfect Buyer
- Case Study #2: Selling Your Practice: One Chance to Do It Right
- Continuity Planning Worksheet
- Practice Emergency Plan FAQs: Questions That Guide the FP Transitions Preparation Discussion
- Due Diligence Checklist
- Tax Treatment of Asset Sales for Buyers and Sellers
- Valuation Methods Table
- Practice Value Worksheet

Index

> "While passion is the catalyst for becoming an independent advisor, David Grau Sr. and the FP Transitions team offer the first practical guide to creating and monetizing real equity value as a business. In an industry where so much has changed, this book exposes the outdated assumptions of a by-gone era, arms you with the facts, and forges a clear path for achieving sustainable success for the future."
>
> — Sharon M. Theall
> *President, Strategic Management Advisors, LLC*

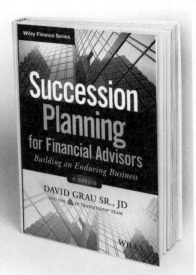

BUILD YOUR LEGACY AND PASS IT ON

Succession planning is the cornerstone of a business strategy geared towards perpetuating income and fueling growth beyond a single advisor's career.

A proper succession plan benefits everyone: the founding advisor, next generation owners, the business as whole and, of course, the clients. This book, *Succession Planning for Financial Advisors,* explores the tools and processes, including:

- Restructuring ownership compensation to support growth and profitability
- Determining a succession timeline based on the unique goals of a founding advisor
- Preparing a business for more than one generation of ownership
- Attracting and retaining next generation talent

Succession planning is about building a business that works for you, perhaps well beyond the traditional retirement age.